# STICK IT!

# STICK IT!

MY LIFE OF SEX, DRUMS, AND ROCK 'N' ROLL

## CARMINE ☠ APPICE

with IAN GITTINS

CHICAGO
REVIEW
PRESS

An A Cappella Book

Published by Chicago Review Press Incorporated
814 North Franklin Street
Chicago, Illinois 60610
ISBN 978-1-61373-552-7

**Library of Congress Cataloging-in-Publication Data**
Appice, Carmine.
Stick it! : a life of sex, drums, and rock 'n' roll / Carmine Appice with Ian Gittins.
pages cm
ISBN 978-1-61373-552-7 (cloth : alk. paper) 1. Appice, Carmine. 2. Rock musicians—United States—Biography. I. Gittins, Ian. II. Title.

ML419.A676A3 2016
786.9'166092—dc23
[B]

2015032307

All photos from the collection of Carmine Appice, unless otherwise noted.
Interior design: Jon Hahn
Interior layout: Nord Compo

Printed in the United States of America
5 4 3 2 1

To Mom and Dad, Nicholas, Bianca, and Leslie.

# CONTENTS

# FOREWORD

Carmine played in my band from the midseventies through to the early eighties. I had liked his previous groups, Vanilla Fudge and Cactus. He was in my band because I found him to be a brilliant drummer. And he wouldn't have been there if he wasn't special.

And almost equally important, Carmine never seemed down. He was always very up and positive. Sometimes he didn't get my British sense of humor, but not his fault: he's a Yank.

There was only one drawback: his sense of style was fucking useless. Absolutely hopeless. He would turn up in these horrible bell-bottom velvet trousers. They might have been acceptable in 1972, but they certainly weren't in the eighties. As for his hair, well, the less said about the parrot-like yellow or orange streaks the better.

Carmine was always good to be around and great to play with, but onstage we had to calm him down when he got too carried away. I called him the Chinese Dentist because he could not resist putting in too many fills. I remember that sometimes we would do "I Don't Want to Talk About It," a simple ballad that just needed him to hold down the beat, but no, he would be putting in all these bloody drum fills! So naturally I would do the only logical thing I could and throw a beer glass at his head. Seriously.

Carmine was so easy to wind up. He would do these long drum solos that he'd finish standing on his stool holding his sticks in the air, which was the cue for his roadie to bang a huge gong behind him for a big dramatic ending. We'd snatch the stick off the roadie or even hide the gong itself, so Carmine was left standing there like a lemon. Then at the end of his solo he would go to the front of the stage and throw his sticks into the crowd, and the road crew would be hiding in the pit to throw two hundred of 'em back at him.

Carmine joined in most enthusiastically with our offstage endeavors like the Sex Police. It worked like this: we would all dress up in white overalls inspired by *A Clockwork Orange* plus T-shirts with "Sex Police" printed on them as we'd charge around hotels winding up anybody in the tour party who had taken a girl back. Given Carmine's habits, he was often in the firing line.

He was also a leading light of the Downstairs Supper Club. We would go out for dinner, eight or nine of us, and halfway through the meal we would all dive under the table and hide. It tended to shock the waiting staff. But I always ended up paying. Carmine never bought dinner. He was tight like that. ("That's not true!" —Carmine)

I have nothing but good to say about Carmine, even though I ended up firing him. God knows why! Maybe that was just how we were back then. He cowrote "Do Ya Think I'm Sexy" with me, which became the fastest-selling song in Warner Brothers history.

I believe people love characters in rock and roll, and Carmine was a real character. He still is! I saw him last at my birthday party, and I am convinced that he was still wearing the same bloody jacket he used to wear in my band. . . .

Rod Stewart

# ACKNOWLEDGMENTS

My thanks to all those who helped with this project:

Leslie Gold, my life partner, for her undying help throughout this book process; for her love, understanding, and insight; and for our great relationship—thirteen years now and going strong. She is my true soulmate and the love of my life. Without her help, the book could not have moved forward as it did. Thanks, baby. XO.

Ian Gittins, my cowriter, for his amazing writing, his diligence, and his experience in the book field. He went above and beyond the call of duty to get the book finished and did everything necessary to see it got released. Amazing job! Thanks, Ian.

Roger Colleti of VH1. Roger hooked me up with VH1 Books and they connected me with my cowriter, Ian. Without these two developments, this book would not be where it is now.

Jacob Hoye, for having the confidence in my life story and pairing me with Ian. What a great team you created.

Nick, my son. He and his sister had to put up with me being on the road for years, but he turned out to be a fine young man of whom I am very proud and whom I love dearly.

Bianca, my daughter. As with my son, she put up with having a dad on the road, but she also turned out to be a focused, go-getting adult whom I'm proud of, love dearly, and support.

My family—Mom and Dad, Frank, Terri, and Vinny.

Mary, my mom, was a music lover who passed away in 1987. She and my father, Charlie, supported all my endeavors in music, even driving me to various shows and wedding gigs when I was too young to drive myself. My mom is missed dearly. My pop, who passed in 2005, was one of the nicest men I've known. Although a hard-working, strict father when I was a kid, he grew to be such a warm, easygoing man as I became an adult. I love both my mother and father and wish they were here to see this book become a reality.

My brother Frank, who put up with me practicing drums while he was trying to study through high school and college. Sorry, Frank! Love you, brother.

My sister, Terri. Since my mother passed, Terri has been the female rock of the family. As a kid she put up with three brothers giving her shit all her life. She is loved dearly by all of us. Love you, Terri.

My brother Vinny. What can I say? He had talent. I helped develop it when he was a kid, and now he takes my gigs! Ha ha! He's a cool guy, and I'm proud to see all he's done with his drumming career. He's almost like my kid! Love you, Vin.

Yuval Taylor at Chicago Review Press, for having the insight to sign me to CRP and for working closely on the book to get it market-ready. Thanks.

Lindsey Schauer at Chicago Review Press, for all her help in getting the book ready for print. Thanks.

For all the photographers who gave me the use of their photos. Thanks, guys. Much love and appreciation.

Paul and Sue Latimer
Neil Slowzower
Leland Bobbe
Alex Solca
Marco Soccoli
Mark Weiss
Michael Sherer

Skip Press, thanks for doing some of the legwork on the book years ago.

Steve Rosen, thanks for your help cleaning up the writing in the early days of the book.

Mike Cusinelli, whose help getting the first deal on the book was key. You rock.

Carol Ross, for helping to manage the marketing and PR on this book—you are doing a great job, as usual.

Dick Benette, my drum teacher and mentor when I was a teenager. I learned so much taking lessons from him. When I grew up, I wanted to be just like him. God bless. Love you, Dick.

Rod Stewart, what can I say? Playing with Rod was the greatest part of my career. In my estimation he is the greatest rock singer/performer—period. I loved working with him as a band member, and I thank him for writing the foreword to the book. You are the best, Rod. Thank you. I send my love to you!

# *Introduction*

# ASK SHARON!

In which our intrepid Drummerdude is decapitated, fired, and almost incinerated by Sharon Osbourne—and all because his name is too big

*It had worked in the sound check. It had* worked great in the sound check. So why the fuck wasn't it working now?

I loved my drum solo on the 1984 US leg of Ozzy Osbourne's *Bark at the Moon* tour. Man, it was quite something. The whole set was genuinely spectacular, like some crazy, big old gothic mansion, but I was pretty sure my jaw-dropping special effects halfway through the set topped it all.

My drums, my famous oversized twenty-four-inch custom kit, sat on top of the sprawling staircase that towered over the stage. It was the best seat in the house. Every night I would smash the shit out of my skins as a manic Ozzy and his band—Jake E. Lee, Bob Daisley, and Don Airey—raced around beneath me. It was a seriously heavy band, the kind of tour I loved.

But the highlight for me, every night, was my big solo. This was what I was all about! The spotlight would fix on me, the stairs would open up, and—thanks to the modern miracle of hydraulics—I would slide with my drums thirty feet down to the stage, a kick-ass, kinetic blur of purple hair, Fu Manchu moustache, glowing drumsticks, and pure adrenalin.

It's the rush that only being onstage in front of thousands of people can give. As pyro exploded extravagantly around me, night after night I got the whole audience chanting and clapping along. It felt great. I felt alive.

Word had been spreading about my special-effect solo. On the brand-new music TV channel MTV, veejay J. J. Jackson was plugging the tour as "Ozzy Osbourne featuring legendary drummer Carmine Appice." Every night had been amazing. In my home city, New York, a few nights earlier, I had heard people yelling, "Carmine! Brooklyn!" and "Carmine! Long Island!" I had felt on top of the world. It was awesome to be appreciated.

But maybe that was the problem on this tour: I was being too appreciated.

Now it was two weeks later, and we were in Cincinnati. The day had not been going well. I had recently started noticing a growing bad feeling toward me from Sharon Osbourne, Ozzy's famously demanding and no-nonsense wife and manager, who had hired me to join the band and play on the tour.

I had known Ozzy from back in the day, 1970 in fact, when my old group Cactus had played a gig with Black Sabbath and we had almost come to blows over a missing lump of pot. But I had never played with him until he and Sharon had contacted me early in '83.

Sharon could not have been more charming when I first met her and Ozzy in London to discuss the tour. She was all sweetness and light. I had explained that when I was on the road in the United States, I held drum classes for wannabe drummers in the early evenings in each city before I played the shows. Sharon had been fine with that. She was also cool with me having my own publicist and selling my own merchandise on the tour.

Or, at least, she said she was.

The European leg of the tour had been great. I was fucking glad that I have never been a big drinker when I saw what happened to anybody from the band or crew who got drunk and passed out: they would wake up with shaved eyebrows or with a giant dick drawn on their faces in marker pen. They wouldn't know until they saw themselves in a mirror hours later, and then they would flip out.

Who was the main culprit behind this shit? Ozzy, of course.

Only one thing had spooked me. Early on during the *Bark at the Moon* dates in England, we had stopped the tour bus to get lunch. The band was still on the bus, and Ozzy and Sharon were in the glass foyer of the restaurant arranging a table. I glanced out the window to see Ozzy clench his fist, pull his arm back, and whack Sharon full in the face!

What the fuck? I couldn't believe it—I mean, I'm Italian, and you just don't treat women like that! I jumped up to get off the bus and get between them, but our bassist, Bob Daisley, grabbed my arm.

"Don't worry about it, Carmine," he told me, nodding toward the brawling couple. "They do it all the time. Just stay out of it."

We all filed off the bus and joined the warring couple in the restaurant. They seemed to have calmed down, and we found a table and started eating. Ten minutes later, to my shock, they were back in the foyer, Sharon slugged Ozzy, and they were smashing each other in the face again. Round two!

Bob was sitting next to me. "See? I told you!" he said, hardly bothering to look up from his burger.

Sharon was a lot bigger in those days than she is now, to say the least, and she could take care of herself with her own fists, but it freaked me out. Yet we got along fine. I hung out at their home in England and played with their baby daughter, Aimee.

Things had changed on the American leg of the tour, though. Sharon was running a tight ship to try to keep Ozzy sober for the shows and introduced a no-visitors-backstage rule. This meant no groupies. Nobody was thrilled about this development—me included, as at the time groupies were a major deal for me. The support band, a young Mötley Crüe, liked it even less, and we soon christened the tour the *No Fun* tour. Its unofficial logo was a limp dick.

But something else was starting to bug Sharon more and more. Me.

As the tour unfolded, I did interviews in the afternoons talking up my drum classes and promoting the tour before heading off to a local music store to teach paradiddles to excited students. Then I would return to the venue for the show. Sharon was getting odd around me—or was I imagining it? I couldn't be sure.

When we hit Cleveland, she saw me backstage before the gig and asked if my preshow drum classes were tiring me out.

I explained to her, "No, let me tell you what I do. I have a little drum kit and fifty kids sit around me and I teach them a few moves, and then they come up on the drums and try what I taught them. I don't even break a sweat—if anything, it fires me up for the shows!" Sharon seemed to accept this, and I thought no more of it.

But then came Cincinnati.

I had done a big newspaper interview a few days before the Cincinnati show, which appeared on the day of the gig. The interviewer had asked what the most spectacular moment of the *Bark at the Moon* tour was, and I had answered honestly: my drum solo! I raved about my drums gliding through the air and the insane pyro at the end. However, I also stressed that it had all been Sharon and Ozzy's idea, not mine.

I guess I didn't stress it enough. Arriving at the venue after my afternoon drum class, I discovered fifty copies of my interview taped to the walls backstage. At first I thought nothing of it. Just another tour prank, right? Ozzy joking and busting my balls again? But then my drum tech, Andre, appeared next to me.

Andre was a six-foot-one stern-looking character who went by the nickname the Viking. If ever anything went wrong, he would stand next to me with his arms folded across his hefty chest and give it to me straight. That was his pose right now.

"C.A.," he told me, "we have a problem."

He held out one of my personal merchandise T-shirts, the ones Sharon let me sell at the shows. It looked like she might have changed her mind. Somebody had used scissors to cut my head out of the picture on the front. It wasn't a one-off—it had been done to every shirt. They were all ruined.

I could not believe it and went rampaging around the building to find the tour manager. I went crazy on his ass: "Who the fuck has done this shit?"

His two-word answer was simplicity itself: "Ask Sharon."

Oh, I intended to! But not right now. It was showtime.

The crowd went wild for us that night, and I was hitting my drums and cymbals so hard it almost hurt. I couldn't get the crap about the T-shirts out of my head, and took my frustrations out on the kit. I was totally primed for my best solo yet.

The moment came. The lights sought me out, and Andre gave me his usual tap on the back to signal the drums were about to drop through the stairs. I switched to playing just my snare for a few seconds so the initial jolt of the riser starting its descent didn't foul up my rhythm. I tensed and waited for the riser to take flight. . . .

Nothing. What the fuck was this?

I was thrown and kept playing the snare as Andre panicked behind me. He was on his walkie-talkie and jumping up and down the fifteen-foot drum-riser ladder to try to fix the problem.

Yet the same thing kept happening: nothing.

Something was badly wrong, and I had to launch into my solo stranded on top of the staircase. The pyro went off as usual, and as I was in the wrong place, I felt the flames crackling way too near to me. *This would be the ultimate way for a drummer to go*, I thought—*in a stage inferno during a solo! Spinal Tap!*

The crowd loved it anyway and cheered and hollered. But as I flailed away in front of twenty thousand fans, I knew that anybody in Cincinnati who had read me in their morning paper talking up my crazy flying solo would think I had been full of shit.

Which, of course, was the whole point. I didn't get to speak to Sharon after the show, as she and Ozzy traveled on their own bus, but as our band bus pulled through the night, I cornered Bob and asked him the question that was killing me: "Would Sharon sabotage her own show just to get back at me?"

"Oh yeah!" Bob nodded without a second's hesitation. "Of course! Getting back at you is more important to her right now than anything—including giving the audience a great gig."

This was crazy shit! I just couldn't process it. These fans had paid hard-earned money to see the show. Would Sharon really cheat them to get revenge on me for a newspaper article she didn't like? I wanted to confront her, but I loved Ozzy and I loved being on the tour. After sleeping on it, I decided to suck it up, keep my head down, and see if I could move on.

Fat chance. Ozzy was oblivious to what was going on, but Sharon had me in her sights and smelled blood. Over the next few days, every time I did a drum class, she would claim I had played badly at the show because I was tired. It was bullshit—but she was fluent in it.

It all came to a head when *Bark at the Moon* hit Texas. Sharon had fired Ozzy's previous drummer, Tommy Aldridge, just under a year earlier. When I bumped into Tommy backstage in Dallas, I thought nothing of it. He lived locally, we were friends, and we had a lot in common.

We were about to have one more thing.

After *Bark at the Moon* hit Houston a few days later, I was chilling out in the dressing room talking about how tight and good we all sounded together and how we had really started to become a great band when I got a message: Sharon wanted to see me.

She was waiting for me in the production office. I greeted her as I walked in: "Hey Sharon, what's going on?"

"I think you know," she replied.

Sharon had a wiseass smirk on her face and was shaking her head side to side like a disappointed schoolmarm. I told her the truth: I had no idea what she was talking about.

"Tommy Aldridge is here because he's joining the tour," she continued primly. "You are fired."

Fired? My mouth hung open beneath my moustache as I stared at Sharon and struggled to take this in. What? Why? What for?

"Your name is too big," she declared with finality. "We want more of a sideman, like Tommy. You should start your own band."

"We have a contract!" I reminded her.

"See you in court!" Sharon said, with a tight little smile. And with that, she was gone.

My departure from the tour was awkward, upsetting, and messy. The other guys were all shocked. We had just played the best show on the tour. It was crazy. Tommy had never even played the songs from the new album. Ozzy was embarrassed. Andre quit the tour in solidarity with me, but Sharon refused to fly him home to Los Angeles—we had to get our own flights.

When I got home I sank into depression. How could this happen? I sat alone in my bedroom watching J. J. Jackson still plugging the Ozzy tour with the legendary Carmine Appice on drums. I was embarrassed. I got FIRED! I tried not to go out; when I did, people would ask me what happened. I didn't know what to say.

Sharon had one last spiteful kick at me. As I watched MTV one day, J. J. Jackson had changed his story and announced I had been kicked off the tour. He read a quote, supposedly from Ozzy: "Carmine had to leave for medical reasons—he was making me sick."

What? I knew there was no way Ozzy would say that. It had Sharon's fingerprints all over it. This was confirmed years later when she quit as the Smashing Pumpkins' manager and said exactly the same thing about Billy Corgan.

Really, you gotta love her.

I sued Ozzy and Sharon for breach of contract and various other shit and settled out of court, but as usual, the only people who got rich out of the lawsuit were the lawyers. I never held it against Ozzy. When I bumped into him a year or two later, he greeted me by saying plaintively, "C.A., I know that you have problems with my missus, but I hope we can still be friends." And we still are.

That was a first for me—being fired while actually out on tour! It had never happened to me before, and thankfully it never has since. It was shocking at the time, but now I just look at it as one low point on what has been an incredible journey of ups and downs through rock and roll.

I guess I feel lucky to have had the career I've had. I was only a teenager when we started trying to push back the boundaries of psychedelic music with Vanilla Fudge. I hung out with Hendrix and spent years rocking out with the, shall we say, *enigmatic* Jeff Beck. When I fetched up with Rod Stewart, Rod recruited me into the rampaging backstage band of merry men known as the Sex Police.

And somehow, along the way, just by being a wild drummer in a rock-and-roll band, I managed to have sex with many hundreds of women—I was only to realize just how many years later—and cowrite million-selling songs. It's not been a bad life for a working-class boy from Brooklyn.

So it's been a crazy ride, and every day I count my blessings that I fell in love with drumming and with music. Because if I hadn't, I may well have ended up like many of my Brooklyn friends—in the Mafia, serving time for murder, or dead.

# 1

# BROOKLYN
# NIGHTS

*In which our wet-behind-the-ears Drummerdude explodes cockroaches, runs with gangs, goes lugging, hurls trucks from unfinished bridges, falls in love with drumming, hangs out with Jimmy James in a hooker's shitty apartment, and gets married*

"*Hey! You kids come back here!*" *No way!* I was out of there! It was 1959, I was thirteen years old, I was being chased at full throttle through the grimy side streets of Brooklyn by New York City cops, and I was terrified.

It wasn't the first time this had happened. In fact, it was getting to be a habit. I had started hanging out with a gang of hoodlums—we called ourselves the Thirty-Eighth Street Park Boys—and far too many evenings were ending with me tearing down the local sidewalks with the cops in hot pursuit, my heart pounding so hard I feared it would explode.

This particular evening had started out, as always, with my mob of adolescents kicking around in Brooklyn, bored and looking for mischief. We had found ourselves under the elevated, old, and now gone BMT line, part of the New York subway system, where some boxcars stood unguarded.

It took us seconds to decide to break into them.

I wasn't one of the main instigators. I was hanging around in the background, nervously keeping watch as the gang leaders smashed open the locks on the car doors and began passing out the cardboard boxes full of radios and other small electrical appliances—at which point, four NYPD cop cars appeared, sirens wailing, and screeched to a halt all around us.

Shit! Here we go again! I was off at full bore, running faster than I even knew I could. My feet pounded on the sidewalk as I zigzagged through the backstreets and alleys. Scared shitless, I tried to lose the burly cop in hot pursuit while one loud thought dominated my panicking mind: *He can't catch me—my parents will kill me!*

That was my teenage life in Brooklyn, or at least a big part of it, and there is no doubt that my mother and father would have been brokenhearted if they had known what I was up to. Because, as far as they were aware, I was an innocent, reasonably well-behaved, God-fearing Italian boy.

I was born on December 15, 1946, and christened Carmine Charles Appice. I am actually a Jr., Carmine Jr., as my dad was also named Carmine, but nobody ever called him that. He had exactly the same name as me, Carmine Charles, but everyone called him Charlie.

We grew up in a little one-bedroom apartment, 1431 Forty-First Street, in the Borough Park area of Brooklyn. I guess it was a typical crowded, chaotic Italian American household. My grandparents had bought a two-unit building and converted it into three units, and they lived on the first floor. My uncle George, aunt Estie, and cousins Linda and Roseanne had a one-bedroom apartment at the front of the second floor.

It was cramped for them, but that was nothing compared to what it was like for us. My father, my mother Mary, my older brother Frank, and I were all squeezed into two rooms and a kitchen at the back of the same floor. When my younger sister, Terri, and brother Vinny were born, that made six of us fighting for space in an apartment built for two.

It meant we had no privacy at all. The sleeping arrangements were crazy. My parents slept on a fold-down sofa bed in the living room, while Frank and I shared my parents' old bed in the bedroom. Terri was an inch away from us on a folding bed, and Vinny slept by Mom and Dad in a crib that was so small, he often kept us awake from banging his head on it.

Frank used to take his eye out at night. That was kind of freaky. He is four years older than me, and just around the time I was born, he got his eye shot out by a bow and arrow. So if you walked into our kitchen at night, there was Frank's glass eye sitting in a solution in a glass by the sink.

Money was tight, and we were living right on top of each other, but I had a pretty happy childhood. My parents were strict-but-not-really-strict in that typical Italian way. My mother loved her kids like crazy, and we could do no wrong in her eyes. My dad had a leather strap to beat us with, but he rarely used it.

My father was a cop for a while, but for most of his life he was a mechanic who fixed oil burners. He was always working overtime to make every cent he could. On weekends he took us to church. My mom stopped going when Frank lost his eye. She reasoned, "What kind of God would let that happen to my son?" But my dad took all of us kids to St. Catherine's Roman Catholic Church every Sunday morning.

I didn't get much out of this ritual. The readings were in Latin and might as well have been beamed in from another planet. We would stop on the way to church to buy fresh-baked buns and pastries from the local bakery. I only got through the services by looking forward to eating the buns afterward.

If I had thought church was bad, my first school experience was even worse. My mom deposited me, aged five, at PS 164 on Forty-Second Street and Fourteenth Avenue, a block from home, and as soon as she left, I went crazy. I screamed at the teacher and kicked her in the shins. She couldn't calm me down, so the principal called my mom to come and pick me up.

Luckily, this kiddie anxiety attack only lasted twenty-four hours, and the next day I played happily in class. My mom loitered anxiously outside the classroom in the hallway until the principal spotted her and told her to go home.

As I grew older, naturally I started looking for ways to get into trouble. We had a cellar under our house, and I would go down there with my Gilbert chemistry set and make gunpowder and rockets out of aluminum cigar cases. When I tried to set one of them off in the backyard, it blew a big hole in the ground. My mother went crazy, yelling her catchphrase: "You son-of-a-bitch bastard!"

Down in the basement my dad had ten-thousand-watt transformers for his work. I'd put wires on the poles and flick a switch, and then a spark would fly across the poles. It was my Frankenstein machine; I thought it was so cool. I also used to use my father's alligator clip wires to electrocute cockroaches and water bugs, until the day I gave myself a huge electric shock that terrified me.

Every summer we would go on vacation to a bungalow that my family had bought in Lakewood, New Jersey. It was great to get out of Brooklyn when it was unbearably hot. I had a bunch of friends down there, and we'd make soapboxes out of wood with old carriage wheels and have soapbox derbies like we'd seen on *Our Gang* and *Little Rascals.*

One time our next-door neighbor, Mr. Comitto, was building a well, and there was a whole load of huge, round concrete shells lying around. My friends and I started climbing onto them and accidentally rolled one down a hill. It smashed to pieces at the bottom against a tree. When Mr. Comitto saw this, he came over to our house and flipped out at me. Naturally, I denied everything. I'm not sure my father believed me, but I got away with it.

Yet most of my bad behavior happened around home. Brooklyn in the 1950s was a wild place to grow up. It was a real melting pot, with Poles, Jews, Puerto Ricans, Italians, and "blacks" all crammed in together. Prejudice ran rampant: we talked about "Polack bastards" and "nigger bastards" as easily as talking about the weather. We knew they were saying similar shit about us.

I used to hang around with my friends after school at a small park called the Thirty-Eighth Street Park (hence the Thirty-Eighth Street Park Boys). Other times we called ourselves the Fifteenth Avenue Midgets. We would go to the local cinema, the Windsor Theater, sneak up to the closed balcony, and set off fireworks, terrifying the audience while *Godzilla* was showing.

Our gang leader was a kid a few years older than me named Joey DeVino. Joey was a real high-energy ass-kicking motherfucker. He didn't give a fuck about anybody or anything and was scared of nothing. He also drank beer, which seemed ultracool to my teenage self, even though I didn't like the taste (in fact, I still don't).

The Fifteenth Avenue Midgets had a range of delinquent activities. We thought the Hassidic Jews looked weird, like aliens, with their big beards, long black coats, and hats, so we pushed them around and pulled their hats off. It seemed like fun at the time.

Another favorite pastime was lugging. Some of the older guys in the gang had cars, or would steal one, and we would speed down a narrow Brooklyn street with a guy hanging out of each car window, holding a lug wrench in his hand, and smashing every parked car's rear window as we went.

Why did we do it? Fuck knows—we were bored and looking for kicks.

There were a few times when our criminal antics took a more sinister, darker turn. One of the worst happened at Coney Island one hot and sticky summer day when I was fourteen.

By then, like any teenage boy, I was perpetually horny and totally obsessed with girls. I would try anything to get my hands on a tit or a pussy, but never seemed to get anywhere and was still a frustrated virgin. At least at Coney Island I could ogle all the chicks in their revealing bathing suits.

Our gang used to always hang out on bay eight at the beach, which we saw as an extension of our turf—Thirty-Eighth Street Park by the sea. We thought we were the kings of that little stretch of sand and ocean, and one day we were delighted when three Puerto Rican chicks came wandering into our bay.

They all looked cool and sexy, with big boobs spilling out of bathing suits that were cut low at the top and high up around the crotch, just how we liked it. They knew they were hot stuff, and as they swaggered to the water we catcalled at them with a stream of sexually suggestive comments.

It started off as harmless joshing and banter, but it soon turned ugly. As the girls stood waist-deep in the tepid, gray Brooklyn water, a bunch of our guys surrounded them. The jokes became verbal abuse and then sexual assault as my friends grabbed at the chicks' tits and tried to pull their suits off. Joey led the attack.

The terrified girls fought back, and two of them managed to escape, running off up the beach screaming insults at us. The third chick was not so lucky, and suddenly two guys lifted her out of the water and pulled the crotch of her suit to one side, revealing her black pubic hairs. The guys then took turns finger-fucking her as she cried hysterically.

How did I feel? I was sorry for the poor girl, but I admit I was also secretly aroused as I watched the fingers sliding in and out of her. But I was way too scared to go and get a piece of the action myself. This was to prove extremely wise.

The chick finally broke free and ran to the boardwalk, yelling at us that she was a Chaplains girl and that we would pay for this. The Chaplains were a notorious black gang with hundreds of members. But so what? We were the kings of bay eight. "Fuck you, spic bitch!" we yelled at her. We thought we were untouchable.

We were wrong. Two hours later, as the afternoon turned into evening, we became aware of black dudes around us—everywhere. It was like the end scene from *The Warriors*. Chaplain gang guys were all along the boardwalk and the borders with bays seven and nine. I swear some even came in from the ocean! We ran to Joey: "Whadda we do?"

Joey might have been a thug, but he also had a weird noble and self-sacrificing side to him. Often if we were deep in the shit, he would avoid a full-on battle by offering to fight the rival gang leader to settle the grudge. If he had to lose and take a beating to save our asses, that was what he'd do.

So the Chaplains got revenge, and Joey got beaten black and blue until his face was swimming in blood. After their head guy finished with Joey, he told the girl who had gotten abused to point out every-one who had molested her. They all had to get down on their knees and apologize as she went along the row slapping their faces hard. Now I was real pleased I had held back!

This was the incident that made me think I should maybe draw back from the gang activities. What had started as fun was getting dangerous. It could easily take over your life, and a lot of guys from the Thirty-Eighth Street Park Boys went on to the Mafia.

The Mafia was everywhere in Brooklyn in the 1950s and '60s. You didn't have to look too hard. I was constantly aware of Italian guys hanging around outside bars, wearing suits and ties or smart black turtleneck sweaters. They were always there, day and night, and clearly didn't have regular jobs. My parents told me to stay away from them because they were gangsters, and I did.

Joey wasn't so careful. He joined the Mafia, got into drugs and gambling, and died young.

So what led my teenage self away from a potential life of crime and onto the straight and narrow? Simple: I fell in love with music—or, more specifically, drumming.

I had always loved music. My brother Frank was really into the doo-wop thing and would listen to "the father of rock and roll," DJ Alan Freed, on WINS on the kitchen radio. Frank was even in a doo-wop group called the Laurels and taught me how to sing harmonies. He bought Elvis, Buddy Holly, and Little Richard records, and I would get into them as well.

When Alan Freed hosted a weeklong rock-and-roll show at the Paramount Theatre in Brooklyn, Frank went but wouldn't take me because it wasn't cool to be seen hanging out with your little brother. So my mother bought me a ticket and went with me instead. I saw some great acts at that show—Chuck Berry, Bo Diddley, Smokey Robinson, and the Ronettes—but what really blew my mind was the drumming.

The house backup band that played with all the artists had two drummers—two drummers!—and it was fucking amazing. I loved watching Ronnie Spector in the Ronettes wiggling her butt in a miniskirt, but I was even more captivated by the beats coming from behind her. How could anybody make a noise that powerful, that immense?

It was my first gig, and from that moment I knew exactly what I wanted to do with my life: I wanted to be a drummer.

I didn't have any drums, of course, but that didn't stop me. From then on, as the hits blared from the radio, I would bang along on my mom's pots and pans.

My cousin Joey had a Blue Pearl Slingerland drum set that I would jump on eagerly every time we went to his house on family visits. My parents took note of how excited I was whenever I played Joey's set, and in 1959 they bought me my own little kit for Christmas from the very first Sam Ash music store, on Utica Avenue in Brooklyn. It cost them fifty-five dollars and was just a bass drum, a snare, and a cymbal, and I thought it was the coolest thing in the world.

From that point on, when I came home from school, all I wanted to do was practice drums. I set them up in our cellar on a platform I made by balancing my grandmother's antique table on top of four concrete blocks. It was my first, primitive stage.

At first I didn't really know what I was doing, and I would just play around with lots of snare-drum stuff. Then I started playing grooves I heard on records and the radio. My grandfather was a shoemaker, and the table he used for repairs was right by my drums. Often he would be working by me, and I'd ask, "Hey, Grandpa, can you bang your hammer to this tempo, and I'll play along?" But Grandpa had no rhythm. Plus, he was deaf.

At fourteen I went to a high school dance where the drummer in the band was amazing. He was about my age but so much more advanced. I got talking to him, and he gave me the number of his drum teacher. The teacher's name was Dick Benette.

I had to ask my parents if I could take drum lessons. This was a big deal since they were raising four kids on my dad's monthly three-hundred-dollar wages, and every dollar counted. But they were both supportive and agreed as long as I promised to really work at it.

The weekly journey to Dick's place in Flatbush took me an hour and could be hairy. I had to get a subway and a bus, and often some black guys from a Coney Island gang would bust my balls. They'd see me with my drumsticks and laugh and dance around the train, saying "Hey, drummer boy—play us a rhythm!" Some weeks they robbed me of my money, and I'd have to borrow my fifty-cent fare to get back home from Dick's house.

It was worth it because Dick was an amazing teacher. He taught me technique and shortcuts as well as how to read drum music and in no time had improved my playing incredibly. His lifestyle also deeply impressed me: he had a beautiful house, drove a Cadillac, and, most impressively, made nearly a thousand dollars per weekend in his own band playing weddings, bar mitzvahs, and jazz gigs.

That was what I wanted: I wanted to be like Dick.

By now I was also playing music in school. My parents told me I needed to get a vocation in case the drumming didn't work out, so I enrolled at the local vocational high school, Grady, to train to be an electrician. I quickly joined the school marching band and orchestra; I was the only person able to read drum music.

Around this time my old man started doing better at work, and so we bought a house and moved around the corner to 1413 Fortieth Street. I liked the fact that it had almost exactly the same address. It was a bigger place, and Frank and I got to share our own room with twin beds. We even got all new furniture in the house.

More important, the Fortieth Street house also had an enclosed brick front porch with windows all around it, and this became the center of my world. I moved my drums into there, and my playing went up a notch in intensity—and volume.

My parents bought a big wood-cabinet stereo that we kept in my and Frank's bedroom next to the porch. I would turn it toward my drums and play along to drum records like "Topsy, Part 2" by Cozy Cole or "Let There Be Drums" by Sandy Nelson, and to jazz albums. Poor Frank would be trying to study at his desk right by the stereo. He still claims I'm the reason he is deaf today.

When the second year of my electrical installation course began at Grady, I was horrified to learn that it was virtually the same as the first year! I couldn't face doing all the same shit again, so I told my parents I wanted to switch to a different school, New Utrecht High, and major in music.

This was great for me because I learned all about music theory and harmony and how to play chords on the piano, which I could transfer to guitar and bass. New Utrecht also had another, very major advantage: it was a coed school, whereas Grady had been all male.

My musical skills were coming along great. The front porch at home was by now a full-on music room. Frank would play a little guitar, I saved up and bought myself a fifty-dollar Kay electric guitar, and the family's Lowery organ also found its way out there. I soon got proficient enough to play them all a little.

Yet even so, for me it was still always about the drums, and one man was emerging as my musical hero and inspiration—Gene Krupa.

I loved everything about Gene. He was the best drummer I had ever heard and a tremendous showman and innovator. My mom told me stories of seeing him at the New York Paramount and everybody dancing in the aisles, and I lapped them up.

The first album I bought was *Gene Krupa & Buddy Rich: Drum Battle*. Even today I can still vividly picture that album sleeve. It had photos of Gene and Buddy at their drum kits, superimposed so that Buddy's stand was going through Gene's bass drum. I worshipped that album and listened to it nonstop until I knew every single solo. It was my bible!

Even more than the record, the movie *The Gene Krupa Story* had an incredible impact on me. I watched all the fans and girls running after him and wanting his autograph, and I dreamed that one day that might be me. Even before I could really play drums, I worked out what my autograph would look like.

I had a friend who lived down the block named Harvey Citron who played acoustic guitar. (Oddly enough, he went on to found a guitar company, Citron Guitars.) He knew a guy named Mario Vitalli who played trumpet and guitar, and the three of us became a band, rehearsing our odd little lineup on the porch.

We called ourselves the Rockatones, and I drew a little rocket ship as our logo. We then became the Vidells. I guess we were just copying; in those days, every band seemed to have the words "tones" or "dell" in its name. Before long, through a friend of my father's in the Bronx, we got our first gig. It was at a Saturday night dance, and we were to be paid $7.50 each.

We packed our instruments in the trunk of my father's big old Plymouth with the huge fins, and he drove us up to the Bronx. We were all nervous, but we played chart hits like "At the Hop" and "Cherry Pink and Apple Blossom White" and people seemed to like us. For me, being onstage and playing to an appreciative audience was incredible. I knew I wanted more.

Slowly, the Vidells started playing a few more gigs: weddings, school dances, church events. The JHC, a Jewish center in Brooklyn, became a regular gig. Eventually we dropped the trumpet and got an electric accordion player who played bass with his left hand and worked the accordion with his right. It was all starting to look promising, but I knew if I was going to take things to the next level, and maybe even one day emulate Gene Krupa, I needed a full professional drum kit.

I was to get one. Luckily, one of our neighbors worked for the legendary Gretsch drum company, which was based near us in Brooklyn. By now I had managed to save some money from the Vidells' weekend gigs. My parents helped me out a little as well, and our family friend got me a deal on Gretsch's Red Sparkle kit.

Now we were talking! My Red Sparkle drums were the shit. I can still remember the dimensions: a 22-by-14-inch bass drum, a 14-by-5-inch wood snare drum, a 13-by-9-inch tom-tom, and a 20-inch Zildjian cymbal on a holder that was mounted on the bass drum at a rakish 40-degree angle. It was fucking beautiful, and I could not have been more proud as I set it up on the front porch.

I wasn't the only person to be impressed. "The little girls understand," as Jim Morrison sang, and as I practiced on my new kit daily, I noticed the local girls my age hanging around outside the house, giggling, dancing, and getting off on my drumming. This I liked. I guess you could say it was a harbinger of what was to come.

My brother Vinny used to kind of look up to me as a kid, and he would occasionally sit at my drum kit and make a racket. It was real cute. Naturally, I had no idea what it would eventually lead to.

With my new drums powering our sound, the Vidells began blowing up. We had some funny little business cards made up—"The Vidells: Music for All Occasions"—and soon the bookings flooded in. Before long we were gigging every weekend and some weeknights.

I soon discovered a strong entrepreneurial side to my nature. One week, three different people contacted me asking to book the Vidells for the same Saturday night. I accepted all three bookings, assembled three different lineups of the band from friends of mine, and took a cut of all the gigs. I ended the night with three hundred dollars—an amazing sum for a seventeen-year-old Brooklyn kid doing nothing illegal!

Around this time I graduated high school. My parents still wanted me to have regular employment, so I got a job working as a runner for a financial company. My heart wasn't in it. I would arrive at work late or half-asleep from a late-night gig the night before, and after a few weeks, I got fired.

A job as a stock boy in a linen supply company in Manhattan was equally short-lived, mainly because my employers grew tired of finding me curled up fast asleep among their products. At this point I told my mother and father I couldn't see the point in doing a job I hated five days a week for forty dollars when I could earn five times more through my life's passion every weekend. They found it hard to argue with the math.

And that was the end of my experience of regular employment. I would never have a day job again.

Instead I continued ramping up my fledgling music career as I began to meet more musicians on the local scene. As well as the Vidells, I did a bunch of shows with a guy named John Dilello, who was an amazing John Coltrane–like saxophonist. Playing jazz gigs with him gave my drumming new depth and resonance.

I also began drumming with a keyboard player named Bobby Spinelli, who became a great friend, and a guitarist named Sammy Cicalo in a group called the 3 Beeets. We played rock and R & B covers, and the most striking thing about us was the leopard-skin jackets we inexplicably chose to wear onstage.

Bobby, Sammy, and I, with another friend named John Zolla, also formed a comedy show-band called the Zany Manhattans. We would play songs like "The Sheikh of Araby" with sheets on our heads, and Sammy—a big, hairy 250-pound motherfucker—would come out in belly-dancer gear that we called his Fatima outfit. It was a goofy concept, but we worked it hard and it did OK.

The 3 Beeets and the Zany Manhattans were fun, but they came to an end when Sammy met a girl and, like a good Italian boy, got married and had to find a day job. To replace him, we brought in a virtuoso guitarist/harmonica player we knew named Ron Leejack and a front man named Dean Parrish, who had even had a couple of solo singles in the chart. We changed the band's name to Thursday's

Children; the psychedelic era was coming in, and we thought it sounded cooler.

Thursday's Children played a bunch of shows at Mafia social clubs in Brooklyn. Obviously, they weren't called that, but they were basically Mob hangouts. They were pretty unprepossessing buildings: usually an old store with the windows painted out so nobody in the street could see what was happening inside.

Once we got inside there would be a bare room with a basic bar, tables and chairs, and a load of gangster-looking guys. They always liked how I beat the hell out of my drums and would call me over and ask what my name was. "Hey, Carmine—a good Italian name!" They were generous, too, and would think nothing of giving us fifty-dollar tips.

We played another gig at a dark and dingy blues club named the Lighthouse on the Upper West Side in Manhattan. Today the area is safe and moneyed, but back then it was a real shithole. The Lighthouse's clientele was a mix of hookers, junkies, drug dealers, and a smattering of genuine music aficionados.

We were booked to play opposite a black guitarist named Jimmy James. I had heard a little about this guy on the club circuit, the rumor being that he was an outrageous guitar player and even played with his teeth. The arrangement was that Jimmy and Thursday's Children would play alternating half-hour sets from 9 PM until 4 AM.

When Jimmy played his first set, I realized all the hype was true. I was fucking blown away. Thursday's Children's guitarist, Ron Lee-jack, played the same kind of fuzz-tone-laden blues-rock guitar, but he didn't begin to have Jimmy's levels of charisma, showmanship, or genius. This was like nothing I had ever seen before.

Halfway through the night, the two acts took a break to give the audience a chance to do some serious drinking, and one of the hookers offered to let us use her place to get high. We didn't know her, but Jimmy and I headed off with her to smoke pot and hang out. The building was a dump, and her apartment was a pigsty, but it was close by and had a cool view of Broadway.

Jimmy and I sat and smoked a big joint together and watched the lowlife goings-on below us. We talked about our dreams of somehow making it in music so we could quit playing scuzzy clubs like the Lighthouse.

We must have looked quite the pair. I was in a three-piece pinstripe suit and polka-dot tie, with my short hair teased up with hairspray, while Jimmy was in flamboyant multicolored gear with wild scarves. His hair was greased back; the Afro that was to become his trademark when he had a far more famous name was yet to come.

The onstage wild man was shy, polite, and soft-spoken off it. In fact, he was almost too soft-spoken; I had to keep asking him to speak up and repeat himself. But Jimmy was fun to hang with, his whole face lit up when he smiled, and as we headed back to the Lighthouse, mildly stoned, I thought what a nice guy he was.

Overall it felt like my life was getting pretty good, and soon it got even better. I was desperate to own a car, and I knew exactly what I wanted: a silver '64 Chevy Impala Super Sport with a 327 engine. I had been carefully saving up my gig money, and by my seventeenth birthday I had $1,200 to put down as a deposit. The car cost $2,950, so I got a bank loan for the rest, with my parents cosigning on the strict understanding that I would make all the repayments.

My Chevy had a license plate that said "Silvercup," and that was what I called her. I loved that car—but I didn't always treat her too well.

By this point in my life, I had mostly cut off my ties to the Thirty-Eighth Street Park Boys. When my old hoodlum friends would call up asking if I wanted to hang out or go kick some Hassidic Jews' asses, I'd tell them "Nah, I have a gig" or "I have to rehearse." But I still liked to let off steam and go crazy sometimes.

Now that I had the car, a whole new routine developed. Most Friday and Saturday nights, Thursday's Children would play a gig, then Bobby Spinelli and I would drop my drums at Bobby's place. It would be about midnight, and we would take off in Silvercup to Mitchell's, a local *American Graffiti*–style carhop diner, to eat cheeseburgers and fries and drink root beer.

A bunch of other guys would be there with their cars, too, and at around two in the morning we would all head up to the Belt Parkway, the main highway through Brooklyn. Around fifteen of us would drive abreast across all the three lanes really slowly to block off the other traffic—not that there was much around at that time of night.

We would come to a halt, somebody would yell "One, two, three, go!" and we would speed off, three cars at a time, turning the Belt into our personal drag strip. We would burn some serious rubber down the parkway for two or three miles, then turn around at an unattended police control-point crossover and race back.

I usually won, except when I raced a guy called Ali. He had a '64 Ford that had a bigger engine than my Chevy but that was also heavier. He would win by half a car, so I would switch Silvercup's carburetor to make her more powerful for the next race. But Ali would do stuff to his car as well and beat me again. It was always close, but I never won. It really pissed me off.

This wasn't the only crazy shit that Silvercup and I got up to. In 1964 they were building the Verrazano Bridge over the Narrows to link Brooklyn with Staten Island. After racing, we would head up there in the middle of the night to hang out.

At the time, the bridge was just a building site. The Brooklyn side was just a two-hundred-foot slab of roadway sticking out over the water. There were wooden fences to keep out intruders but no security guard, so it was easy to move the blockade and drive onto the bridge.

One particular night I went with a bunch of friends and smoked pot at the edge of the construction as we gazed 150 feet down into the Narrows. Desperate for kicks, we spotted a work truck full of five-foot-long gas canisters and decided to throw a few of them over the edge.

"Wheeee!" The first canister emitted a high-pitched squeal like a bomb out of a World War II movie as it arrowed through the air, followed by a resounding splash as it hit the water. So did the next nine or ten we hurled down. But we were seeking bigger thrills than this and had a bright idea: Why not push the whole truck over?

Once we had dreamt up this plan, there was no way we were going to back out. One guy used his battered old car to push the truck to the edge of the bridge, and then around ten of us put our shoulders to the tailgate and heaved. It was hard work, but eventually it pitched over the side. There was an eerie silence.

Not for long. The thirty or forty canisters left on the truck fell loose and emitted the same piercing hissing noise as they cartwheeled toward the river. One by one they smacked into the Narrows, but their impact was nothing compared to the almighty smash that the five-ton truck made as it hit the water and slowly sank.

It was so loud that we were sure the cops would come, so we leapt into our cars and hightailed it out of there, saving the laughs and congratulations for when we were safely back at Mitchell's. Our vandalism even made the local TV news, but nobody suspected us and we got away with it.

Silvercup wasn't just a source of illicit thrills for me; she also gave a major boost to my love life. Brooklyn girls liked being driven around in a gleaming '64 Chevy, and Bobby and I would cruise the streets looking for good-looking chicks. We sprinkled Aqua Velva aftershave on the rug by the heater so that the scent would permeate the car. "Wow!" girls told us as they climbed in. "This car smells great!"

Yet by then I didn't need a new car or sweet-smelling eau de toilette to get women. I had learned an important fact, and one that was to transform my life for the better for years—decades—to come: chicks love musicians. Some of them—and this was a hugely welcome revelation—particularly love drummers.

When Thursday's Children began playing the New York club circuit when I was just seventeen, I was still a hapless virgin. After a year on the scene, I had slept with more than three hundred chicks.

At first it was weird to have so many girls showing interest in me, but I quickly got used to it. As the band started playing shows most evenings, it became normal to have a different chick every night of the week. Sometimes it was two. I would have a quickie with a girl in the back of the club, then another one would take me back to her apartment after the show.

Nobody ever forgets the first time they had sex, and I'm no exception. We played a gig in Manhattan, and after the show Bobby and I got talking to two girls in the club. Eventually my chick said the words every man longs to hear: "Do you want to come back to our place?"

She lived in Queens, so we all jumped in Silvercup and headed out there. I had assumed "our place" meant the two girls shared an apartment, but when we arrived it transpired my new lady friend lived with her husband, a soldier who wouldn't return from the local army base until six in the morning.

By then it was 3 AM, so Bobby and his girl stayed in the living room, while our hostess and I vanished to the bedroom. We got down to some heavy petting, which was normally as far as I was allowed to go, but this chick pulled me on top of her and we went all the way. One thought dominated my mind: *Wow! This is cool!*

As usual for first-timers, I didn't last very long, and I had just got my rocks off and was regaining my breath when Bobby and the other woman ran in the room. The friend got straight to the point: "Your husband is home!"

"I thought he was working late!" my chick gasped and turned to her illicit guests. "Out the window!"

So like in some bad movie, Bobby and I ran around gathering our clothes and leapt out the window in our boxer shorts. Luckily, we were on the ground floor, so it was only a three-foot drop. Crouching double, we hid between two parked cars, threw our clothes on, ran to Silvercup, and got the hell out of there.

And what was the name of the angel who took me on this rite of passage and turned me from a boy into a man? I'm sorry to confess that I don't have a clue.

After my first time, the chicks began piling up at a crazy rate. Thursday's Children got a regular four-nights-a-week gig at a Greenwich Village club called Fox's Corner. A blonde named Mary used to hang out there. She was four years older than me, much more sophisticated, and trained me in the arts of loving: taking baths together, different sexual positions, blow jobs, and the like. Naturally, I was a very willing student.

My liaisons with Mary were to come to a dramatic end. One night in Fox's Corner I was packing my gear away when a guy came up to me, pointed at her across the room, and said, "I hear you're dating her."

"Well I'm screwing the hell out of her!" I told him.

"Not any more you're not," he said, and suddenly I had a gun pointing at my head as he told me that his Mafia boss was also fucking around with Mary. I finished packing up my drums and never went to Fox's Corner again.

Most of the girls I met were just wham, bam, thank you ma'am, but some encounters were plain weird. One Spanish lady invited me up to her place, where she had a little dog. As we got down to business, she confessed that she often put food on her pussy so the dog would lick it off and lick her out at the same time. It grossed me out so much that I made my excuses and left.

A woman from out of town took me to her hotel and said, "Let me get more comfortable." I liked the sound of that but was less enthusiastic when she whipped off her false eyelashes and wig, a hugely padded bra, and even a false butt. She was haggard by now, so when she went to the bathroom, I quickly split.

While I was leading this new life as a teenage rock-and-roll Casanova, I was still living at home. I never took girls there, and my father would bust my balls if I rolled in at seven in the morning as he was getting ready for work. I would invent some crazy story about Silvercup breaking down, to no avail: "You can tell your mother that shit—I know what you've been up to!"

The other extraordinary element of my rampant promiscuity was that I had a girlfriend.

I had met Marion in around tenth grade at high school, and we started dating. We used to fight a lot. One night we were having a huge argument, she ran into the bathroom and I put my hand right through a painted door that I thought was wood but turned out to be glass. I had to have stitches and played that night's gig with a splint. But we normally made up and by now had been together around three years.

Marion had no idea about my serial cheating, and to me it didn't seem anything unusual. I was young, and it was the Brooklyn way—maybe we were copying the Mafia guys, who all had wives at home and gangster groupies on the go? Marion lived at home with her father, so I would go around there for a coffee and then head off into the night to start partying.

Overall I couldn't find much fault with my life in 1964. I was having a great time playing drums, screwing chicks, and racing my car—what wasn't to love? But then something came along that I knew could very easily tear my playhouse down.

By '64, America was getting sucked deeper into Vietnam, and with my eighteenth birthday rapidly nearing, I knew that I would get drafted. I didn't know or care about the war, to the despair of my father, who would tell me, "You've got to watch the news! Read the newspapers!"

I knew one thing about Vietnam: I didn't want to go there. So when my draft papers and an appointment for a physical examination arrived, I put a plan into operation. I didn't shave for days, I stayed up for two nights solid beforehand, and I smoked a load of pot before leaving for my interview. By the time I got there, I looked terrible and was out of my fucking tree.

I walked in the door, and the recruiting sergeant asked me if I did any drugs. He didn't seem at all fazed when I replied that I smoked pot. "Everybody does," he replied. Clearly I was going to have to up the ante.

The soldier handed me a sheet of paper with a list of questions asking if I had taken heroin, cocaine, acid, amphetamines, and so on. I had never even seen any of them, but I checked every box. This time the sergeant did look a little shocked, and sent me off to see the army psychiatrist.

As the doc asked me questions, I bit my nails, twitched, and blurted out random answers that bore no relation to what he had asked me. As an actor, I must have convinced in my role as a basket case, as the recruiters rated me a 4F: a nervous wreck who under no circumstances should be allowed to own a gun or fight for his country. Some friends having the same interview as me were there for three hours. I was in and out in thirty minutes.

While I avoided going to war, Vietnam had one large impact on my life: I married Marion. It was easier to avoid the draft if you had a family, so when the papers arrived, I proposed to her. She accepted. After I fooled the recruiters, I was all for calling it off, but my horrified parents made clear that this was not an option.

They had already booked a local catering hall and a band and invited two hundred guests, and there was no way they were going to cancel all that. In fact, my mother put it very directly, as was her habit: "I went to all this trouble to organize this. We're going through with it, you son of a bitch!" So the big Brooklyn Italian wedding went ahead, with a very reluctant groom at its core.

Suddenly I was nineteen years old and married.

If I am honest, this unwanted development had no real effect on my lifestyle. I continued screwing around and gigging with Thursday's Children. And I had just played a show at a pokey little hole-in-the-wall in Garfield, New Jersey, called the Choo Choo Club when two guys named Mark and Tim asked me to join their band. It was called the Pigeons.

# 2

# A SUPREME WAY
# TO FUDGE REALITY

*In which Drummerdude flies from the Pigeons to Vanilla Fudge, is managed by the Mob, trashes his first hotel room, becomes an international rock star, encounters a charming young maiden named Suck-A-Luck, and goes native in swinging London*

 *Mark Stein was a big, wide-bodied guy with* kinky, curly hair and a slightly crazed stare. Tim Bogert wore black-rimmed glasses and looked at first glance like a bit of a bookworm. As we talked in the Choo Choo Club, it became clear that these two intense guys were on a mission: to get me to take wing from Thursday's Children and fly to the Pigeons.

At first I wasn't sure. Everything was pretty great in my life. Thursday's Children were making good money, or so we thought, and I was enjoying the buzz and the security of being in a group with my best friends. But I had to hand it to Mark and Tim; they sure were persistent—and persuasive.

They were also very complimentary, falling over themselves to tell me they loved that I not only had a great drumming technique—particularly my right foot, they noted—but also sang. This appealed to them, they said, as the current Pigeons drummer wasn't very technical, which was holding them back.

"We want to make it!" Mark enthused. "We want to draw big crowds and try this new music that's happening on Long Island and have hit records!" He also told me they had a manager who was willing to put the band on a salary so that they could concentrate on playing music.

This was all new to me, and it sounded like a major leap from Thursday's Children's fun but amateurish shtick. Yet it took me by surprise. I had never thought about my future too hard, assuming I would eke out a comfortable living through music like Dick Benette. But hit records? A salary? They had my attention and my interest. I gave Mark and Tim my phone number and told them I'd think about it.

They called me up a few days later, told me they had already fired their drummer, and invited me to a rehearsal to check them out. Mark was on keyboards and sang lead vocals, while Tim was on bass and sang. A good-looking, shaggy-haired Italian American guitarist and singer named Vince Martell rounded out the band.

As they rehearsed, it took me no time at all to realize they were all talented as fuck.

We jammed a little, and it blew me away. Tim was the first bassist I had ever played with, and what a way to start! He was one emotional and innovative musician. Mark was a great B3 organ player, and when he opened his mouth, it knocked me backward. He was an incredible singer with so much soul.

Vince—or Vinny, as everybody called him—was a really nice guy, a pretty solid guitarist, and a great rhythm guitar player. They were all easy to play with, and when we sang harmonies on rockier versions of R & B/soul classics, like Wilson Pickett's "In the Midnight Hour" and the Temptations' "It's Growing," I felt goose bumps on my arms. Shit, this could be special!

So that was it. I was in. I was a Pigeon.

Now it was time to meet our manager, at which point I did a sharp double take. I may not have heard of the Pigeons before they flocked my way, but I had met their manager before—and he had fucking terrified me.

A couple of months earlier, Thursday's Children had played a bunch of shows at a huge Long Island club called the Shell House. For our last show there, it was under new management and had gained a clientele of what looked like serious Mafia guys. It had also changed its name to the Action House.

when we had so many gigs booked that we ended up staying in the Orphanage for six weeks.

Jerry also accompanied us when the Pigeons went even further afield. Phil had bought us a van to get around, and in November '66 he booked us a bunch of dates at a club in Miami. We drove all the way down with our gear. None of us had traveled much, so we were pretty naive. I remember we stopped for a burger at a McDonalds. A board outside read, "Three Million Burgers Sold!" and we thought it meant the burgers had all been sold from that branch!

We stayed down in Florida for four weeks, and we were such crazy young fuckers that we went wild. We met some local girls, and one night after the gig they invited us back to their house to party. As we left the party, stoned, in the early hours, we spotted hundreds of giant water bugs swarming down a manhole cover in the street outside.

We lifted up the cover to see thousands of bugs and cockroaches wriggling around. They looked utterly disgusting, and our collective band mind quickly reached a decision: there would have to be a Great Bug Massacre. As luck would have it, we had bought some Fourth of July–style fireworks in Miami a few days earlier. We made a time bomb by taping four cherry bombs to a cigarette, which would burn down and light the fuses, and lowered it into the manhole.

We were safely in the van when our bomb exploded, blowing the manhole cover into the air. It sounded like I had ended up in Vietnam after all. We raced off.

When we returned to the party an hour later, the cockroaches and bugs were all over the outside of the three-story apartment, the cars, the sidewalk—and the indestructible little bastards were still alive! It was gross.

The Great Bug Massacre gave us a taste for pranks down in Miami. The next morning we honed in on Tim. He and I were sharing a hotel room, as we would do for years. Tim is as blind as a bat without his specs, so we picked orange peels and other shit out of the garbage, hid his glasses, and when he woke up told him, "Hey, Tim! Jerry made you some breakfast!"

Tim slouched over to the table and was about to start eating the garbage when we told him we were only kidding and gave him his glasses. He put them on, yelled "You fucks!" and flipped the table over in anger. Getting carried away, we smashed up the beds, the closets, the television; in no time, before we knew it, we had trashed the room.

We surveyed the damage. Realizing we were in deep shit, we locked the room door with the chain and exited through the window. When they saw what we had done, the hotel called the cops, who issued warrants for our arrests. (The next time we came to Florida, by which time we had changed our band name and were playing way bigger venues, someone busted our balls and told us the warrants were still valid and the police were looking for us after the show. We were so paranoid that Mark Stein and I spent the hours leading up to our flight out hiding in a bathroom at the airport.)

Phil and Chubby didn't mind us doing shit like that as long as we were working hard to get our sound together. In fact, we had formed a nice relationship with our wiseguy management team. They were lovely guys as long as you stayed on their side and never crossed them.

Over time I learned a little more about Phil. He and Chubby had started out stealing hubcaps as kids in Brooklyn but began making serious money via real estate and, shall we say, other means. By the time I joined the Pigeons, he owned huge properties all over Brooklyn, Queens, and Long Island and was a multimillionaire.

Phil was clearly a smart businessman with obvious Mob affiliations. He carried himself that way, and in any case it was no big deal to have Mafia links in New York back then. Yet as the Pigeons carried on rehearsing in the Action House, we started to realize that Phil might actually be more connected than we had imagined.

We didn't care. Frankly, I was more concerned with the band and cleaning up my personal life. Spending all my time out on Long Island, I hardly ever saw Marion. The few nights I was home, she would go to bed early because she had work the next day, and I would sit up alone, bored, watching TV, eating pizza, and gaining weight.

Now that I knew I wasn't bound for Vietnam, what was the point in being married? When the Pigeons returned from Florida, I filed for an annulment. Our marriage had lasted nine months. Marion was upset, but having been a reluctant nineteen-year-old groom, I was now twenty, single again, and delighted to be so.

The Pigeons were still playing slowed-down, rearranged versions of R & B and Motown classics during our daily Action House rehearsals. That kind of thing was big in New York and Long Island at the time. The Vagrants and the Rich Kids were just two of the groups who were doing it, and we would mess around in rehearsals, making big productions out of songs like "Out of My Head" by Little Anthony and the Imperials.

One night Mark and Tim had a brainwave about another number we could rework in that vein. Their inspiration was to rocket us out of the Action House and change all of our lives forever. And, like all great ideas, it could not have been fucking simpler.

We used to hang out at a club called Cheetah in Manhattan now and then, and one night at the start of '67, Mark and Tim were sitting outside the Cheetah in a car, smoking a joint. They had the car radio on, and when Diana Ross and the Supremes' "You Keep Me Hangin' On" came on, a lightbulb went on over their heads. Shit, the Pigeons should rearrange this song and give it some drama!

They came into our next rehearsal really buzzed, and when they shared the idea with Vinny and me, we loved it. As a band, we believed a song's music should match the lyrics, and that song's just didn't. The Supremes' music was all fast and happy, but the words weren't. You don't sing "Set me free, why don't you?" if you're in a good place, right?

Mark had the original arrangement idea, and we started fucking around musically with it to bring out the emotion in the lyrics. We moved the bridge chords around, we wrote a new melody, but most of all we put in all these huge, dramatic buildups and crescendos—and, of course, we slowed the pace of the song down to a crawl. We threw the kitchen sink at it.

While we were knocking "Keep Me Hangin' On" into shape, we were also working on heavyweight, bluesy psychedelic covers of a bunch of other tracks, such as the Beatles' "Ticket to Ride" and "Eleanor Rigby" and Curtis Mayfield's "People Get Ready." We were paying our dues by playing loads of East Coast dates and sleeping on people's floors to save money.

Phil wanted us to make a demo tape and told one of his people, Shelly Finkle (who, oddly enough, was years later to manage Mike

Tyson), to get ahold of Shadow Morton, the young New York producer who had written and produced big hits like "Remember (Walking in the Sand)" and "Leader of the Pack" for the Shangri-Las.

This was to prove easier said than done.

When Shelly first called Shadow, he simply wasn't interested in coming to Long Island to see some starting-out band that he had never heard of. Shelly turned up at his Manhattan studio with a limo and two bottles of whisky and drove him out to the Action House to see us. Shadow loved our arrangements, particularly on "You Keep Me Hangin' On," and agreed to produce a demo.

By now the Pigeons were generally acknowledged to be a good, tight live band. But we had never done any recording, so we were anxious when we turned up at the studio. Also, Shadow was a big deal. He was only slightly older than us, with wild, tousled long hair. He was eccentric and liked a drink. After we ran through "Hangin' On" in the studio, he nodded and said, "OK, let's play it for the engineer."

We did the song again, really still warming up, but the engineer had the tape rolling and we nailed it in one take, in mono. That was the version that would come to be heard all over the world. When we finished, Shadow played it back to us and we all had the same reaction: "Wow! That sounds fucking amazing!"

It did. It still does. Nowadays I call it the seven-and-a-half minutes that changed my life, but of course I didn't know that then. I was just blown away by how amazing my drums sounded—so big and so powerful.

Phil was a great businessman, and he was always confident that we would make it. He would tell me, "If you're not a millionaire by twenty-five, I'll give you a blow job!" That was a fucking incentive to succeed right there! But he didn't know the music industry, so Shadow and Phil's big-shot entertainment lawyer, Stevens H. Weiss, went off to get us a record deal.

Our demo got plenty of interest, and in April 1967 the Pigeons signed to Atlantic Records. There was one drawback, however: Atlantic Records didn't want to sign "the Pigeons." Ahmet Ertegun, the label's founder and president, didn't like our name and told us we had to change it. We didn't mind; in fact, I had always thought the Pigeons was a weird thing to be called but had just gone along with it.

We tried to think up a new name but were getting nowhere until we played a gig at the Page 2 club in Long Island and ended up talking to a chick named Dee Dee who worked there. She told us how her grandfather used to call her Vanilla Fudge. Then she looked at us and added, "Maybe you guys should call yourselves that—you're like white soul music."

Vanilla Fudge! We liked it. We told Phil, and he liked it. We told Atlantic, and they liked it, too. Vanilla Fudge it was.

Shadow had also taken our demo to Scott Muni, the New York radio DJ who was then playing all the progressive rock and underground sounds like the Beatles, Jimi Hendrix, and Jefferson Airplane on WOR-FM. He started spinning it on the air, as did Murray the K.

I'll never forget the first time I heard "Keep Me Hangin' On" on the radio. I couldn't take Jerry to my parents' place, so Phil would let us use one of the apartments he owned. I was on the way there with her in my Chevy when it came on the air. It was an incredible moment. All I could think was, *Wow, I wonder how many people are listening to this.* Like a good Italian boy, I phoned my mother to see if she had heard it; she was as excited as I was.

It felt like we were making it. I guess "You Keep Me Hangin' On" didn't sound like anything else out there at the time, and it captured people's imaginations. Listeners started phoning the station, asking what the song was and who this weird band Vanilla Fudge were.

Because of this interest, WOR-FM entered us into a just-for-fun contest they did on-air, where they played three new songs and asked listeners to call in and say which they liked the most. The DJ put us up against the Beatles and the Beach Boys, probably the two biggest bands in America right then—and, don't forget, our track was only a demo!

We had just played a gig in Poughkeepsie, in upstate New York, and were about to sleep on a friend's floor when Phil phoned us up. "Hey, you guys won the radio contest!" he told us. "You beat the fucking Beach Boys and the Beatles!" Our manager was really stoked, and so were we.

It was on the same trip to Poughkeepsie that I wandered into a pawnshop and spent five dollars on a twenty-six-inch bass drum. I refinished it at home to match my Red Sparkle kit. As some people have been kind enough to say that it revolutionized the sound of drums in rock music, I guess I should consider it five bucks well spent.

Atlantic knew they had to capitalize on the buzz around us and rushed out two versions of "You Keep Me Hangin' On" in June—our initial seven-minute epic and a more radio-friendly three-minute edit. DJs played them like crazy, and that summer of 1967, we seemed to hear them everywhere we went.

At this point, everything was going at warp speed. Had it really only been nine months since I had joined an anonymous Long Island bar band named the Pigeons? Now we were Vanilla Fudge, we had a huge record corporation behind us, and we had a single zooming up the *Billboard* and *Cashbox* charts.

I didn't know how the fuck it had all happened, but I knew that I loved it.

In between gigs, we finished off our self-titled debut album with Shadow. As well as the Supremes and Beatles numbers, we also included heavy-ass rearrangements of "She's Not There" by the Zombies and even Sonny and Cher's "Bang Bang."

There was one weird thing about that album. Everybody in the band had long hair, at least shoulder length, but a few local groups at the time were wearing it shorter and cleaning up their looks, and we did the same. So when our group photo appeared on the album sleeve, we looked clean-cut and collegiate, like the other Long Island bands. That didn't last.

Next we had another major rock-and-roll rite of passage: our first West Coast tour. Despite being twenty years old, my sole trip outside the New York tristate area before that point had been to Florida with the Pigeons, but now Vanilla Fudge had July dates booked in Portland, Oregon—as the support act to the Mamas and the Papas, no less.

Before we flew west, I finished with Jerry. She had started demanding that we get married, and given my recent marital history, I figured I was way too young to start treading that path again. Plus, maybe I had an inkling that very soon, female company would not be hard to come by.

Vanilla Fudge got a night flight to Oregon because it was the cheapest option. I had never been on a plane before, so of course Phil took full advantage, busting my balls by sitting behind me, smashing the back of my seat, and yelling out "Oh, fuck!" as if something was wrong and the plane was going to crash. I was shit-scared but pretended not to be.

The slapstick continued when we arrived in the early hours. Phil had appointed himself our tour manager but had no directional sense and drove the rental car around in circles for hours, for some reason spending some time in a train yard. When we eventually found our hotel, it was a real fleapit, and we were crammed in three to a room—even Mobster millionaire Phil.

On our first West Coast morning, we ate breakfast through the haze of our virgin jetlag and then headed off to check out the venue. The first gig was at Portland Coliseum, which held ten thousand people or so—way more than we had ever played to before. We all stood out front and read the marquee. "The Mamas and the Papas," it proclaimed in huge letters, and beneath it, all itty-bitty: "Vanilla Fudge."

As we stood enjoying the sight of our name in lights—even tiny ones—a car drove past. Spotting us on the sidewalk, the guys inside yelled out, "Vanilla Fudge? Vanilla Shit!" Way to spoil our buzz! We were outraged and, like the New York punks we were, went chasing after the car, flipping the bird and yelling, "Fuck you! Come back here, assholes!" Needless to say, they didn't come back.

The Mamas and the Papas and Vanilla Fudge weren't a great fit. They were all about peace and love; we were noise and full-on aggression. We were psyched for the show, but at first the fans, who were used to the laid-back Californian sound of the likes of the Byrds and Buffalo Springfield, didn't know what to make of us with our New York noise.

After a couple of numbers, Mark said something like, "Right, now we're going to do another song," and it drew a few isolated boos from the crowd. This pissed him off, and he flew off the handle: "Look, we flew three thousand miles to give you this show, and we are going to give it you whether you like it or not!" To our surprise, this rebuke drew a round of applause. It was a turning point for the gig, and the crowd even demanded an encore, to our delight.

Next we drove to Seattle, where they were hipper to Vanilla Fudge, even to the extent that a local radio station declared it to be Vanilla Fudge Day. Nevertheless, our first show there was kind of lame. We supported Sonny and Cher, who were boring, at a big outdoor gig where the crowd was stuck fifty feet away on the other side of a lake.

We had another Seattle show a few days later at the Eagles Ballroom and went down the night before to check out the venue. The Yardbirds were on and blew us away, especially when we went backstage after the show and found they were nice guys. It was the first time we met Jimmy Page. We were to get to know him very well in years to come.

Our own show there was an eye-opener, in more ways than one. It was the first time we happened across West Coast hippie chicks in see-through tops with no bras, and our eyes were popping out like cartoon characters. If that was what peace and love was all about, we wanted in!

In fact, that West Coast trip was our initiation into the world of groupies. We had a single on the *Billboard* chart, an album poised for release and getting a big push, and we were making a name for ourselves. Suddenly there was no shortage of girls wanting to hang out with Vanilla Fudge.

Seattle was a great example. We were staying at a cool hotel called the University Inn and met some girls who were happy to come back and party with us. We were all smoking pot and having sex with the chicks when Vinny, who was my roommate on that trip, announced he was going to take a bath with his girl.

They vanished into the bathroom, but in their stoned and aroused state, they forgot to turn the faucet off. Soon water was cascading not just over the side of the bath but under the door and all through the bedroom. The floor became a lake, and to our addled minds it made sense to try to mop up the water with the bedsheets. Cue one fucking great mess.

One of our roadies, who was totally wired on pot, declared that he was going to catch the elevator down to the lobby in the nude. The band trooped down to see him stumble into reception stark naked, together with a chick in just her bra and panties. The hotel manager kicked us out on the spot.

In years to come, our love of groupies and hotel trashing led to us being thrown out of a crazy number of hotels. It was fucking dumb behavior, but we were young, reckless, and rock and roll. We just figured, why shouldn't we do what the fuck we want? Of course, we never realized until our accountants told us years later that, via Atlantic, we were *paying* for all the damage.

Unknown to us, we were also paying for the stretch limo the record company sent to LAX the next morning to meet us as we flew in from Seattle to Los Angeles. The car took us straight to the Century Plaza, the most expensive hotel in the city.

Man, I fell in love with L.A. the second I set eyes on it. So this was why they called California the golden state! I loved the haze of sun that shimmered over the city, the palm trees, the cool cars, and the beautiful women. To my naive young eyes, the famous Hollywood sign high in the hills looked impossibly glamorous.

Faced with a free day before playing the Whisky a Go-Go, we rented a car, checked out Venice Beach, and zoomed down Sunset Strip, excited young tourists in the City of Angels. We also did some radio interviews and audaciously informed L.A. on-air that we intended to have the mother of all parties on our floor at the Century Plaza. When we got back to the hotel, we found five hundred excited fans waiting in the lobby.

Fuck! Had our lives suddenly changed or what?

We had a rather more exclusive party in mind, so we picked out a bunch of the hottest chicks and took them up to our floor. We decided to take a shortcut to see which of them were up for sex. Gathering them in one bedroom, the four of us disappeared into the bathroom, emerging a minute later . . . butt naked.

A couple of girls freaked and ran out of the room. Most of them didn't. Let's just call it a process of natural selection.

We had an amazing sex party with the girls who were left, all swapping partners and getting into all kinds of shit, and then decided that we were hungry and would treat our guests to a meal. We phoned room service and ordered ten steak dinners, not even bothering to check out what they cost—again, we assumed Atlantic was footing the bill.

Phil was slightly more clued in, and when he saw the cost of our ten-person sex-party dinner, he decided we had better downsize from the Century Plaza, and pronto. The next morning we moved en masse to a hotel on Sunset Strip near the Whisky a Go-Go, where we were due to play that night.

Vanilla Fudge's initiation into the world of free love was set to continue. We spent the evening before our Whisky show hanging out in the club with two sexy groupie chicks, although they didn't come back with us that night. The following evening was a different story. We played an awesome gig to a packed Whisky crowd who really got what we were trying to do. I didn't care much for our support act, though—some band called Alice Cooper, who had a cheesy panto-horror stage set and were throwing rubber chickens around. I could tell they were never going to get anywhere.

After the show, the two girls came back to our hotel, and we were all sitting around with them in a bedroom, stoned, telling them how much we would like to have sex with them.

"Well, I'm really hungry," one of the chicks yawned.

Yes, we told her, but we'd love to fuck your brains out!

"That's cool, but I'd like a hamburger first," she drawled.

Talk about an offer we couldn't refuse! We called down to room service for a burger. While we were waiting she started giving blow jobs to everybody in the room—band, roadies, whoever. We were waiting in line with our dicks in our hands, like a porn film.

The girl took a break when her burger arrived, but then a truly debauched night ensued. We had two adjoining hotel rooms, and the second chick decided she was as happy to fuck all comers as her friend was to suck them. They took a room each. After finishing her burger, Suck-A-Luck, as we christened the first girl, would give expert head to a guy—or sometimes two at a time—as her friend waited next door.

As soon as one of us got a hard-on, he transferred next door to fuck the other chick, while Suck-A-Luck turned her hand and her mouth to her next client. It was a great system. We were all high from the nonstop reefers, and we went on until about 5 AM.

When we woke up, we did it all again before breakfast.

This West Coast trip was cool! It was amazing to me how many girls wanted to have sex with us just because we were in a band that was getting well known! That 1967 trip established firmly in my mind the idea that sex was a major part of life on the road. Soon we all felt like we needed at least one girl per day just to feed our egos.

From L.A. we swung down to Huntington Beach to play at a club called the Golden Bear. This was a must to play for upcoming bands visiting L.A. and was a cool hippie joint that was perfect for us. We were booked into a Ramada Inn on Highway 1, and I was just waking up after our first night there when there was a knock at my door.

"Maid service!"

The maid came in—and wow! She was eighteen and beautiful, with a cute little pumpkin-like face and an amazing body. I had been doing well with girls lately, so I started calling her Pumpkin and hitting on her. At first she said she couldn't fool around with guests, but in no time she had stopped trying to make my bed and was climbing into it.

The last leg of the mini-tour found us back in L.A., where Suck-A-Luck and her pal rejoined us for a repeat performance. We all wanted to stay in California forever, but after a last frenzy of sun, sex, and buying hippie threads on Sunset, we got the plane back to New York.

In truth, our life there was cool, too. Vinny and I started sharing an apartment right on the ocean in Long Beach, Long Island. It wasn't far from the Action House, and by now the band was pretty much spending every spare moment at Phil's club.

You couldn't blame us! We were treated like kings there. Phil made sure we ate and drank for free, and every night was full of guys coming up to us to tell us how they loved our music and what great musicians we were and girls looking at us like they wanted to fuck us—and normally doing it.

What was not to like?

The end of summer saw the release of the *Vanilla Fudge* album, and in its second week it jumped from number two hundred to number thirty-three on the chart, which gave our fast-developing egos another boost. We made a whistle-stop return trip to the West Coast for another two weeks of wild shows, increasingly inventive hotel-room trashing, and groupie antics.

Playing the Cheetah Club in Santa Monica, I tried to bounce my drumstick off the snare and catch it, succeeding only in smacking myself above my eye with the stick. I had to play the next show with a gauze patch, sunglasses, and blood running down my face. We also played the Anaheim Convention Center, proving a hard act to follow for headliners the Bee Gees.

Out in California, we met Neil Young, Stephen Stills, and the rest of Buffalo Springfield backstage at the Bee Gees show, and they told us the West Coast bands really respected Vanilla Fudge. That meant a lot to us; we had no idea, as we were in our own little bubble of Long Island and the Action House.

If the West Coast had been exciting for us, what happened next blew our minds: Vanilla Fudge were going to England.

This was a massive deal for us. At the time, Britain seemed like the center of the rock-and-roll world, and the British Invasion had made bands like the Beatles, the Rolling Stones, and the Animals into superstars in the United States. We took limos to the airport, and there were fans waiting to see us off. We were buzzing.

The flight to Europe was so fucking long that we were going out of our minds. I got sick and spent the landing puking down the toilet. Still, we were psyched to be in London, and now we just needed a guy to be our roadie/tour manager and show us the cool places to go. We quickly found one.

With a name like Bruce Wayne, his nickname had to be Batman. Bruce was an English roadie with wild permed hair that stuck out as if he had put his fingers in an electric socket. We hired him for our dates, and he made it his mission to teach us the dos and don'ts of England—important stuff like the fact that you could buy White Castle–like American burgers in joints called Wimpy Bars.

"You Keep Me Hangin' On" was in the top twenty in Britain at the time, so people knew who Vanilla Fudge were. We had three London shows lined up, but first we played some warm-up gigs in the English Midlands. Typical American tourists, we loved playing Nottingham, as it gave us a chance to drop by Sherwood Forest, where Robin Hood—Robin fucking Hood!—came from. We got a great reaction at those Midlands shows, and the whole experience was really exciting.

I was even more excited by the beautiful girl with black hair and enormous tits who I met at our show in Leicester and spent the night with. All my life I have been a sucker for a big pair of tits. I'm hardly the first man to feel this way, but I have luckily had more chances than most to indulge my preference.

Back in London, Bruce Wayne introduced us to a city-center private members' club called the Speakeasy. It probably held about three hundred people and at that time was the hip hangout for major bands, singers, and anybody in music. And it was there, on one of our first nights in London, that I met the guy who was to bring both joy and grief to my musical career for decades to come.

The first thing I noticed about Jeff Beck was the hair. He had that weird pineapple cut that a few English bands seemed to like. It towered so high on his head that it hid the fact that he was actually not all that tall and was a skinny guy with pretty rough skin. But it was a real thrill to meet this English guy who was already a big guitar hero in the Yardbirds.

Jeff appeared shy and was very soft-spoken, but he seemed to be into Vanilla Fudge, and one night down at the Speakeasy, he, Tim Bogert, and I had an impromptu jam. It rocked! The three of us clearly had great chemistry, but I can't claim we got any clairvoyant vision of our joint musical future. We were just chilling and having fun.

Vanilla Fudge weren't the only American hopefuls trying to get a toehold in England. As "You Keep Me Hangin' On" had been tearing up the chart in the States, we had kept hearing about a wild new guitarist called Jimi Hendrix who did crazy stuff like set his guitar on fire. Hendrix seemed to be everywhere, wowing the Monterey Pop Festival and being kicked off a joint tour with the Monkees because of his way-out music and lewd antics.

One summer's day in New York, I had been flicking through a music magazine and happened across a picture of Hendrix playing his guitar with his teeth. My jaw dropped. He had a huge Afro, but I recognized him as Jimmy James, my acquaintance from the hooker's filthy apartment on Broadway.

I hadn't seen him since, but one evening at the Speakeasy I noticed lots of people crowding around someone. It was Jimi. When the crowd moved away, I went over to say hi. We reminisced about the hooker's pit, I told him that I was now in Vanilla Fudge, and he said that he had heard our stuff and dug it. Jimmy James was still a sweet, quietly spoken guy, but now he had a real aura; nobody could doubt that he was a rock star.

The Who wrote a song about the Speakeasy, with a chorus that ran "Speakeasy, drink easy, pull easy," but initially this was not true for Vanilla Fudge. We were desperate to screw English chicks, but although we had had some success in the Midlands, London girls just did not want to know us.

London chicks were polished, reserved, and classy—and Vanilla Fudge were none of those things. Barely out of our teens, we were brash, loud, and excitable, and some people found our aggressive New York manners (or lack of them) obnoxious. We even overheard a few muttered comments about "loud-mouthed Americans."

Our first London gig was a place called the Finsbury Park Theatre (which later became the famous Rainbow Theatre). We played with Traffic and the Herd, Peter Frampton's band. We got to meet Frampton (whom we had never heard of at the time), plus Steve Winwood and Jim Capaldi, whom we knew of because we loved Traffic. They were all cool.

The second show, at the Speakeasy, was a way bigger deal for us. The venue was so packed it was impossible to move in the crowd. Huddled in our tiny dressing room preshow, we kept hearing fresh bulletins about stars who were supposedly there: The Beatles had turned up! The Rolling Stones were in the club! Oh, and the Who were there, too! The audience was rammed in so tight that the Queen of England could have been there, for all we knew.

Nervous and high on adrenaline and good-quality London pot, we were a fucking nuclear blast that night. When we played "Hangin' On" and did the dynamic break leading up to the organ section, the place went wild. It was the most extreme reaction we had ever had, and it was the night that made our name in London. Our Speakeasy mutilation of "Eleanor Rigby" was later to turn up on a seminal sixties UK art film titled *Popcorn*, alongside Mick Jagger, Hendrix, and Joe Cocker.

That night everybody wanted to talk to me about my Red Sparkle drum set with its custom twenty-six-by-fifteen-inch bass drum. Not even serious A-list drummers had seen one that big before. Keith Moon, Jim Capaldi, and Jimi Hendrix's drummer, Mitch Mitchell, all sought me out to rave about my kit.

This was all awesome, but as four horny young New Yorkers, it seemed just as important to us that after our ice-breaking, wild Speakeasy set, London's girls were willing to party with us. It was at this point that we came up against an intractable enemy—our hotel.

Vanilla Fudge were totally fixated on taking our pursuit of free love international, and our hotel was just as intent on stopping us from doing it. The management had some weird house rule against women who were not guests going up to the rooms, and the jerk-off front-desk staff were determined to enforce it. When we did manage to sneak a girl in, the manager found out and came up to our rooms to tell her to leave. We reacted in the only way we knew: we screamed, threw shit around, and got kicked out.

Luckily, the place we transferred to had a more modern attitude toward rock-star guests entertaining female admirers, which was convenient, because we gained a few more after we played our last London show, supporting the Who at the Saville Theatre in front of three thousand people.

We had seen Hendrix in the same theater the week before, with his towering stack of Marshall amps, and realized that we would need the same power to blow away a crowd as big as that. All we had shipped from the States was my drum kit and a couple of amps—no way would they be enough for this cavernous venue.

Our English superhero, Bruce Wayne, again came to our rescue, negotiating a deal for us to borrow the Yardbirds' huge Vox backline. We opened our set with a spotlight trained on the Vanilla Fudge logo on my bass drum. The red pilot lights from a mountain of amps twinkled all around us. We played one of our best-ever shows, and when I sang "People Get Ready" a cappella, apart from Mark's organ, you could have heard a pin drop. It was an amazing, colossal show—a whole bunch of reviews said we even upstaged the Who.

Our reverse British Invasion had been a fucking blast. We ended our trip with a serious shopping trip to Carnaby Street, the home of London's happening hippie and mod gear. By the end of the UK trip, I was sleeping with a girl named Pauline, who worked the switchboard in our last hotel. (So they *were* more liberal than the previous establishment!) She promised to keep sending me new clothes after I had left, which I thought was really cool.

We were expanding our minds and our horizons. New York and Long Island used to be all we knew; now we felt like we had conquered London. Vanilla Fudge were on top of the world. And the view was about to get even more spectacular.

# 3

# WHY IS HITLER ON OUR ALBUM?

*In which Drummerdude begins his forty-year Fu Manchu impersonation, buys contraband from Henry Hill, is terrified of a Mob capo, becomes expert at "the Finale," accidentally makes a preposterous album starring JFK and the Nuremburg rally, and assures Jimi Hendrix that Electric Ladyland is OK*

*When Vanilla Fudge landed back in New York* and swaggered off the London plane, we looked like some wild new English band. I guess we had gone a little native. I was a vision of fuck-knows-what in a lush red velvet jacket with a high collar, and the entire band was a riot of paisley shirts, velvet pants, scarves, stripy sport coats, and layered haircuts.

At the time, you couldn't buy these hip English clothes in the States. We couldn't get enough of them. Luckily, my British hotel friend Pauline kept her promise to keep me supplied, so every few weeks I mailed her fifty dollars to ensure that flowery shirts and crazy pants kept winging their way from Carnaby Street to Long Island.

My other major image change was my moustache. In the late sixties, facial hair was in, and initially I grew a fairly ordinary moustache. I didn't much care for it and decided the whole Fu Manchu look would be better. More than forty years on, that comical but cool appendage remains my visual catchphrase.

As my look changed beyond recognition, so did my life. I drove over to Brooklyn to see my parents, and when I stepped out of the car in my new sartorial elegance, the neighborhood all came out to watch. The local kids would crowd around me, and suddenly my mother was a local celebrity just for being my mother! She loved it.

I had left an old drum kit at my parents' house, and on one visit home around that time, my little brother, Vinny, jumped on the kit and said, "Look what I can do!" I knew he used to play my kit, but he had gotten real good. I was impressed and fixed him up to take lessons with my old tutor, Dick Benette.

Life had suddenly gotten totally awesome. For me it was all about being a rock star, appearing on TV and in magazines, and living in my apartment right on the beach, with all my bills paid for me by our accountant/lawyer. I wasn't quite twenty-one years old, and I was having an absolute fucking blast.

So it was kind of bizarre that I should also get a steady girlfriend at that time, but that was exactly what I went and did.

One night at the Action House, I got talking to a really attractive chick named Arlene. Cool, voluptuous, and a chic dresser in all of the latest mod clothes, she was about my age but still in school. She was also a very talented painter and soon became a regular overnight stayer at my beach apartment.

There were still all kinds of Mafia guys hanging out around the Action House, although we didn't have too many direct dealings with them. Phil had always told us that we should respect those guys, and one of them in particular—Paul "Paulie" Vario, the don of Long Island and boss of one of the main New York mobs.

Like Phil needed to tell us that! We were hardly going to disrespect the Mob men. But Phil's words came back to me one night when Vinny Martell and I were in my car driving home from the studio and a big Caddy pulled up alongside us. I glanced over. Inside were Paulie and a couple of his henchmen.

They gestured for Vinny to roll down the passenger window, which he did. The back window of the Caddy went down at the same time. "Who is that?" asked Paulie. "Carmine?"

"Yeah, it's Carmine and Vinny from Vanilla Fudge," replied Vinny.

"Yo, Vinny, Carmine—come over to my house and have a drink!" said Paulie.

This was clearly a command and not a suggestion, so Vinny and I followed the Caddy through the night streets. We were—let's be honest—shitting ourselves and freaking out. "Let's have one drink and get the hell out of there!" I told Vinny. "What if the cops come or another Mob does a hit?"

Paulie's home was a mansion in a gated enclosure, with guards both by the gates and near the house doors. As we passed them, I noticed they were carrying assault rifles. Shit! Now I really did not want to be there! I felt like an extra in a gangster movie.

Once inside, Vinny and I had one drink and lasted maybe half an hour of laughing, joking, and shooting the shit with our hosts before making our excuses and telling them we had to be in the studio early with the Fudge the next day. I could not have felt more relieved to leave. Phil heard about our house call and told us, "You guys done good!" I was just pleased we never had to make a return visit.

Another regular visitor to the club was a cohort of Phil's named Henry. Henry always had an eye out for a new way to make a buck, not to mention a constant stream of goods and accessories that had come his way by unspecified means and that he was keen to unload onto us at bargain prices.

One typical afternoon, Henry turned up at my home, called me over to his Cadillac, and opened up the trunk. "Yo, Carmine!" he said. "I got some stuff. It fell off a truck!"

Inside the trunk were Revox tape machines, fur coats, portable TVs, and all kinds of other stuff. I knew the tape machines went for around seven hundred dollars in the stores. "How much for those?" I asked him.

"A hundred dollars."

"Any guarantee?"

"I guarantee if it breaks, I'll give you a new one."

That was good enough for me. I bought two of them. And what was Henry's last name? Hill—the Henry Hill who was to become one of America's most notorious mobsters after being played by Ray Liotta in Scorsese's classic movie *Goodfellas*. When Henry ratted and became a federal witness against the Mob, Phil was horrified. "A piece of shit," he called him.

Yet I have to admit that Phil and his Mafia connections were good for us. We always felt looked after, and we always knew we'd get paid. No promoter was going to cross the Mob!

At one point, as Fudge continued to get bigger, Phil heard that one of the New York Mafia families wanted protection money from the big rock bands. Phil, Paulie, and our attorney, Steve Weiss, went for a sit-down with the heads of that family and managed to talk them down from taking 5 percent of our gross profit to taking 1 percent. That saved us a lot of money!

After that sit-down, Phil told us that we owed Paulie a favor—just like in the movies, right? We had to play a show at his club in Brooklyn without getting paid. It grossed tens of thousands of dollars, all of which went straight to Paulie. That was just how the music business was back then, until the Mob got wise, left the bands alone, and infiltrated the record companies instead.

Thankfully, on a day-to-day basis we were largely in ignorance about all this. In the fall of '67 we went back on the road, playing gigs with Steppenwolf, Frank Zappa and the Mothers of Invention, and the Chamber Brothers. Yet I was far more excited by our hometown gig at the Felt Forum at Madison Square Garden supported by one of my all-time heroes: Buddy Rich.

Actually *excited* isn't quite the right word. I was terrified. Whenever I saw Buddy on TV being interviewed by someone like Johnny Carson, he always seemed to be a total fucking asshole. As a jazzman, he made no bones about hating "rock drummers." Plus, he was the best drummer in the world! How could I hope to follow him with my solo?

Phil Basile managed to calm me down, explaining that it was cool to have my hero supporting us. But I was still nervous as hell on the night. I watched Buddy's set from a hidden spot at the side of the stage, and his technique was unbelievable. I literally could not believe some of the shit he was doing.

Even so, the crowd's reaction to Buddy was good but not great, and when I did my solo with Fudge later, I actually went down better. I wasn't stupid enough to think I was a better drummer than Buddy Rich. I knew he was from a different generation and some Fudge fans might not even have heard of him. Plus, of course, he was not a rock drummer. Still, getting a better reaction made me feel proud. Did I talk to him that night? No, I didn't dare go near him!

Tim and I were starting to become known as quite the badass rhythm section in Vanilla Fudge, with critics praising us for our energy, range, and tightness. The fans seemed to love what we were doing, too.

They showed their love in various ways. By now the sexual revolution was in full swing, and although we still met naive girls who weren't too sure what sex was all about but were very willing to learn, we increasingly encountered way more self-confident chicks who were part of what was by now being called the "groupie" phenomenon.

Tim and I were still sharing hotel rooms, but that never curtailed our sexual adventures. If anything, it enhanced them. If one of us was in bed with a girl, the other would usually jump in the bed and get involved. Occasionally the chick would freak out. Usually they didn't.

Like a proper rhythm section, Tim and I began playing together and making some very sweet music. When it came to girls, we had different desires. Tim liked full sex with our groupies, but I was nervous about catching the clap or some other disease and giving it to Arlene, so would normally settle for a blow job.

We would often have threesomes with a chick, and finessed our routine into something that we called the Finale. To put it at its simplest, we would try to work it so that we all came at the same time. There would be a writhing pile of flesh that would—ahem—climax something like this:

"Tim, are you almost ready?"

"Not yet, C.A.! In a minute!"

"Hey, honey, are you ready?"

"Yeah, yeah, nearly there. . . ."

"OK, right, let's do it!"

Then—wham, bam—we would all orgasm together! Tim and I were weirdly proud of the Finale, and it was something that we did for many years.

And we never hated ourselves in the morning.

As 1967 closed, Vanilla Fudge felt as if we had lived through our dream year. A record deal, a hit album, awesome shows not just up and down the East Coast but also on the West Coast and in England—how could we even hope to top that?

Well, we found out how when we were asked to play the *Ed Sullivan Show*.

It's impossible in today's multimedia age to get across what a big deal the *Ed Sullivan Show* was back then. On a Sunday night you turned on CBS and you watched it; it was kinda compulsory. It made careers. I had seen Elvis and the Beatles on there. Playing it was like the official stamp of approval that you had arrived.

Our big date was January 14, 1968, and in the days leading up to it we thought and talked of nothing else. We stayed in a hotel by the Ed Sullivan Theater and had to go down to the theater for the four days running up to the show to rehearse "You Keep Me Hangin' On," a song we had by then played hundreds of times and knew backward.

It's a sign of how important that show was that we didn't mind getting paid less than our going price. We only got five thousand dollars, but doing *Ed Sullivan* was all about the prestige. All my family would be watching, my friends—everyone I knew. My parents were so proud, and it made me feel really good that they got to see their son on this show.

After the Sunday afternoon dress rehearsal, when Ed appeared in our plush dressing room for a few words of small talk, we were psyched and ready to go. This confidence lasted until the elevator ride down to the studio theater, when I asked the uniformed guy running the elevator how many people would be watching the show.

"Oh, about fifty million," he casually replied.

Fuck! Suddenly my heart was beating as loud as my drums, my mouth had run dry, my head was spinning; I guess it was what nowadays you would call a panic attack. But there was no time for that as we took our places under the harsh stage lights. We were only getting one shot. Fifty million people! This was it.

We had brought our own Batman, Bruce Wayne, back from England with us and insisted he be in the sound booth for our performance. He knew how the song would sound and would tell the show's producers if anything was wrong, which gave us confidence. Once Mark had hit the tune's opening organ note and we were underway, our nerves dissipated; it just felt like playing a gig.

We got into it and even did our usual crazy, dramatic moves. At one point I jumped up on a music break and attacked my left cymbal. We got a mixed reaction in the studio. Ed Sullivan was really an icon of Middle America, and half of the old, square-looking crowd looked like they'd rather be listening to Sinatra or Tony Bennett.

Luckily, there were also some younger kids in the studio, so we went down well with them, and the reviews were amazing. Critics raved about us, and the next day we clocked up a quarter of a million single and album sales. And as the days and weeks passed, they just kept on selling.

It seemed like we were invincible. For a whole year everything Vanilla Fudge touched turned to gold. From this rarefied position, surely it was impossible to fuck up our new status as one of the hippest, most critically and commercially successful bands in America?

Well, we found a way. We promptly recorded one of the most ludicrous, overblown, and downright fucking stupid albums in the history of music.

The *Vanilla Fudge* album had been kept off the top of the chart by the Beatles' *Sgt. Pepper's Lonely Hearts Club Band*. The Rolling Stones had recently delivered *Their Satanic Majesties Request*. Concept albums were all the rage, and Shadow Morton decided that Vanilla Fudge should have a piece of the action.

Our wunderkind producer came up with the concept behind *The Beat Goes On*. Even now, having lived with the record for nearly forty years, I find it hard to explain—to understand—exactly what that fucking concept actually *was*. I guess the idea that there is always music, no matter what is going on in the world, is about as close as we are likely to get.

Shadow was totally into this big idea—whatever it was—and Ahmet Ertegun from Atlantic was right there with him. We just went along with it. These were two major record-industry guys, and for all of our recent success, we were still basically wet-behind-the-ears punks. They must know what they're doing, we just assumed.

The recording sessions were weird from the start. We certainly weren't trying to write any music. We had an array of rented instruments, and when we got into the studio each day, Shadow would give us all specific, peculiar instructions.

"I need you to play something from the thirteenth century," he would tell us or, "I want something that sounds like gothic blues from the 1920s." "I need a death march!" He even got us playing Beethoven's *Moonlight Sonata*. We had no idea how all this shit was going to hold together, so we just tried to follow his directions as best we could and keep him happy.

Shadow had us playing snatches of Beatles songs like "I Want to Hold Your Hand" and "She Loves You" but told us to do them straight rather than our usual slowed-down, fucked-up reinterpretations. We covered Elvis's "Hound Dog," "In the Mood" by Glenn Miller, even Cole Porter's "Don't Fence Me In." Why? We had no idea.

Sometimes Shadow would get a little trippy music going in the studio and then record our answers to would-be profound questions.

What did we think God thinks of "Eleanor Rigby"?

What did we think of President Johnson?

What does poetry say?

What did we think of the Beatles' interest in Indian meditation?

Did we like ice cream?

We would just say the first thing we thought of, but Shadow seemed satisfied with our halting responses. When he pointed the mic at me, I blurted out, "I'm not a talker, I just play drums, so listen to my drums if you want to hear me talk!" Then I gave a weird little cackle. It sounds dumb now, but what did I know? I was just a kid with no clue what was going on.

What I did know was that when I heard the finished record, I was horrified. Shadow had really gone to town. Without telling us, he had mixed in all sorts of bizarre news and audio clips: John F. Kennedy speeches, Hitler addressing a rally, Nazis yelling "Sieg Heil!" protesters shouting "Black Power!" There were snatches of Mozart, Beethoven, and Franklin Roosevelt.

*What was this shit?*

Even listening to it now—which, let me tell you, I rarely fucking do—*The Beat Goes On* sounds like an album that even Spinal Tap would be wary of making. Yet Shadow and Ahmet loved it and kept telling us it was going to be the next big thing and as big as the Beatles. What were they smoking? Or was that where the problems started?

The band's reaction to the finished record was mixed. Tim, Phil, and I hated it from the start. We were three pretty down-to-earth guys, and our reaction can best be summarized as "Oh my God! What the hell is this?" Mark and Vinny, who made up the artsy wing of the group, liked it. They claim now that they never did, but that's not how I remember it.

The world knew a turkey when it heard one. The success of our first album and our level of fame at that point meant that a lot of fans went out and bought *The Beat Goes On* as soon as it came out—it even hit the top twenty. But as soon as people started hearing it, it went tumbling down the *Billboard* chart, and returns started flooding into the record label.

This was the first real bad luck to hit Vanilla Fudge, and it was a major disaster. No sales meant no royalties, which, in fact, landed us in debt to the label. Even more serious, we realized that a complete fiasco like this could kill our careers stone dead. We were in danger of becoming a laughingstock.

There was only one way to get rid of this albatross around the Fudge's neck: we had to record a new album and get it out right away.

We went back into the studio with Shadow, but this time the sessions could not have been more different from *The Beat Goes On*. Even before that record appeared, Vanilla Fudge had been getting shit in the press from critics who sneered that we never wrote our own songs and only did cover versions. This criticism had always seemed unfair to me; we invariably rearranged other artists' songs so radically, including writing passages of new music, that our versions were never anything like the original. Also, our follow-up to "Keep Me Hangin' On," "Where Is My Mind," was an original song that had gone top fifty.

Still, it was an issue that had to be addressed. We decided to return to the raw energy and sound of our first album, but with all our own material.

The album was to be called *Renaissance*, because we knew we needed a rebirth. We all wrote songs for it. I penned my first-ever tune, "Faceless People," on the old Lowery organ my parents had bought me. It was about the many, many people you meet out on the road and how they all seem to merge into one. I've never thought myself a great lyricist, but at the time I felt the song was quite deep.

Mark Stein and I cowrote a song called "Paradise"; he had a chorus and I had a verse, so we stuck them together. Tim and Mark wrote a song together, Vince wrote one, and Shadow gave us a number called "The Spell That Comes After" by his friend Essra Mohawk. We did include one cover, "Seasons of the Witch" by Donovan, which ended up being the album's lead-off single.

Atlantic rushed *Renaissance* out in June '68, and it did pretty well, reaching the top twenty, which meant that for a short while we had three albums on the chart (although *The Beat Goes On* was unsurprisingly rapidly plummeting downward). Then the label rereleased "You Keep Me Hangin' On," and it hit number six on the singles chart. We had survived our career crisis—thank fuck!

Atlantic promoted the single's reissue with joint trade magazine ads with Cream's "Sunshine of Your Love," and we did two gigs with Cream, in Houston and Dallas. I heard that Ginger Baker, a very strange man, was peeping at me through a curtain during my drum solo. The word was also that he was refusing to go onstage unless the promoters gave him a white limo with a crate of beer and two black hookers. As for his playing, I knew Ginger was a good drummer, but he didn't blow me away. (I guess that was what the black hookers were doing to him!)

The Houston trip was more memorable for me for Tim's extracurricular activities in our shared room at the Holiday Inn. He appeared after the show with a massively fat chick, and when she went to the bathroom, I shared my misgivings with him.

"Tim, what the fuck are you doing with her?"

"I just feel like fucking a fat chick," he explained.

Tim got his wish. She turned out to have a thing about using butter as a lube, and they were at it all night. The Butter Queen—as she was soon christened—screamed and yelled until dawn as I tossed and turned in my bed and shouted back at her to shut the fuck up so I could sleep.

There were not many fat chicks when Vanilla Fudge fetched up in Honolulu soon after to play a festival along with Creedence Clearwater Revival. It was our first time in Hawaii, and there were so many gorgeous women that we thought we had died and gone to paradise.

The island was just so laid-back. One afternoon I was swimming with Mark on Waikiki Beach by our hotel when two insanely beautiful women offered to take us to a natural swimming hole. When we said we would grab our shoes from the hotel first, they told us not to bother, as it was a car ride and then a very short walk away.

Yeah, right! Once we got to the other side of Oahu, the "short walk" turned out to be half an hour down a rutted track, and our soles were cut to ribbons. The girls wove us some rough-and-ready "shoes" out of exotic leaves, but still our feet were killing us.

When we got there, it was worth it. There was an amazing pool with a picturesque waterfall cascading into it and vines hanging from the trees. This was a long fucking way from Brooklyn! We expected to see Tarzan come swinging by! The idyllic scene got even better when the chicks produced some Hawaiian pot known locally as the Voice of God, stripped, and took us skinny-dipping.

The only cloud hanging over this perfect experience was the prospect of the long, painful hike back to the chicks' car. Enter Batman! As we left the water hole, as if by magic, the roar of a motorbike engine filled the air, and Bruce Wayne emerged over the horizon on a rented bike. We had never been so pleased to see our English superhero.

We loved being on the road, but our next live venture was to be a real trip. Phil arranged for us to go back on tour with my old friend Jimmy James, a.k.a. the Jimi Hendrix Experience.

This Stateside tour lasted a few weeks and also included English psychedelic band Soft Machine and an Irish group called Heir Apparent to open up the bill. Mostly, though, I was stoked to catch up with Hendrix and watch his amazing playing firsthand again.

Jimi didn't have it all his own way on that tour. Vanilla Fudge were on top of our game and really tight by now, and at a few of the gigs we blew Jimi clean off the stage. Obviously, we were biased, but it wasn't just us who thought so—some of the reviews at the time said that we had upstaged Hendrix.

This was quite some accolade, because on that tour Jimi was on the best form of his life and playing out of his skin. He was such an incredible showman, with the whole routine of playing with his teeth and behind his neck and just wrenching noises out of six strings that you could not believe. Tim and I used to stand on the side of the stage during his set and then walk back to our dressing room with "Voodoo Child" still ringing in our ears.

It's amazing to think how we used to tour in those days. We would fly everywhere, so our trucks would pull up to the belly of the plane and unload all the gear, including the Hammond B3 organ and Jimi's Marshall stacks. They were just standard commercial flights, so our tour would take over half of the plane. Some passengers loved it, while others were less impressed with our rock-star antics.

But that tour was a blast. In San Diego, Tim and I, Mitch and Noel (from Jimi's band), and a couple of guys from Heir Apparent rented motorized sailboats from the Hilton where we were staying and took them out on the hotel lake. When the management caught us busting Noel's balls by ramming his boat with ours, trying to capsize him, we narrowly avoided being kicked out of yet another hotel.

Tim had a girlfriend in L.A. who came down to see us, bringing a load of pot and chicks with her—one was Sally Struthers, who went on to play Gloria in *All in the Family*. We had a cool time hanging out with them. It was a lot nicer than our gig a few days later at the Hollywood Bowl.

Vinny still quietly had his thing about wanting to be a guitar hero, but Vanilla Fudge were never really that sort of band. We were more like a rhythm section orchestral band, driven by Tim and I. And in any case, Vinny never truly had the chops to be a Clapton or a Jeff Beck.

Being on the road with the greatest guitar hero of all—Hendrix—must have subconsciously made Vinny even more frustrated. Who knows? Before we played the Hollywood Bowl, he did a whole load of acid backstage—whether he intended to or somebody spiked his drink, I don't know to this day—and decided that this was going to be his night.

We only had a forty-five-minute set, and early in it Vinny had what was supposed to be an eight-bar solo. It seemed to go on for fucking ever. He was in his own distant galaxy, firing out these crazy licks we had never heard him play before that had nothing to do with the song. The promoters cut our set short. I don't think we even got to play "You Keep Me Hangin' On."

Backstage we were all mad as hell at Vinny, which led into a big shouting match. But he just said what he always said about shit like that: "Oh, I guess I just got into it." Plus, of course, he was off his head on acid. What could we do?

By contrast, Jimi was kicking ass even by his standards. He was electric that night. The fans got so carried away that they started jumping in a big water fountain in front of the stage. The Hollywood Bowl management started flipping out, and Jimi had to stop playing and tell people to get out because if any of the lights in the fountain were to smash, they would get electrocuted to a crisp.

Atlanta was also a wild night. Ted Nugent was opening up the bill with his band, the Amboy Dukes, and told me before the show that he was going to play the guitar with his teeth.

"But that's Hendrix's thing!" I told him.

"So what?" said Ted. "Everybody here who doesn't know that will see me do it first and think that Hendrix is copying me!" He did it, as well.

I'll give him this: Nugent has always had huge balls.

On that tour, like most of the others, we would get to the gig and find a load of groupies waiting backstage. You would pick out whichever one you wanted, take her back to the hotel, and the party would begin. In Atlanta I met a beautiful chick named Brenda with—naturally—enormous tits. She claimed to be a virgin, but going by the evidence of our several hours of sexual gymnastics, she was a very quick learner.

Yet my most memorable moment of the Hendrix tour came in Jimi's hometown of Seattle. He had just finished his *Electric Ladyland* album, and he invited us back to his hotel room to listen to it and tell him what we thought of it.

I can still picture the bedroom: a real old-fashioned-type hotel room with high ceilings and windows so tall they made you feel cold. As well as the Fudge, there were members of Soft Machine and Heir Apparent, roadies, and groupies all crowded in the room, drinking, smoking pot, and taking acid as Jimi dropped the needle on the record.

Hendrix was obviously a rock superstar by now, but underneath it all he was the same shy, quiet Jimmy James I had shot the breeze with in the New York hooker's apartment two years earlier. And at first he looked twitchy and nervous at this impromptu playback party—which was weird, as it had been his idea.

Imagine being one of the very first people ever to hear *Electric Ladyland*, and imagine Hendrix anxiously asking you if you liked it as you listened. I felt privileged to be there. As one by one we all honestly told Jimi how awesome this music was, he visibly relaxed, and his face became wreathed in smiles. That was an afternoon I will never forget.

Decades after that tour, a Hendrix biography came out that said Jimi had at one point wanted us off that tour because we were blowing him off the stage and had asked his manager to try to arrange it. It doesn't sound like the Jimi I knew. There's no way of knowing now if it is true, but I prefer to believe it isn't. And I think I'm right.

When the tour ended, it was time for Vanilla Fudge to record our own next album, and we went straight into the Record Plant in New York. We were to record on a twelve-track machine for the first time, which was a big deal for us; it was the only studio in the city that had this technology. The recording sessions were to prove eventful, hedonistic . . . and debauched.

Around the corner from the Record Plant was a club called the Scene, and we would head down there, pick up groupies, and take them back to the studio. We would put them in a side room, which quickly became the place we all went to get blow jobs between takes. We encouraged the chicks to walk around with their tits out and showed porn films on the studio wall via an eight-millimeter projector.

By now Jeff Beck had a new band, the Jeff Beck Group, with Rod Stewart on vocals and Ronnie Wood on bass. We got a call one day asking if these two English guys could come down to watch us record, as they were big Fudge fans. Rod and Ronnie turned up with their pineapple haircuts, sat quietly and shyly in the corner, and hardly said a word. As first encounters go, it could hardly have been more misleading.

The album, which was to become *Near the Beginning*, was taking shape and was a pretty unorthodox beast. For one thing, it only had four songs on it.

We decided to give the album one studio side and one live side. On side one we took Junior Walker & the All Stars' "Shotgun" and gave it the Vanilla Fudge heavy treatment and also covered Lee Hazelwood's "Some Velvet Morning." Then we added a song I had written called "Where Is Happiness."

Side two was a different story. Ever since our early Rhode Island gigs at Dorian's, our crowds had gone mental for a number called "The Break Song." It had big solos, which were hip at the time. Even after we had got big we had carried on playing it live because it always went down so well.

Tim's playing on "The Break Song" was particularly amazing. He would bang the bass with his fists, yank on the strings, and run his hands up and down the neck to get the craziest sounds he could out of it. He even used a guitar fuzz tone: the end result sounded like an elephant in heat. People seemed to love my drum solo, as well.

We decided to record the track live at our gig at the Shrine Auditorium in Los Angeles to get L.A. back on board. This was a tactical calculation; *The Beat Goes On* appeared to have gone down even worse in that city than everywhere else, if that was possible.

I remember the night we recorded the track well for two reasons. One was that Richie Havens opened for us. Richie was a soulful human being with a distinctive gap in his mouth where two front teeth were missing, and he would attack his acoustic guitar with such aggression that you thought the strings were going to break. He never had a proper band, but even on his own he would always rock the crowd. He was a cool guy.

What else do I remember of that night? I met a gorgeous chick with huge tits and smoked some great pot with her before the gig. It meant that I was really high as we played "The Break Song." Our only difficulty was cutting it down from twenty-eight minutes to twenty-four to fit on the record.

The *Vanilla Fudge* album (powered by the rerelease of "You Keep Me Hangin' On") and *Renaissance* were both still riding high on the *Billboard* chart, so there was no need to rush *Near the Beginning* out, and we decided to release it early in '69. At the end of '68, we took off on a short tour of the West Coast and Southwest with a brand-new, unknown support act to whom we were giving a few dates as a favor.

Their name was Led Zeppelin.

# 4

# THIS BUSINESS
# IS FULL OF SHARKS

*In which Drummerdude unwittingly pays for an obscure band called Led Zeppelin to support him, advises Robert Plant to move around onstage a bit more, gets John Bonham a decent drum kit, fails to get it up for the Plaster Casters, and has a front-row seat for rock and roll's most infamous fishy tale*

*While the Fudge had been getting huge in* the States, our old friends the Yardbirds had been splitting up in Britain, and Jimmy Page had been busy assembling another band. We didn't know too much about Led Zeppelin before we played our first dates with them, nor had we given them too much thought.

What we also didn't know was that we were paying for them to be on the bill! Our first date was at the Denver Auditorium Arena on December 26, 1968. The two groups shared the same agent, a guy named Ron Terry, who apparently rang up the Denver promoter, Barry Fey, and told him he wanted to add this band nobody had heard of to the bill.

"We don't need them. The show is sold out," Barry told him.

Ron was relentless with Barry, telling him the fee would only be $1,500, but Barry refused to budge. Then Ron had an idea: "Hey, if you pay $750, Vanilla Fudge will pay the other $750."

I didn't find out about this until Barry told me about it nearly a quarter of a century later. Fuck knows how many other shows we paid for Led Zeppelin to play with us!

I'd love to say that Zeppelin seemed an amazing and life-changing band the first time we set eyes on them . . . but they didn't. When we turned up at the Auditorium Arena, they were already on and didn't seem to be going down all that great. There were about 7,500 people at our sold-out show, and a few pockets of fans were booing them and chanting, "Bring on the Fudge!"

This was harsh, because they didn't sound bad, but nobody had heard of any of them, apart from Jimmy. At that point, John Paul Jones was a session musician, and John Bonham was just a kid. Robert Plant stood stock still onstage; I even took it upon myself to tell him he should move around a bit more.

Zeppelin mostly kept to themselves offstage for those few dates. One of their party, though, was familiar to us. Their English tour manager, Richard Cole, a friend of Bruce Wayne, had worked for the Fudge six months earlier. A rangy guy with a strong London Cockney accent, he always wore a long black coat that made him look like a mortician, so we called him Mort. He was a nice guy with us, always up for a laugh. If he had an evil side, that only came out later, with Zeppelin.

More tellingly, on that first Zep tour I also formed a friendship with their wild-man drummer, Bonham, that was to stand the test of time. It may sound a little weird, but he was the nicest, kindest, gentlest guy to be around, a true English gentleman—until the demon drink passed his lips.

Back in '68 he was pretty wide-eyed and excited about it all—and he loved my drum set. I had picked up a sponsorship from Ludwig that summer and really gone to town. They had got me the first natural-wood kit ever made. As my massive bass drum sounded so good and loud, I thought having the rest of the kit bigger would do the same, and ordered a complete oversize kit: two twenty-six-inch bass drums, a tom-tom that was a marching tenor drum, two huge floor toms, a deep snare drum—the works.

It looked pretty wild, and Bonham freaked out when he saw it, staying on my case and asking me to get him a similar deal with Ludwig. I talked Zeppelin up to Ludwig, saying, "I think they might be big." Just call me Nostradamus, right? Ludwig agreed, and a few months later Bonham had an identical set to mine, even down to the two-bass-drum setup (although he soon dropped that).

Ludwig's roster at the time was Ringo Starr, Mitch Mitchell, Ginger Baker, Dino Danelli of the Rascals, and me. It soon became clear that Bonham was the equal of any of us. Hearing the debut Zeppelin album before our tour, I was blown away by his playing, and told him I loved one triplet pattern he played with his right foot.

His answer surprised me: "I got that from you."

"Eh? I've never done that!" I said. Bonham reacted by telling me that I had done it on the first Fudge album. I had no idea what he was talking about, but I went back, listened to the album, and he was right. He had taken what I did and enhanced it. Well, they say imitation is the sincerest form of flattery, right?

Not that I minded. I took plenty of tricks from Gene Krupa, Buddy Rich, and countless others over the years. As jazz drummer Joe Morello said, "We all steal from each other. Nobody has it all." It's just how it goes.

We were out with Zeppelin again the following month when they and another new English band, Jethro Tull, opened up for Vanilla Fudge at a couple of shows at a Chicago club called the Kinetic Playground. A few years later that bill would have filled a stadium, but there we were, all squeezed into a tatty old venue that maybe held 2,500 people.

I'll never forget how cool those Chicago shows were. Bonham, Tull drummer Clive Bunker, and I had a great time hanging out together and swapping stories. We hung around side stage and threw spitballs at each other during our sets. During Zeppelin's show, Bonham was goofing on me, mimicking my stick twirls and the way I always grabbed my cymbals.

Offstage there was plenty of groupie action—I met a teenage chick who gave us all blow jobs in the back of our tour van. We had also heard about the Plaster Casters, the Chicago groupies who had just cast Hendrix's erect dick in plaster and were now doing it to all the visiting rock stars, and decided to make their acquaintance.

Sadly, when we got there, they just didn't do it for me and I couldn't get it up. So, like a bad actor, I remained uncast.

With our *Near the Beginning* album out and doing well, we went back on the *Ed Sullivan Show* to play its lead single, "Shotgun." The day had an inauspicious start. Mark and Vinny had been getting on each other's nerves, and when Vinny showed up at the hotel room they were sharing, Mark greeted him with a punch in the face! The funny thing was that Mark hurt his hand doing it, and Vinny had to lend him money to get it bandaged up in a hospital so we could play the show.

Apart from the intraband violence, our second *Ed Sullivan Show* appearance was OK, though it didn't have the impact of the first time around. But the album was doing well, "Shotgun" was heading up the chart, and Vanilla Fudge got asked to star in a couple of commercials.

A few bands thought doing shit like that was a sell-out, but we just figured, what the hell? The more things we had going on, the better! First was a TV ad for Braniff Airlines. We had to walk through the door of a makeshift plane and say, "Hi, we're Vanilla Fudge—when you've got it, flaunt it!"

Next came a radio commercial for Coca-Cola, who asked us to write two songs using lyrical ideas they gave us. I remember it had to say "Things go better with Coke." We wrote the songs and turned up at the studio, where all the Coke execs were waiting—and Vinny fell violently ill and couldn't play.

Phil called up our attorney, Stevens H. Weiss, who dealt with all the major artists, and he told us that Jeff Beck happened to be in New York and would play the session. Wow! How fucking cool was that? The recording was awesome, and Tim and I were in heaven riffing off Jeff's incredible playing. I guess you could call it a sign of things to come.

The weird thing with the Coke songs was that I ended up singing lead vocals on one of the tracks, and Tim did the same on the other. I have no idea why Mark Stein didn't sing either of them—after all, he was the voice of the band!

Around this time Deep Purple appeared with their debut album, *Shades of Deep Purple*, and it was obvious they were copying our style of music and arrangements. They had the same organ sound and slowed-down psychedelic cover versions as Fudge, and they were saying a lot of nice things about us in the rock press.

We figured imitation was the kindest form of flattery and took them out on tour with us in Canada, which was great. We would jump onstage with them and jam during "Hush," and they would do the same with us during some of our songs. We got on well, and within a year, they were massive.

We also did a few dates around this time with Three Dog Night, who were also just getting big. They had also taken musical tips from us—particularly our way with harmony and vibrato—but they had made it very much their own trip. It was their first tour, and they weren't really too sure what the hell was going on.

They soon got used to us going into their dressing room and turning over their table of food and drinks at the end of the night, but I could tell some of our antics with groupies came as a shock to them. But by the time we got to Tulsa, Oklahoma, and were swapping chicks between bands, they had got the hang of it.

We played a whole heap of promotional TV appearances. We would fly to California to do *The David Frost Show* or *The Dick Cavett Show*. We also went on *The Merv Griffin Show*, and at the rehearsal a guy wandered over and started admiring my maple-wood drum set. He told me he was the drummer with the NBC Orchestra.

"Great! What's your name?" I asked him.

"My name is Louie."

"Oh, hi, Louie. How you doing? My name's Carmine."

"I play double bass drums, too," he told me.

We chatted for a while. Then he said, "When you're in L.A., give me a call. I'd like to get together with you." He wrote his name and number on a piece of paper, but I didn't look at it until I was getting changed in the dressing room and it fell out of my pocket.

"Louie Bellson."

*Louie Bellson?* This was amazing to me! Here was a guy I had listened to my whole life, playing with people like Benny Goodman and Duke Ellington. He was the first drummer ever to play double bass drums, and for me he was a hero up there with Gene Krupa and Buddy Rich. Half-dressed, I ran back outside to find him again.

"Louie Bellson! Why the hell didn't you tell me you were Louie Bellson?" I asked, grabbing his hand.

"Ah, I don't like to throw my weight around," he answered—which is a measure of just what a cool guy he was. After that initial meeting, we always kept in touch.

When I was home, I was still seeing Arlene. I bought a house in Oceanside in Nassau County, and when I wasn't touring she would live with me there with a kitten, Tiny Little Baby, or Tiny for short, that she gave me. It was the first pet I'd ever had, and I loved that cat. When I was on the road, the pair of them would go back to her parents' place in Long Island.

Looking back, this was weird: I must have cheated on Arlene a thousand times with chicks and groupies while I was away, yet she never seemed to suspect a thing, or at least never let me know if she suspected anything. And I never thought she would. I assumed I was bulletproof. We all did back then.

So it was the height of stupidity to take Arlene to see a new movie called *Groupie*, all about the new wave of girls who lived to fuck musicians. What could possibly go wrong, right?

Arlene and I settled into our seats, popcorn in hands, and imagine my horror when up on the big screen loomed Brenda, the virgin I had met on the Atlanta tour with Hendrix. It seemed that after our tryst, she had thrown herself whole-heartedly into her new vocation and was now a big player on the groupie scene.

"Who was the first rock star you went with?" the interviewer asked her.

"Oh, that was someone from Vanilla Fudge," she coyly replied.

"*Who was that?*" Arlene hissed at me in the dark.

"Beats me!" I gulped. "It must have been Tim!" Tim rarely had a steady girlfriend, so he was a natural choice as a scapegoat. Luckily, she believed me—or she pretended to.

Yet if you want to talk groupie action, there is one tour that has passed into legend: the Led Zeppelin and Vanilla Fudge trek across America in the summer of 1969.

This was the third time we had been out with Zeppelin that year, and by now they were unrecognizable from the gawky, awkward band we had taken on the road six months earlier. No longer static, Robert Plant was now prowling the stage like a wild man (he had taken my advice, right?), Jimmy Page was wrenching impossible sounds from his guitar, and my pal Bonham had his own oversize Ludwig kit.

Zeppelin were honkin' live now. They were phenomenal, and with a rocketing reputation on both sides of the Atlantic, they were no longer our support band. This was a coheadlining tour, meaning that we topped the bill on alternate nights.

Vanilla Fudge had blown superstars like Jimi Hendrix and the Who off the stage before, and now we had to watch that the same thing didn't happen to us. Before our eyes, Led Zeppelin were turning into the best rock-and-roll band in the world. It was both exciting and intimidating to watch.

That tour was a riot in all the right ways. Despite our healthy competitive rivalry, we got on great with Zeppelin. They were like our British brothers. We drove each other to ever more extreme heights onstage, and when we hung out backstage or at the hotel, there was serious debauchery.

People have this idea that Led Zeppelin were the most carnal and hedonistic of all the bands, like a traveling Caligula circus, but that's not totally true. The band had its moments, but often Bonham and Plant had their women on the road with them and kept a low profile. The majority of the partying was about Bonham's drinking when his wife wasn't around and the sexual antics of the road crew, led by Richard Cole, their notorious on-the-road troublemaker and ringleader.

When the tour rolled through Texas, Tim's old friend the Butter Queen showed up again. She was still big and fat but seemed to have made it her mission to find gorgeous young local and Mexican chicks for us to party with when we were in town, and showed up at our hotel with two nubile friends in tow.

The three of them sucked and fucked their way through a roomful of musicians and roadies, one of whom produced a Polaroid camera. Pictorial highlights included a photo of a string of sperm from my dick to the Butter Queen's mouth and one of her with butter in her ass and crotch. It was totally gross, and I can hardly believe we did that stuff.

Don't go flicking to this book's photo spread to see the photos—thankfully, they are long gone.

Other antics included trying to visit Jimmy Page in his room in the middle of the night. He refused to let us in, so we set off a fire extinguisher under his door. Jimmy was unharmed, but his favorite boots were ruined.

Zeppelin were not on the bill when we played a huge New York show at the Singer Bowl in Queens supported by the Jeff Beck Group, Ten Years After, and the Edgar Hawkins Singers. Jimmy Page and Jeff Beck were old school friends, and when the Beck Group, including Rod Stewart and Ronnie Wood, were on, Zeppelin decided to jam with them.

I joined them on my drums, but just as we were getting into the jam, John Bonham stood up behind his kit, stripped totally nude, and played the rest of the set naked. It was vintage Bonzo, and he didn't seem to mind getting arrested when he came offstage.

That was one night Vanilla Fudge had a very hard support act to follow. Even my watching parents only wanted to talk about Bonham. "Why did he *do* that?" my mother asked me. I told her in all honestly that I had no idea.

Yet the wildest night by far of the Zeppelin/Vanilla Fudge tour, and the one that has passed into rock-and-roll infamy, happened one balmy summer's evening in Seattle.

Some people call the Seattle Pop Festival of July 1969 "the forgotten Woodstock." As well as the Fudge and Zeppelin, there were a whole bunch of other artists on the bill: the Doors, the Byrds, Santana, Flying Burrito Brothers, Alice Cooper, Ike and Tina Turner. Fifty thousand people showed up. It was a big deal.

We were hanging out with Zeppelin, and we were doing most of the hanging at the Edgewater Inn. Now, the cool thing about the Edgewater was that you could fish right out of the window. It was famous for it. The hotel was right on Elliott Bay in Puget Sound, and it rented out fishing poles from the lobby.

I hadn't been doing too much fishing. I was way more interested in getting high on the strong local pot. After the Fudge played the festival, we had a day off, and we had such a nice laid-back vibe going that we decided to stay around for a bit of rest and relaxation.

As was my habit, I had been making local friends. On the day of our show, I had met a chick hanging around the hotel. What was her name? You know, to this day I can't remember. She was short, with wavy brown hair and small tits. She didn't say a lot, but you know what they say, right?

It's always the quiet ones.

We got talking at the Edgewater, and I offered the chick a lift to the gig. I had a limo all to myself that day, and we had hardly even closed the door behind us before she leaned across the back seat, lowered her head into my lap, unzipped me, and eased my dick into her mouth. I don't think the driver had even turned his engine on—but she sure turned me on!

This girl knew what she was doing. She wrapped her pouting, luscious lips around me—I can't remember her name, but I can still picture those big blow job lips—and she gave me the best time it is humanly possible to have in a car driving through Seattle. When I came, I'm surprised I didn't take her head off.

It sounds wild now, but at the time this kind of thing was no big deal. Vanilla Fudge would get sucked off in limos all the time: on the way to gigs, on the way back to the hotel, en route to the airport. I remember another girl at a festival one time jumping into my car as we were about to pull away.

"I'll give you a blow job if you don't come in my mouth," she promised me.

"Well, what am I going to do with it?" I asked her. I could see no good reason to stain the limo's upholstery.

"I have an envelope," she said, and produced one from her bag. I wondered if she always carried one for that purpose.

"OK, maybe I'll mail it to you afterward!" I told her. So that's what we did. I came into an envelope. I don't believe I ever did get around to mailing it to her.

But, anyway, back to Seattle. Zep and Jim Morrison were watching from the side of the stage as the Fudge played the festival. It was insane to see the crowd stretching back to the horizon. When I got to my limo to go back to the hotel, the same girl was waiting for me. She didn't vary her shtick. As soon as we pulled away, my dick was back in her mouth. I had to give it to her: she was an artist. She got me off twice more on the forty-five-minute drive back to the Edgewater.

Her lips were clamped around me for the entire journey, and by the time I got back I needed a break. So I sent her down to one of the roadies. Or, rather, I did our usual routine: took her down to his room, told her I would be back shortly, and vanished. She didn't have a room at the hotel, so I assume she must have slept there. I can't say I gave it too much thought.

The next day came, and the Fudge and Zeppelin started getting nicely blasted. We made John Paul Jones's room our base camp, and John Paul, Robert Plant and his wife Maureen, Tim Bogert, and I were all hanging out there in the late afternoon.

The room was nothing special: a couch, a TV, standard-issue flowery curtains, and a matching bedspread. We were all smoking that strong local pot, the wine was spiked, and we were kicking back, listening to music and watching the cruise ships and speedboats in the bay through the big picture window.

There was a knock at the door. Shit! We all hit panic mode and scrambled to hide the pot, pick up the spare roaches scattered around, and spray air freshener in a doomed attempt to smother the pungent smell of marijuana suffusing the room. Cautiously, John Paul opened the door.

It was her.

It was the blow job chick, and she had come dressed for groupie business: seriously short cut-off jeans; a flowery, see-through chiffon blouse; and, it was clear, no bra. I must have told her in the limo the previous day that Mark Stein had camera gear with him, because she sat on the bed and started saying the same thing over and over: "I want to make a movie with you guys."

She was even higher than the rest of us and was messing with my pot buzz, so I wanted to get away. I went to the next room, where I could hear yelling and laughter, and found Bonham and his wife Pat, Richard Cole, Zep roadie Clive Coulson, and Bruce Wayne having a fine old time.

They were as wasted as we were and were fishing out of the Edgewater window. They must have been doing something right, because the bathtub was a wriggling mini-aquarium of fish. And arrowing through the middle of them was a two-foot-long, dead-eyed, ferocious-looking creature: a mud shark.

I sat with those guys for a few minutes and told them about this crazy chick next door. Then I went back to John Paul's room, using our secret knock to tell them it was one of the tour party. The mood was mellower in there by then, and the girl had stopped banging on about making movies, so we put on the first Delaney and Bonnie album.

We had just switched to Joe Cocker's first record, and Robert was saying how much he liked it, when there was another knock on the door. We went into panic mode again, making stoned and hapless attempts to hide the evidence of our all-day party. Just like the first time, we really needn't have bothered.

Bonham came bursting into the room with Cole, Coulson, and Bruce Wayne. Behind them trailed Mark Stein holding his Super 8 camera and lights, and looking like he sure wasn't set on filming a holiday video of the sailboats bobbing up and down in the harbor.

One second we were all blissed out in peace, love, and a cloud of dope smoke. The next, it was carnage. Richard and Bruce were the ringleaders, and they started straight in on the blow job chick sitting quietly on the bed.

"You want to make a fucking movie?" they asked her. "OK, let's do it right now! Take your clothes off!"

Meek as could be, the girl obediently stripped until she was naked. We were all giggling nervously, unsure what was going on—and that was when I realized the invaders from next door had brought their new pet, the mud shark, with them.

"What the fuck are you going to do with that?" I asked.

I got an answer I did not expect.

Richard and Bruce threw the chick down so she was lying on the bed. Mark had by now got his camera rolling and the lights gleaming, and under their harsh glare Richard held the shark by the tail and started whipping the girl with it, beating her again and again as she writhed around the bed.

Man, it must have hurt her! The shark had these protruding, vicious teeth like little razor blades, and every time it slapped against her, its teeth ripped her skin and left tiny blood-red scars all over her back. The poor chick looked like a pincushion—and the wildest thing was that she was bucking and screaming with pleasure, as if she was about to come.

Was this really happening? Mark was getting it all on celluloid, and he moved his camera in closer as Richard and Bruce pulled the girl's legs open and shoved the thrashing shark up inside her. The chick was laughing as she came repeatedly.

By now it was total anarchy in John Paul's room, and we were all doubled up with laughter as the insane scene developed. The shark was right up in the girl, its tail flailing between her thighs, which were drenched in the juices of her cum. We were rooted to the spot, transfixed and howling.

The bedroom door was open, and a few of us were by now in fits of hysterics in the doorway. Hearing our racket, the Edgewater manager ran down the corridor from the lobby to see what all the noise was. He burst into the room, scattering the crowd by now gathered inside the door, and gasped at a mental scene: a stoned, naked girl, covered in tiny blood spots, being pleasured by a mud shark.

"You people are fucking crazy!" he yelled. "Stop this at once!" And we dispersed like insects when a rock is lifted, capering down the corridor to our own rooms.

John Paul and Tim came back to my room with me, and we wept with laughter as we replayed what had just happened. Slowly our hysteria began to dissolve, and we came down from our weird, twisted high. We even called room service and ordered crumpets and English tea. Very civilized, right?

"Where did that bird go? I wonder if she's still in my room," pondered John Paul.

There was a knock on my door. I opened it, and there she was! By now she was dressed in John Paul's robe. She had gotten up, taken a shower, put it on, and wandered down the hall after us.

John Paul freaked out: "Get that dressing gown off, you bitch! I don't want your slutty germs on it!" So much for the gallant English gentleman! Without a word, she obeyed him and sat naked on the bed as we ate the crumpets. A relative calm descended.

Scene two! Action!

There was another knock at the door, and Richard Cole and Bruce Wayne barged their way in with a couple more roadies. They looked demented. They were carrying one of the hotel fishing poles from their room, and they told the girl to spread-eagle herself on the bed—which, submissive as ever, she did.

"We're going fishing," Richard told me, totally matter-of-fact. "We're going to stick this fishing hook up her cunt and see if we catch anything."

"You can't do that!" I told him, aghast. "Are you guys crazy? You'll kill her! A fishing hook isn't made to be put up a pussy. If you're going to do that, at least use something the right shape, like . . ."

My eyes cast around the room and fastened on a condiment bottle on the room-service tray. "Like this ketchup bottle."

It says a lot about the fucked-up mental state we were in at that moment that this seemed to me like a sensible compromise! Richard agreed. He laid the girl down on the bed and handed her a swab of butter left over from the crumpets.

"Put this on your pussy," he ordered her.

The crazed chick rubbed butter all over her crotch, snatched the ketchup bottle, and began feverishly fucking herself with it—in, out, in, out, in, out. She was moaning orgasmically again. She seemed to like it even more when Richard took his belt off and began whipping her.

This was all too much for John Paul, who left in disgust. I think I would have split as well, if we had not been in my room. Instead, still drunk and stoned, I was getting semi-turned-on by the depraved scene in front of me: this wild girl jerking off with a ketchup bottle.

Richard was now in movie-director mode, telling a roadie to stick his dick in her mouth and then come all over her face. The guy pulled down his zipper, and she started blowing him as she got herself off. Some of the other roadies did the same, and in no time the oblivious chick had cum all over her face, chest, and legs. She had butter all over her lower half and was still jerking off with the ketchup bottle when Richard put down his belt, took out his dick, and pissed all over her.

I know what you're thinking: animals, right? And I guess at that minute none of us seemed human, least of all the girl, who was still moaning with pleasure and getting off, even when a certain someone—let's call him Richard Cole—provided the coup de grace by climbing on the bed, dropping his pants, and shitting on her chest.

Let me tell you, this all reads as sick to me now as it does to you. But at the time, as the crap hit the crazy chick's chest with a sloppy thud, I could only think one thing: *That is my bed!* My bed—by then awash with shit, piss, semen, butter, ketchup, and one panting nymphomaniac.

I grabbed my suitcase and stuffed my clothes into it. "Tim, I'm moving into your room," I declared, and we high-tailed it out of there into Tim's adjoining room.

We were chilling a couple of hours later when one of our roadies called the room. "Guess where I am right now," he said. "I'm in bed with that chick who wants to be in a movie!"

"What?" I asked him. "Do you know what this chick just did?"

"Yes, I heard," he said. "But it's OK. She took a shower."

Wow! That must have been some shower.

The next day we flew out of Seattle and passed through Chicago, where I ran into Frank Zappa at O'Hare Airport. I knew Frank from our shows with the Mothers of Invention and—still high from the Seattle weed—I gabbled the whole story of what had gone down at the Edgewater Inn to him.

"Wow, that sounds crazy," said Frank, who was clearly taking mental notes, because a couple of years later his next record, *Fillmore East: June 1971*, had a song called "The Mud Shark" that related the whole sordid tale, including the following line: "Let's say you were a rock-and-roll band called the Vanilla Fudge / Let's say one night you checked into the Edgewater Inn with an eight-millimeter video camera."

Thanks a lot, Frank!

Of course, due to that song, to Richard Cole writing a book, and to general word of mouth, the mud shark incident is now the most infamous story of rock-and-roll debauchery ever. Some even say it's apocryphal; it never even happened. Well, let me tell you, it did. And for better or worse, I had a front-row seat.

What happened to this notorious X-rated classic? Well, a friend of Vanilla Fudge named Randy Pratt bought a Super 8 film from some guy who claimed it was Mark's original forty years later, but when he developed it, it was too old and there was nothing on it.

I reckon this was probably for the best. Morbid curiosity aside, that is one action movie that, older and wiser, I really would not like to see. And whatever happened to the chick? Oddly enough, years later she called in to a radio show I was on. She had moved to Alaska, raised a family, and lived happily ever after.

I wish her well. Believe it or not, she was a nice girl.

# 5

# THE CACTUS WITH THE PRICKS ON THE INSIDE

In which Drummerdude has his fill of Fudge, is busted for drugs while wearing ladies' bikini bottoms, forms Cactus with a gun-toting, knife-wielding singer, jams with Joplin, learns Hendrix's rude name for Led Zeppelin—and is devastated when Jimi dies

*Vanilla Fudge's summer of '69 tour with* Led Zeppelin had also witnessed another major development. It may not have entered into global rock-and-roll folklore like the mud shark incident, but one particular conversation was to have a major impact on the band's future—or, rather, our lack of one.

Backstage at the Singer Bowl in Queens, just before he went on and stripped off, John Bonham took Tim and me aside and told us how much his friend Jeff Beck loved us as a rhythm section. He said Jeff admired our tight playing and instinctive rapport and had enjoyed our Coke-commercial session as much as we had. Bonham added that Jeff, Rod, and Ronnie were about to exit their separate ways out of the Jeff Beck Group—and that Beck would love to form a band with us.

This news blew our minds. It also came at a good time. Tim and I were growing tired of the Fudge. Touring with Zeppelin had shown us how we wanted to play heavier, harder, bluesy rock and roll. We were over Vinny's too-long guitar solos, and we were especially over Mark's organ and Fudge's slowed-down rearrangements.

Don't forget, this was the era of the supergroup, when artists would break up successful bands and form new groups, as Eric Clapton, Steve Winwood, and Ginger Baker had done with Blind Faith. Suddenly all we wanted to do was quit the Fudge and form a supergroup with Jeff.

Bonham gave Tim and I Jeff's phone number, and we called him up. The conversation went like a dream. Jeff confirmed that he would love'to start a band with the two of us.

Did he think Rod Stewart might join as well, we asked him.

"Maybe," Jeff told us.

Wow! This was really fucking taking shape! Suddenly Tim and I had this cool secret, and we couldn't wait to get started!

For now, we kept our heads down and carried on with Vanilla Fudge business. This was to include our first on-the-road drugs bust. All the big bands were getting busted around then—the Beatles, the Rolling Stones, Hendrix—and I guess we had known our time would come. The scene of the crime turned out to be Montreal, Canada.

We played a weird show there at an outdoor expo. The venue had a bizarre layout, with huge concrete stairs leading up to the stage, meaning the audience was a long way from the action, and two songs in, Tim yelled to the crowd to move in closer to the band.

Some fans took him too literally, and immediately thousands of people were pushing past the overwhelmed security, up the stone stairs, and onto the stage. Mark Stein was stranded on top of his organ, surrounded by a mob of rabid fans grabbing at him.

It was out of control, and once security had rescued Mark, we had to run backstage, fans throwing themselves at us as we went. There followed an hour-long wait as riot police arrived and pushed the crowd back into place. Then we played an amazing gig.

I guess the local police may have taken this incident personally, because it wasn't the last that we were to see of them. That night we partied at the hotel. Tim and I smoked all our pot and then checked with Mark and Vinny next door to see whether they had any more. They said they hadn't, and so we crashed out.

At six the next morning, we woke up to the crack of splintering wood as a team of armed cops burst through our locked bedroom door, yelling, "Put your hands up!" They didn't just bust the lock; they took the door clean off its fucking hinges. They introduced themselves as the Royal Canadian Mounted Police and made Tim and I stand motionless as they searched our room for narcotics.

This was embarrassing for us for a few reasons. In those days I tended to wear chicks' bikini underwear—I just liked the feel of it better than the guys' stuff—and Tim always slept butt naked. So having been fast asleep thirty seconds earlier, there we were: Tim totally nude and me in girls' dainty bikini panties, with our hands over our heads, being barked at by Canadian Mounties.

We were also shit-scared. As the Mounties roamed around our room, I had visions of us spending months—even years—in a Canadian jail, even though I was reasonably sure they wouldn't find anything. Tim and I always got rid of our pipes and roaches before going to sleep, just in case—but that wouldn't help if they planted some on us!

Thankfully, they let us go after realizing we were clean, but Mark Stein wasn't so lucky. Our singer had been holding out on us, got busted, and was led off to the police station in handcuffs. Talk about instant karma! Our tour manager, Paco, was also arrested after the cops found a joint he had hurriedly shoved up his butt. Thanks to our lawyer, Stevens H. Weiss, they got off with a fine and probation—but it was a sobering episode for us.

After this North American tour, we had European dates planned, and going from the sublime to the ridiculous, a few weeks after coheadlining with Zeppelin, Vanilla Fudge found ourselves competing in a talent contest in Italy.

Fuck knows what it was all about. Someone at Atlantic Records had figured it was a good idea, and suddenly there we were in a stupidly expensive hotel in Venice to take part in some televised festival that we had never heard of and knew nothing about. We were there for three days and were scheduled to play one song—"Some Velvet Morning" from the *Near the Beginning* album—on the festival's second night.

On the first evening, we headed down to check out the venue. It was a weird scene: Italian-speaking aristocrats in tuxedos and ball gowns wafting around a beautiful old opera house. We felt like fish out of water in our hippie gear and so headed back to the hotel. The rooms didn't even have televisions, so I phoned Arlene and ended up getting into a crazy argument that went on for hours. When I got the room bill, I saw that fight had cost me four hundred dollars. Thank fuck Phil was there, as usual, to bail me out by paying the bill.

With three days to kill in what felt like a luxury prison, we went stir crazy. When we discovered a gay guy who was connected to the festival hanging around the hotel, we dragged him to the pool and threw him in fully clothed, followed by assorted chairs and tables. The hotel management was not impressed by this, nor by our habit of strolling into the lobby, dropping our pants, and mooning the other guests.

Tim proved better at killing time, befriending some chick from our record label, taking her to our room, and fucking her brains out. When the second night came around, we went back to the opera house and played "Some Velvet Morning" on live television. We didn't give the contest a second thought; we just wanted to get the fuck out of Venice.

So, naturally, we won the competition and had to go up onstage to receive our prize of a beautiful golden gondola in a gold box. But where the fuck was Vinny? We ran around the building trying to find him for the presentation ceremony as the Italian organizers screamed at us. We couldn't locate him, so Bruce Wayne posed as Vinny in the winners' photos. We later found that he had fallen asleep in an upstairs stairwell out of sheer boredom!

The next day, we rearranged the hotel, moving lobby furniture between floors and unraveling toilet paper all the way from the elevator to the waiting limos. The newspaper headlines celebrating our victory yelled "Vanilla Fudge Primo!" and Batman beamed out of the front pages, mistakenly identified as Vinny.

There were fans screaming at the airport as we jetted out, but Tim and I couldn't have cared less. We just wanted to get to England.

Jeff Beck picked Tim and me up from our swanky Savoy Hotel suite, and we cruised around swinging London in his Mini Cooper 1200. Jeff told us that he and Rod Stewart had fallen out, so Rod wouldn't be in our band. This was definitely a setback, but we figured we'd start out as a trio and find another singer.

We were still psyched about being in a band with Jeff. The three of us played a couple of impromptu jams at the Speakeasy. One of them was so wild that I literally destroyed the drum kit by hitting it too hard. The drum's heads and cymbals were smashed to bits, and the high hat cymbals finished up inside out. We realized once more just how powerful this band could be.

Jeff, Tim, and I picked up a couple of chicks, took them back to the Savoy, partied, and laid waste to our suite. Beck held back a bit from this. Hotel wrecking wasn't his thing, and he looked a little shocked as the beds and televisions flew across the room. But Tim and I left London on a high and feeling good about the future.

We even had a name for this new group: Cactus. That was my idea. I had seen a drive-in movie theater in Arizona called the Cactus Drive-In and thought it was a great name for a band.

Tim and I had a few last Vanilla Fudge dates to honor, and so we arranged to meet Jeff in New York a few weeks later with Phil and Jeff's manager, Peter Grant, who also managed Led Zeppelin, to firm up the business side of things. From London we flew back to Europe to play Montreux, Switzerland, at the casino that was to burn down soon afterward and be immortalized by Deep Purple in "Smoke on the Water."

Fudge were clearly in our death throes. The thrill had gone, and we just weren't getting along. We were promoting our fifth album, *Rock and Roll*, but the chemistry had been so bad when we recorded it that we couldn't even be in the studio together. Tim and I would do our bits, and then Mark and Vinny would go in and do theirs. I guess the fans could tell, as it did worse than all of our previous albums.

When Tim and I told Mark and Vinny we were quitting the band, they were shocked. Fudge had just been offered big money to tour Japan, but Tim and I refused to go, as we were so desperate to get started on Cactus. Mark and Vinny were really pissed off with us, but they didn't try to talk us into staying. They could see our minds were made up. The die was cast.

Tim and I flew back to New York from Europe excited to meet Jeff again and get our contracts signed—but we were hit by a bombshell. The day before he was due to fly out with his manager, Jeff was in a bad car accident in England in one of his hot rods and fractured his skull. He would be out of action for months, maybe a year or so.

Working with Jeff was suddenly on the back burner, and Tim and I realized we were in a bit of a spot. We had broken up Vanilla Fudge and now didn't have anything to replace it with. Where did we go from here?

We decided to do a few more dates with Fudge just to keep our heads above the water financially, while at the same time trying to get a new band going. So we started auditioning musicians, rehearsing like mad during the week, and playing still fairly lucrative gigs with Fudge on the weekends.

Our main priority was obviously to find a new guitarist to take the place of Jeff. Those were pretty big fucking shoes to fill! We ran across a guy from Detroit named Terry Kelly and jammed with him for a few days. He could play when he wasn't drugged out of his brain—which unfortunately wasn't very often.

Our next attempt was more productive. A New York musician friend, Duane Hitchings, recommended Jim McCarty, who had been with Mitch Ryder and the Detroit Wheels and played with the Buddy Miles Express. Jim was good friends with Hendrix, a great guitarist, and probably the nearest thing that America had to a Jeff Beck.

Jim was from Detroit but was living in San Francisco. After talking on the phone, we flew him out to Long Island to meet us. He was well over six feet tall, as skinny as a scarecrow, and had a definite penchant for the rock-and-roll lifestyle. But he was also easygoing, cool to hang with, and, most importantly, a phenomenal guitarist. As soon as we started playing together, Tim and I looked at each other, loving how his energy flow and lightning guitar riffs gelled with us. Yep, this was our guy.

Now we just needed a singer, and Jim recommended one of his Detroit friends, Rusty Day. Rusty had sung in Ted Nugent's band, the Amboy Dukes, who had played many gigs with Fudge, and we knew he was a cool front man. Rusty was a funny dude but not somebody you would want to cross. He always carried guns and knives and had that badass edge that a great rock-and-roll singer needs.

So that was it. Cactus was ready to roll!

Before we gave birth to the new band, we had to lay the old one to rest. One of the last dates I played with Vanilla Fudge was down in

Florida at the Palm Beach Pop Festival. They were billing it as a three-day Woodstock South, with the Rolling Stones, Johnny Winter, Jefferson Airplane, and the Byrds all hauling their asses down to Florida.

Janis Joplin was also there, and we put a jam together with the Fudge; Johnny Winter on guitar, and Janis on vocals. The crowd was really getting their rocks off, and as we played a long, stoned slow blues, Janis walked to each of us, one by one, grooving and telling us, "Kick ass, you mother! Do it!"

During the guitar solo in the jam, Janis was moving and shaking by my drums, drinking from a bottle. Suddenly she jammed the bottle into my mouth, nearly knocking my teeth out, and tilted it up so high that a river of liquor flowed down my throat. In a few seconds the jolt of the slug of booze was so intense that I got a head rush and thought I was going to fall off my stool. The booze tasted sickly, and it turned out to be Southern Comfort, which I had never tried before but which Janis cheerfully drank by the gallon. After our jam, she gave me a hug and a kiss on the cheek, said, "You rock, baby!" and wandered off. What a mad woman.

While that was our last big show, we truly brought the curtain down on Vanilla Fudge at the same place where it all began—the Action House. There were two thousand people crammed into Phil's Long Island club that night and nearly as many locked outside, clamoring to get in.

That was an amazing night. It was hugely emotional to look out at the faces of people who had supported the Fudge right from the start. Yet Tim and I knew we were doing the right thing. Our big farewell night tugged at the heartstrings, but that same heart told me it was time to move on.

Incidentally, it wasn't too long after that goodbye gig that the Action House burned down. Phil did OK from the insurance, and there were a lot of rumors knocking around that the Mob had started the fire deliberately. Years later, when I saw Ray Liotta as Henry Hill torching a club in *Goodfellas*, I wondered if that was based on the Action House.

Phil was to manage Cactus, and the band's rehearsal sessions were magic from the start. Everything just clicked into place right away, and the energy we were generating was such a contrast to the negative, jaded last days of the Fudge.

Jim was an incredibly fast guitarist, and Rusty had this knack for coming up with amazing lyrics off the top of his head as we jammed. He was anti-war, anti-police, anti-Establishment—anti-everything really. Because our music was so heavy, Atlantic had the idea of billing us in ads as "the American Led Zeppelin," but to me we were more of a punk rock band like the MC5.

We played one gig to test out our sound and material—at a sold-out festival with Hendrix in a stadium in Philadelphia in front of fifteen thousand people. We were nervous beforehand but decided to play only new songs, nothing by Vanilla Fudge, and the fantastic reception we got blew us away.

We had written our self-titled debut album very quickly. There were a couple of covers—including Mose Allison's "Parchman Farm," where I did a crazily fast double-bass-drum shuffle that was so fast it sounded like a runaway freight train. I wasn't a blues fan, but the kick-ass speed and energy made it a great song. We also did Willie Dixon's "You Can't Judge a Book by the Cover." But other than those, it was all original material. We recorded it in a studio with our stage Marshall amps and all of Tim's cabinets. It was like standing next to a jet engine in a tiny room. No wonder I'm half-deaf today.

The *Cactus* album was an ass-kicker from beginning to end, and we couldn't wait to play it live. We played two phenomenal gigs in Texas with the Who. We only had a forty-five-minute slot at the first show, at Dallas Coliseum, but went down great and even got to play an encore.

After the show, Cactus, our entourage, and a few groupies were sitting on our dressing room floor passing around a bong when through the fog of dope smoke we saw two Dallas cops standing in the doorway. The pungent smell of marijuana was impossible to miss, and the officers marched in and started to frisk everyone.

Shit! This was not good. Pot was a big no-no in Texas in those days, and the prospect of going to a state jail there terrified us more than anywhere else. The last thing we needed was good ol' boy jailbirds running their hands through our long hair, asking if we were boys or girls, and telling us we were mighty purty. It was even scarier than the Montreal bust with the Fudge.

Luckily, the promoter, Terry Bassett, a good friend of Phil's and thus presumably connected, persuaded the cops to let us off. As my heart pounded with relief, I could have kissed him. That was a close one!

Our next port of call was the Atlanta International Pop Festival. This was a big deal, with the promoters tearing down the fence Woodstock-style and letting close to half a million people in to see Hendrix, the Allman Brothers, Procol Harum, and B. B. King.

Our set was amazing. I'll never forget the sight when Rusty told a quarter of a million fans in Atlanta to get up and dance and the sea of people stretching to the horizon broke into crazy waves. When he told them all to say "Yeah!" the roar that bounced back hurt our ears.

Atlanta was a cool festival, not least because somebody had spiked the punch and wine backstage with mescaline, which meant we spent our entire time on the site in a euphoric haze. Unfortunately, it also meant we missed Hendrix playing "The Star Spangled Banner" at midnight on the Fourth of July as fireworks went off, which has gone down as a legendary moment in rock history.

Because Jim McCarty was good friends with Hendrix, I tended to see more of Jimi in my time in Cactus than I did when I was in Vanilla Fudge. When he was in New York, he stayed in the Chelsea Hotel in Manhattan. That was Jimi for you; he might have been one of the world's biggest rock stars, but he didn't even own a place to live. He just lived out of hotels, rode around in limos, and spent all his money on his recording studio.

Mostly Jimi loved to jam. I would bump into him at Steve Paul's the Scene club just off Eighth Avenue. It was a cool venue and always had happening acts playing: Buddy Miles Express, Terry Reid, Brian Auger, Mike Bloomfield, and so on.

For the last hour each night, before the club closed at 4 AM, it would have a star-studded jam session with whoever happened to be there. I would climb onstage and suddenly find myself jamming with any of Jimi Hendrix, Janis Joplin, Eric Clapton, Steve Winwood, Jack Bruce, or Johnny and Edgar Winter.

When the club closed its doors, we would pile around the corner to the Recording Plant studio, which Hendrix used to rent out around the clock when he was in New York. We would smoke pot and jam until the sun came up. Then I would fall exhausted into my Jaguar XKE and head back to my home in Oceanside. I guess the law went easier on DUIs in those days!

At other times, I would go with Jim and hang out with Hendrix at the Chelsea. His room was a real hippie pad, with incense sticks burning and colorful art posters and cloths hanging on the dimly lit walls, and Jimi was the same shy, intense, quiet but friendly guy he had always been.

One of the few times I ever heard Jimi be less than cool about another musician was when I mentioned Led Zeppelin to him. He frowned and told me, "I call them Excess Baggage." He thought they weren't original and ripped off other artists, including him. This shocked me; it was so out of character for him.

We also discovered that we had a girlfriend in common—or, rather, a groupie. Every time I was in Tampa I used to get with a beautiful Native American–looking chick named Alaina, and one day, when I mentioned her to Jimi, he said that he did the same.

This freaked me out—partly because I really liked Alaina and hadn't known she was a groupie working the circuit, but mainly because this was Jimi Hendrix! I was going with the same girl as Jimi Hendrix! But I could hardly complain. After all, I still had poor Arlene waiting patiently at home for me.

Rusty Day was turning out to be quite the shamanic front man for Cactus. He used to tell me, "An audience is a bunch of sheep. They need to be directed and told what to do." And as a super-charismatic guy, he could easily get them eating out of his hands.

This could lead to trouble. At a show with Hendrix at the Boston Garden, we were supposed to play forty-five minutes but ran well over an hour, mainly because Rusty kept whipping up the crowd. The Garden was a seated venue, but Rusty had this thing about the audience being a "free entity" who could do whatever they wanted— sing, dance, get high—and so kept telling the crowd to stand up.

When the audience obeyed, the police would bark at them to sit down, and Rusty would yell in his harsh Detroit tones for them to stand back up: "Get up! Rock and roll! This is a revolution! Fuck the po-lice!"

As we finally got offstage, four or five cops were waiting and arrested Rusty on the spot. Ten thousand fans were yelling for an encore, and we pleaded with the police to let Rusty go back on. There was no chance of that, so we had to muddle our way through a song as a trio, with Tim and I singing vocals. Our lawyer, Steve Weiss, then had to get Rusty released.

Up in Ontario, Canada, we played at Strawberry Fields Festival with Sly & the Family Stone, Jethro Tull, Grand Funk Railroad, and Alice Cooper. That particular weekend, Cactus's onstage attractions were as way-out as Alice's—and if you ask me, far more exciting than dolls and guillotines!

At that festival we had met a young lady at the hotel who was so in love with our album that she was happy to strip and dive into the pool naked, except for five Cactus stickers on her tits, ass cheeks, and pussy. Those stickers were great. Our original album artwork had featured a cactus that looked like a dick and two balls. Atlantic didn't let us use it, but we liked it so much that we made up thousands of stickers featuring the original, vetoed artwork.

Our new friend modeled them so delightfully that we christened her the Cactus Queen. When we played our theme song, "Cactus Boogie," at the Strawberry Fields Festival, we brought her out onstage with us in her sticker outfit. Unsurprisingly, the crowd went nuts.

It was time for Cactus to hit Europe, and we did a few dates with Ginger Baker's Air Force. We became good friends with Graham Bond, their legendary saxophonist and keyboard player, who must have weighed three hundred pounds and always wore huge capes. Graham was a character, a true English eccentric, and always stood out from the crowd, especially when he was with his equally wild wife, Diana, who dressed like a gypsy woman.

Ginger, though, had always been fucking nuts. One night in London before our tour began, Cactus were hanging out in the Speakeasy, and Rusty spotted Ginger at the bar. Rusty went over and politely introduced himself.

"Hello, Ginger. I'm Rusty Day. I play with Tim Bogert and Carmine Appice in Cactus, and I'd like to say what a big fan I am of yours."

Ginger turned to him with a sneer: "Why don't you go talk to yourself?"

Now, this is typical of Ginger's attitude toward life and other human beings, but it was not a wise way for anybody to talk to Rusty, a wild man who packed knives and pistols and was not afraid to use them. Somehow Rusty controlled himself from punching Ginger out, but it was a close thing.

A few weeks later, when Cactus and Ginger Baker's Air Force were out on tour together, we were due at a festival in Germany. Together with other bands playing the same festival, such as Sly & the Family Stone, we all flew en masse into Hamburg.

We always used to smoke hash in the bathrooms on planes, and as we came in to land, we realized we still had a lot left. There was no way we could take it through customs, so we simply ate it. Shortly afterward, an army of stoned, buzzing, and confused rock stars descended on passport control; luckily, the promoters shepherded us through without a hitch.

From Hamburg we all got a train to the festival, but somehow Ginger and Rusty got separated from the tour party and had to travel to the site together in a Mini Cooper. After the incident at the Speakeasy, we were expecting murder on the Autobahn. God knows what the atmosphere was like in that Mini Cooper, but the two of them got to the festival in one piece.

That was when the trouble started. All the bands were staying in the same hotel and seemed in the mood to do serious damage to the place. The lobby was soon full of broken lamps, and we were all being loud, obnoxious rock stars; when I found a worm in my steak at dinner, I reacted by flinging my food across the room.

The hoity-toity hotel staff were freaking out, and things were no better when we arrived at the festival. Phil Basile greeted us, looking serious, and informed us that we might not be able to go on, as a group of bikers called the Rockers, a kind of German take on the Hell's Angels, was causing trouble on the site.

As he finished speaking, we heard a burst of rapid gunfire and hit the ground as if we were in a movie. A promoter ran in and told us to get out pronto; the Rockers had machine guns and were shooting the place up. As the firing paused, we made a mad dash for the Mini Cooper and floored it.

Phil was made of sterner stuff. Our Mobster manager wanted to go back for our fucking money! We told him to forget it and that we should escape to Hamburg or London, but he was having none of it. Driving back to near the site, he literally crawled along the ground to the promoters' office, then came sprinting back to the car from what by then sounded like a war zone. I'm not sure he had our money.

Later on that same tour, Cactus had a date in Montreux, missed our commercial flight, and decided to hire a six-passenger, two-engine private plane over the Swiss Alps. It was one terrifying flight. The turbulence was unreal, and as the tiny plane bounced and shuddered through the air horribly close to the mountaintops, I was sure we were going to die.

We were crashing through fog, or clouds—we had no idea which it was. Every now and then a jagged mountain peak reared up in the cockpit window. I swear at one point we were flying sideways. Thoughts of Buddy Holly's last flight filled my head. I even started praying. When we set down safely, I kissed the ground.

The Montreux promoter was the famous Claude Knobs, who had also promoted Vanilla Fudge. Rory Gallagher and Taste were also on the bill, and he persuaded them to play for longer to fill in for us. When Cactus finally arrived, we were too tired and traumatized from the flight to play a full set, so we jumped onstage and jammed with Taste.

One of our last European appearances that summer of 1970 was at the legendary Isle of Wight Festival in England. More than half a million people made their way to this small island off the south coast for the nearest that Europe came to its own Woodstock.

Hendrix was the big draw, but the whole lineup was amazing, with the Doors, the Who, Joni Mitchell, Miles Davis, Chicago, and scores of other huge stars appearing over four days. There were mountains of pot, acid, and mescaline, plenty of which found its way into the backstage wine. Cactus hung out at the festival for days.

We performed on the Friday evening, two days before Jimi, and he watched us from the side of the stage. Later that night, in a big communal backstage tent-cum-changing-room, Hendrix and Jim McCarty sat down with acoustic guitars and jammed some far-out blues. I'll never forget how captivating it was. The entire tent was mesmerized.

Hendrix was due to play on Sunday night and finally went on in the early hours of Monday morning. He had some technical problems, but he was sounding fucking awesome when, after watching a few songs, we had to split.

I was never to see him again. Three weeks later, he was dead.

Even nearly fifty years on, I can't begin to say how much this freaked me out. Hendrix did his share of acid and pot and mescaline, but so what? We all did! We never expected anyone to overdose from it. Like I said, we all thought we were invincible back then.

Jim McCarty had spent a few days with Jimi in London after the Isle of Wight and said he had seemed normal, with no hint of depression or weird stuff going down. After the news broke, we just wandered around mouthing clichés about how we couldn't believe it. We were all in shock.

I was still in a daze shortly afterward when I went down to Electric Lady Studios to watch Mitch Mitchell rerecord his drum parts for *The Cry of Love*, the first posthumous Hendrix album. We talked about what a unique talent Jimi had been and what a waste his death was—but even talking for hours, we couldn't find the right words for how we really felt and for the emptiness within us.

The irony was that when Jimi died, his album and concert sales were in a bit of a lull, and his profligate, crazy lifestyle meant he didn't have much money—certainly not after all his hotel and limo bills had been paid! Of course, his legend means that his estate is now worth more than a hundred million dollars. Not that it's any good to him.

How do I feel about Jimi now? It feels weird to visit the Hendrix exhibition at the Rock and Roll Hall of Fame and see fans staring in awe and wonder at guitars that I saw him play and at clothes that I remember him wearing as we sat talking or jamming deep into the night. And more often than I think of Jimi Hendrix the ultimate rock star, I remember shy, quiet Jimmy James.

Ultimately, I feel privileged to have known him, and proud to have called him a friend. We have not seen Jimi Hendrix's like again. I don't think we ever will.

# 6

# WELCOME CACTUS SINGERS!

In which Drummerdude is arrested on a catnip bust, takes a public dump, writes a book, trashes more hotels, is impressed by the sex appeal and stamina of the Faces, rescues a rock god from a Caribbean beach, and answers a siren call from Jeff Beck

 *Cactus were mean muthas. We all came* from the kind of backgrounds where you had to know how to look after yourself; in particular, Rusty Day often seemed a hair trigger away from acts of intense violence. Black Sabbath, from the industrial English city of Birmingham, didn't take any shit, either.

Getting us together was always likely to spell trouble.

We played a show with Sabbath and their wild-man singer, Ozzy Osbourne, at the Sunshine Inn in Asbury Park in November 1970. Their second album, *Paranoid*, had just been number one in Britain and was a huge hit in America, and they were getting to be seriously big news.

On the afternoon of the gig, an ounce of pot went missing from the Cactus dressing room. For us, this was a major larceny—as bad as stealing money. One of our roadies, Michael Spina, who was a little guy, went to Sabbath's dressing room and asked if they had taken it. They denied it and punched him out.

This needled us, and in no time both bands were up in each other's faces yelling. It looked as if a full-on fistfight was set to kick off. Rusty was right in the middle of it, and I was terrified that he would pull one of his guns or knives from his personal arsenal.

The club owners came running down and calmed the whole thing down, but the bands were still brooding as we hit the stage that night. The winner was the audience, as we both went for broke musically, trying to blow our rivals away.

*Circus* magazine got wind of the argument, and turned it into a huge "Cactus and Black Sabbath at War!" deal. It caused a major bad vibe between the bands for a year or two, which was kind of ironic given that Ozzy's and my paths were to cross again so many times over the years.

The other funny thing about the fight was that it meant nobody in Cactus or Sabbath gave even a thought to the unknown New Jersey singer-songwriter opening the bill that night—some guy named Bruce Springsteen with his band Steel Mill.

Then again, we played with so many new artists, and most of them sank without a trace. Who was to know who would be the exception? Another time, shortly afterward, Cactus had to pull a gig in Boston after Tim had a motorcycle crash, and fans were instead entertained by a little-known group called Aerosmith. Years later, Steven Tyler told me it was a pivotal night in their career.

Cactus were still young guys, and I can't pretend that we were any less prone to screwing around and on-the-road adventures than were Fudge. One particularly messed-up evening came after a college gig in Syracuse, New York. The show was awesome, like a runaway freight train, and we got invited to a party afterward. We could have a drink, smoke some pot, meet some women—what could possibly go wrong?

The four Cactus members were drinking wine out of a gallon jug when we realized that it had been spiked with mescaline. This did not mix well with the superstrength pot we were also smoking. It pissed us off, as we were so high that we were being assholes, so no women wanted to talk to us—plus, we had a flight early the following morning.

It all put us in the mood for mischief.

Our tour manager, Mark, drove Cactus from the party back to our hotel through thick snow. We had a rent-a-truck sitting in the parking lot that was out of action with engine trouble. When Mark got out of the car, leaving Rusty in the front passenger seat, Tim, who was next to me in the back, suggested to Rusty that he drive the car right into the truck.

Never one to pass up a fucked-up idea, Rusty threw the car into drive and headed for the truck. I leapt from the backseat, reached across Rusty, and slammed the vehicle into reverse as it smashed into the truck. As the dented car skidded backward, I jumped out and ran for the safety of the hotel.

Looking out of my room's window, I saw Rusty still in the car and watched in stoned disbelief as he rammed it back into drive and smashed it into the back of the truck. This was an even stupider idea than it looked, as we still needed the car to get to our flight out of there the next morning!

Mark managed to ease the vehicle out from where it was, by now wedged under the box of the truck, and we all reconvened in my room to play guitar, smoke more pot, and try to come down from the mescaline. We were as wasted as it's possible to get, which made what happened next all the more bizarre.

Somebody went to use the bathroom, and the toilet flush wasn't working properly; it just kept running. I wasn't aware that Tim had any great plumbing skills, but he announced that he would fix the problem and headed into the bathroom with Jim in tow. A violent series of bangs and crashes ensued.

We looked into the door to see that the entire bathroom had been comprehensively trashed: shower, tiles, bathtub, toilet. A loose pipe was jerking around the room, shooting water everywhere. As I gaped at the damage, the bedroom phone rang. Jim picked it up to find nobody there. Naturally, his reaction to this was to douse the phone in lighter fluid and set it on fire.

So we had a damaged and useless rent-a-truck buried in three feet of snow, a rent-a-car we had deliberately smashed up, a trashed bathroom, and a hotel telephone impersonating a pile of cinders. This was going to be trouble, and we had to get as far away from it as possible as quickly as we could.

The next morning, still groggy and high from the mescaline and the pot, we jumped into the battered rent-a-car—which was somehow still running—and told Mark, "Let's get out of this state!" Our tour manager burst out laughing and dropped his bombshell: "Have you forgotten? You all *live* in this state!"

Fuck! Our wasted minds had failed to process that Syracuse really isn't all that far from Long Island. We managed to get to the airport and out of town before the police could reach us with their arrest warrant, but Steve Weiss had to pull yet more sharp moves to mollify the law and pay off the hotel.

Back in New York City, we went into Electric Lady to make our second album, which was to be called *One Way . . . or Another*. The recording process started off with the wrong kind of hit for me. On the way to rehearsal in my Jaguar XKE, I smashed into a woman in a big Chrysler who made a crazy turn in front of me. I gripped the steering wheel hard at the moment of impact, and the doctor who treated me told me the effect was like if I had smashed my arms with a metal hammer. We had to delay the album sessions and cancel a load of gigs.

When we finally got going, things started looking up. For some reason a woman named Jo-Jo was hanging around the studio. She was the ex-wife of Denny Laine, who was in Wings with Paul McCartney, and she and I had a short affair. Because she was Denny's ex, she felt like a conquest. She was pretty wild, and I remember lots of blow jobs in the studio.

We had another exciting Beatles-related visitation one day in Electric Lady when the studio door opened and in walked George Harrison. A Beatle! In our studio! I could not have been more excited if Jesus Christ had materialized in front of us.

It was kind of weird, as somebody had once told me that George was a big Vanilla Fudge fan. But I didn't dare to ask him, and he didn't look as if he recognized Tim or me.

Jim McCarty was clearly equally thrown by our unexpected guest. "What's the name of the band?" George asked him, in his soft Liverpool drawl.

"Hi! I'm Jim McCarty!" our guitarist replied. When I jumped in and said we were Cactus, George nodded, mumbled some comment to our engineer, Eddie Kramer, and strolled out. We had met rock royalty.

Making the album was a riot, and way more fun than the first record. We had our full stage setup in the famous Studio A and went in with an outline of songs, then wrote most of them in there.

The sessions were fluid, speedy, and productive and gave birth to what became one of our signature tunes: "Big Mama Boogie." It started off as just McCarty on acoustic guitar and Rusty playing baritone harp and yowling his crazy lyrics: "I'm from Detroit, where the boogie was born / I been boogyin' since '51." Then we all piled in with a full-on noise assault and made a monster.

With the album recorded, it was time to get back out on the road. We played tours with Ten Years After and Ted Nugent. Ted was a real smart businessman. Everyone knows he never drinks or takes drugs, but he also took his own motor home and trailer on tour to avoid paying for hotels and flights. Ted would be making five grand a night and paying his band a few hundred dollars per week in salary.

Cactus always did well in Ohio, particularly in Cleveland. It was a regular gig for us, and one weekend in '71 we flew in on a Saturday afternoon, with a free evening to kill before a theater show that Sunday night. Or, rather, we were going to have a free night, until Frune the Loon stepped in.

Frune the Loon was a wild guy who was one of our roadies, and a distant relative of mine. I didn't know him until he started working for us, but he turned out to be my cousin's cousin. He was a good-looking guy with curly Peter Frampton hair, and he got plenty of chicks. But he was also kind of crazy. We could tell him to do anything—"Frune, go moon those people over there" or "Throw a bucket of water over that guy"—and he would just do it, without a second thought.

For most of the flight to Cleveland I was asleep, but the rest of the band and crew were partying hard—cocaine, acid, all sorts of shit. They played a trick on Frune and gave him a bag of catnip, telling him it was strong pot.

In those days we used to always smoke joints in the bathroom on planes and then pour cologne on the floor to disguise the smell. Frune headed off to the john to smoke his catnip. When he came out, he bumped into a stewardess and offered her a toke on his joint!

The stewardess told the captain what had happened, and I woke up to discover everybody quickly disposing of whatever stash they were carrying. Poor old Frune might only have been dispensing catnip, but that didn't mean we wouldn't face consequences for his dumb actions.

Sure enough, we emerged at the gate in Cleveland to find a bunch of guys waiting for us. Still groggy from my sleep, I assumed they were fans. When one of them asked me, "Are you in Cactus?" I cheerily answered, "Yeah!" expecting to be asked for my autograph.

"OK, get over there!" he brusquely told me, producing a police badge. "You're under arrest." They arrested everybody—even the drivers the promoters had sent to the airport to collect us.

No matter how many times we got busted, it always freaked me out, and this was a grim situation, especially when we got herded into a windowless paddy wagon. Somebody had the idea that it might help us relax if we tried meditation, and so the whole van chanted "om" as we bumped along. We almost started enjoying the journey—until we got to jail.

The cooler in the downtown Cleveland police station was an ancient shithouse that turned my stomach. The cops shoved us into a concrete holding area with filthy stone beds, and a toilet fastened to the wall that had a layer of crud all over the seat.

Some in the party were still pretty high, so for the first couple of hours we kept our spirits up by singing Beatles and doo-wop songs, but then depression and panic began to set in. How the fuck were we going to get out of here? Would we make our gig? Had the tour manager spoken to Phil? It was Saturday night, so our wiseguy manager would be driving between his three or four Long Island nightclubs. This was decades before cell phones; he could be impossible to get hold of.

We tried to explain to the cops that our supposed pot was only catnip. They didn't care. They would have to test it in their lab, which wasn't open on weekends. As we digested the grisly news that we could be stuck in that hellhole until Monday, they offered us cheese sandwiches.

Sometimes food goes right through you. Unlucky for me, this was one of those occasions. I fought my insides desperately but eventually had to take the most embarrassing dump of my life, on the most revolting toilet I had ever seen, in front of the whole band and crew, with hardly enough paper to wipe my ass. As I glared at Frune the Loon, I seriously contemplated adding another charge to my rap sheet: homicide.

Thankfully, in the early hours of Sunday morning, the cops announced they were letting us go—all apart from Frune and another poor roadie who had picked up one of his catnip spliffs. As we left the jail, reporters crowded around us yelling questions, and the next day we were the lead story in the Cleveland *Plain Dealer*: "Rock Group Cactus Busted!"

The upside to this scandal was that our gig completely sold out that day. The downside was that the news traveled back to New York, where my parents flipped. I had to phone my mother and talk her down. Frune got released when the police lab opened and discovered the joints really *were* catnip.

With half of our road crew still in jail, we had to help set up our own gear for the show, but the gig went well. Our opening act was Long John Baldry, the blues singer who first discovered Rod Stewart before Jeff Beck took Rod under his wing and led him to worldwide fame.

The funny thing was I usually enjoyed Cleveland gigs because I had met a girl named Nancy on an early trip to Youngstown, and every time we went to Ohio she would come along for the ride. Nancy was nice looking, with big boobs—as I have explained, my favorite type—and we always had great sex.

She came with me one time when we moved on from Ohio up to Toronto. After a cool show at the Massey Hall, some guy came backstage and invited Cactus to a party at Roshdale, which was like a social experiment: a twenty-story-high apartment building where the authorities tolerated soft drugs. Consequently, it was full of hippies and drug addicts.

When we walked into the party, I had never seen anything like it in my life. As well as incense, people were burning hash—just passing around huge blocks of it the size of your hand. In a bedroom, hippies had a huge bowl of hash attached via a pipe to a vacuum cleaner! No joke, the hash smoke was about two inches thick—it smelled like the room was on fire.

We opened the apartment door, and the thick smoke rolled out into every crevice of the apartment building's hallway. I smoked so much that my lungs hurt. Unfortunately, I got so high that I couldn't perform sexually back at our hotel later and passed out. It certainly wasn't worth Nancy's time traveling up from Cleveland!

For some reason, Southern chicks always seemed to be up for groupie action, and we met a real live one in Kentucky. After a sold-out theater show in Louisville, everybody headed back to our suite for a party. We had loads of mescaline and pot, and soon everybody was pretty gone.

I met a girl who we soon nicknamed Long Tall Sally after one of our songs. She had a beautiful body, and by the time we were in the suite, she was wearing a 1940s smoking jacket with nothing beneath it. The two of us went down to the roadies' room to smoke some pot alone before going back to my room.

I went to the bathroom in the roadies' room and reemerged to find the rest of the band and the crew had materialized and turned off the main room lights. They all started humming "om," just like in the Cleveland paddy wagon. Sally was kneeling on the bed, and suddenly all the guys gathered around her and started touching her. She melted into the bed and lay on her back.

Sally was as high as a kite, and as a load of hands helped her off with her robe, it was clear she was excited. What followed was just pornography. One guy started kissing her; two were fondling her tits; one moved in on her crotch and started eating her out. In no time, Sally had a hard-on in each hand; we even put Vaseline on her feet so we could fuck her toes.

She must have got guys off twenty times during that all-night gang bang and was still smiling the next morning when we dropped her off at her house on the way to the airport. I will never forget looking back at Long Tall Sally as she did the walk of shame to her front door and seeing a giant cum stain all over the back of her robe.

That was an extreme night even for us, but at this point we were having a total blast in Cactus. The gigs were awesome, and every night on tour seemed to get better and better. The crowds always loved "Big Mama Boogie," during which Rusty would get so carried away that I lost count of how many times he got arrested.

The shows were nearly always followed by an orgy—and if we weren't screwing chicks, we were destroying hotel rooms. The invention of Krazy Glue was great for us, and we progressed from gluing chairs to ceilings to turning whole hotel suites upside down.

For some reason, a Hilton in San Antonio, Texas, seemed to get the worst of our attentions. Every time we stayed there, we ended up heaving TV sets and wrought-iron chairs and tables off our balconies into the canal below. In the morning we would sit and eat breakfast on the terrace with whichever chicks we had picked up the night before and laugh at all the items of hotel furniture in the bottom of the canal.

Of course, like all spoiled rock stars, we were paying for all of the damage ourselves through our record label, management, and accountant. I could never work out why the San Antonio Hilton kept letting us go back, but maybe it was because they knew they could basically redecorate their hotel at our expense!

I wasn't partying nonstop every night on the road, however. In fact, during one period on the road in 1971 when an addictive new enthusiasm had gripped me, I became positively studious.

Ever since I had strolled into a Sam Ash music store in Long Island and flicked through a terrible beginners' book of rock drumming, I always wondered why the few drum-instruction books that existed were so awful. Ambitiously, I decided that I would correct the situation.

For a month or so of Cactus dates, after the show I would retire to my hotel room (alone!) every night to work on the book that was to become *The Realistic Rock Drum Method*. Remembering how I had first learned to play grooves, I aimed to write a book that would take an absolute beginner to the point where he could play with a band. I enjoyed writing it and was pleased when a publisher agreed to put it out and to pay me a five-hundred-dollar advance.

To my delight, the book came out to great reviews. The Ludwig drum company, my long-term sponsor, suggested I start doing drum clinics to promote the book and teach students to play drums. I loved the idea, especially after my first clinic, at a Sam Ash store in New York, attracted around seven hundred fans.

So from then on, whenever I was on tour with a band, I would also stage drum clinics on days off. Eventually I even started doing drum clinic tours. I guess in a funny kind of way, I was making history—no other well-known rock musician had done anything like this. Not that I was trying to make history. I was just enjoying teaching.

The early seventies was an era when bands released two albums a year, rather than one every two years like today, so as soon as Cactus had toured *One Way . . . or Another*, we went back into the studio to record the follow-up. It was titled *Restrictions*, and it featured a song called "Mean Night in Cleveland" about our catnip bust.

Then we went straight back on the road—and if our exploits in Vanilla Fudge and Cactus had been pretty debauched and rock and roll to that point, now they were about to go up—or I guess I should say down—to another level.

It was time to say welcome to Sodom and Gomorrah—otherwise known as touring with the Faces.

We soon realized that Rod Stewart and Ronnie Wood were nothing like the two shy, pineapple-topped little mice who had dropped in on Vanilla Fudge's recording studio and hardly said a word. What we had there were two larger-than-life English jokesters who would do anything for a laugh.

Rod and Woody—they were quite the double act. Even more than us, they were living the life and loving it. They were full-on rock superstars, good-looking guys with those cute English accents that American chicks couldn't get enough of, and the number of women they pulled was unbelievable.

The Faces would generally book a whole floor of whatever hotel they were in, and it would turn into a nonstop-party-cum-orgy for the length of their stay. The first time Tim and I went over to visit them, there were ten chicks in Rod and Ronnie's room, and the Faces' tour manager, Pete Buckland, was picking them up and throwing them all on the bed.

We all eagerly leapt on and joined them, and everybody jumped up and down on the bed until it broke in two. Tim celebrated by grabbing a chair and smashing it into a plaster wall, where it hung like some freaky art installation. That set the tone for the two bands' time together.

The Faces had a bar onstage as part of their set, and Cactus would go and sit at it during their show, drink brandy and Cokes, and get totally wrecked. But the Faces were about more than hedonism and debauchery. They were also a fantastic live band.

I'll never forget playing with them at Madison Square Garden. A band called Bull Angus opened for us. I had a quick chat with their New Jersey drummer, a guy named Tico Torres. Of course, he was to go on to fame and success with Bon Jovi.

After Cactus's set, I took a hit of mescaline and went out into the crowd to watch the Faces. They were amazing that night. "Maggie May" was the big song, and as they launched into it and twenty thousand fans jumped and sang along, the Garden's new floor, built on steel girders so it had more give, vibrated under us.

Blurry from the mescaline, I initially thought I was tripping, but then I realized that the Faces were so awesome that night that Madison Square Garden itself was dancing! Up there with Hendrix, it was one of the best rock-and-roll shows I have ever seen.

Rod and Ronnie knew how good they were, and, as with us, that confidence and cockiness could spill over into brattish arrogance—especially where women were concerned. If a groupie chick came backstage wearing a short skirt or lace or fishnet nylons, we would just yank them right off. We were the absolute epitome of spoiled, obnoxious rock stars.

I remember at one gig in Chicago, two beautiful twins with huge tits were in the dressing room. They had tank tops with no bras, and every time we went past, we pulled their tops down so they were bare breasted. I was on a mission to get both of them in bed but had to settle for one of them, as one of the Faces nabbed the other one.

It's hard to say which was our greater passion—fucking chicks or fucking up hotel rooms. It got to the point where Phil Basile told Mark, our tour manager, to write down in a book everything that we broke, to ensure that the individual culprit paid, and not the band as a whole. When Tim and I heard about this, we busted Mark's balls.

We would ask him over to our room, and he'd pen a meticulous inventory as we trashed the joint:

*Tim: One lamp, one bureau.*

*Carmine: One mirror, one television, one picture frame . . .*

In Akron, Ohio, Faces tour manager Pete Buckland and one of their roadies smashed up two of our rooms, and we swore to exact revenge. Finding their rent-a-car with its doors unlocked, we removed all the knobs, ashtrays, and sun visors; let the air out of the tires; ripped wires out of the engine; and stole the hubcaps. To finish off, we backed our own rent-a-car into its side, leaving it caved in. The vandalized vehicle was a wreck.

Other favorite activities included filling buckets with water then knocking on somebody's room door and, when they opened it, throwing it over them. To give it an edge, we normally pissed in the water first. One time in Washington, DC, we water-bombed Tim in bed with a groupie after a roadie climbed up the outside of the hotel to his balcony—on the fifth floor!

Pulling fuses out of fuse boxes to slam rooms into darkness was also fun. Probably unsurprisingly, Cactus soon began getting barred from hotels and then from entire hotel chains. That was the case after a stay at a Holiday Inn in Georgia. It had all started so well: we had arrived to find a sweet sign outside announcing, "Welcome Cactus Singers!"

The hotel management wasn't so welcoming, however, after a wild night that saw the band and crew charging naked up and down corridors, throwing water everywhere. Next morning, with cops on the way, we headed fast across the state border into North Carolina. Having jumped straight out of the shower, Tim Bogert was in only a towel as our getaway rent-a-car burned rubber out of Georgia, and we had to stop at an abandoned train yard for him to get dressed.

We were having great fun with the Faces, but not everybody in our camp was happy. Jim McCarty was growing fed up with playing with Cactus—specifically of playing with Tim. Tim plays his bass as a lead instrument, and it can leave a guitarist feeling crowded out. Frustrated, Jim quit, leaving us needing a replacement.

We found our new man by a weird route. Right after Jim quit, we did a radio interview in Rochester and announced that we were going to a local club to jam and look for a new guitarist. The club was crammed with hopeful applicants, of which a guy named Werner Fritzschings was easily the best. We didn't find out until years later that when he joined, Werner was only seventeen years old.

We were also getting grief from Atlantic about Rusty, although he was an amazing front man. The label thought he was trouble—which was true—and they didn't like his rebel-rousing antics or his voice, which they said "wasn't commercial." After Jim left, they increased the pressure on us to drop our singer.

I thought Rusty brought a lot to the group, but he was getting more and more unhinged. Phil Basile was of the opinion that if the record company didn't like our singer, they wouldn't back us properly, and so we kicked Rusty out, which pissed him off severely, to say the least.

Rusty was one of a kind and a true loose cannon. I loved the guy, but we lost touch after Cactus. When I heard ten years later that both Rusty and his twelve-year-old son had been shot dead in Florida after a drug deal went wrong, I was very sad but not really surprised.

Rusty's replacement was to be a guy named Pete French, whom we brought in from Atomic Rooster, a group we had played with at various gigs and festivals. Having seen how well the Faces had done with a good-looking English singer, we decided to try the same formula—and aped their sound even more by bringing in an old friend, Duane Hitchings, on keyboards.

Our lineup had changed, but the fun and games with the Faces went on when we both played the Mar y Sol festival in Puerto Rico. This Brooklyn boy had never seen anything like it. We flew in to a private airport in the middle of a thick tropical jungle, and I warily disembarked, expecting to see gorillas and tigers.

There were around twenty bands playing the festival, including the J. Geils Band; the Allman Brothers; and Emerson, Lake & Palmer. They were all booked into the same incredibly exclusive hotel, with its own beautiful beach, surrounded by palm trees, leading to a turquoise sea—a true exotic paradise.

When we arrived, the hotel snootily informed us that the lobby and restaurant were out of bounds to anybody not wearing a sport jacket. A fucking sport jacket! Nobody in Cactus even owned a jacket.

We explained that they were set to have twenty rock bands staying there, so they may need to relax that rule.

Backstage at the festival was insane. Everybody was snorting cocaine. Thankfully, it's not a drug that has ever done much for me, but I joined in this one big time—only to discover that it was actually a line of mescaline. Great! Now I knew we would be up all night until our set the following afternoon!

Already buzzing, we met a beautiful, tanned bikini-clad chick who wanted a photo with the band. "Sure," we told her, "if you take off your top and show us your tits!" She was happy to do it, and that picture, of us fondling a grinning topless girl, turned up in *Rolling Stone*. In fact, it popped up everywhere over the years—it haunted us.

Back at the hotel, the management was realizing that the lack of smart-casual attire was the least of their problems. Rock stars wandered stoned through the lobby, girls in tow. The hotel's louvre doors were getting smashed. I trashed Tim's when he wouldn't let me into his room because he had a chick in there.

By now I was seriously wired. I managed to get it on with a chick I had met at the festival, but when she passed out after we had sex, I was still way too high to sleep. After sitting by the edge of the ocean for the rest of the night, I had breakfast at the hotel's balcony restaurant and freaked myself out thinking how easy it would be to jump off and kill myself.

I was weak, trembling, and in a bad way as Cactus helicoptered to the festival and took the stage. The emcee was a radio-DJ friend of ours from New York, Alex Bennett, who introduced us by saying, "Now, after completing a tour of wrecking Holiday Inns across America . . . here's Cactus!"

The sun was just setting on this paradise island, the vast crowd stretched to the twilit horizon, and we played an amazing set. Pete worked the crowd as well as Rusty had, Duane's keyboards sounded immense through the Marshall stacks, and the Puerto Ricans went crazy for us—as they did for the Faces that wild, balmy night.

The next day I thought the hotel maître d' would have a seizure when a massive interband food fight broke out and bread rolls were bouncing off the chandeliers and the few remaining louvre doors. Even legendary music mogul Clive Davis was involved. The hotel staff were going from room to room demanding to check for damage by the time we checked out and went for one last look at the beach.

We spotted a skinny, pineapple-topped silhouette loitering in between the palm trees. It was a rock superstar: the Faces had somehow managed to leave the island without Rod, who was wandering the beach disconsolately with no money to get to the airport, let alone buy a ticket. Luckily, Phil Basile was never short of ready cash and loaned Rod his airfare to wherever he was heading.

The Mar y Sol festival had been quite an adventure, and not just for us. Local media reported there had been accidental deaths, a murder, and several rapes over the weekend. The event ended with an arrest warrant out for the promoter, who fled the island.

We always figured the Faces were the rowdiest, most anarchic touring companions imaginable—before we met Badfinger, whom the Beatles had signed to Apple a few years earlier. We played a three-week alternate-headlining tour with them in '72, and on the first night, Badfinger ran onstage at the end of our set and splattered us with custard pies.

Seeking revenge, we did the most stupid thing imaginable: we filled a fifty-five-gallon metal oil drum with water, piss, and beer; carried it to the side of the stage; and threw it at Badfinger while they were playing. With all of the guitars, amps, and mics plugged in, we could have electrocuted them—but we weren't scientists, right? We were dumbass rock and rollers!

When Badfinger and Cactus hit Texas, we wandered into a huge bar holding about a thousand people, all of whom seemed to be dressed up with cowboy hats. We were in our usual rockers' gear and had hardly sat down with our beers before the heckles began: "Queers!" "Faggots!" We told a few people to fuck off, then decided the odds were not on our side and made a strategic retreat to recommence one of our favorite pastimes—smashing up the San Antonio Hilton.

The Badfinger dates were a lot of fun, and it was sad for me to see what happened to them over the ensuing years. First their singer, Pete Ham, hanged himself after their financial situation became desperate.

Their guitarist, Tom Evans, did the same a few years later, which I found unbelievable; Tom was such an easygoing, fun-loving guy.

Yet the Badfinger tour also proved to be the last hurrah for Cactus. We were getting along OK, but a new album, *'Ot 'n' Sweaty*, half of which was recorded live at the festival in Puerto Rico, did not do well, and Atlantic seemed to be looking for an excuse to drop the band.

Over in England, Jeff Beck had recuperated from his car crash and was touring the second incarnation of his Jeff Beck Band, with Cozy Powell on drums. He was ready to revisit our planned joint project, and when his people phoned Tim and me to ask if we felt the same, there was only going to be one answer.

It was time to lay Cactus to rest. Suddenly—and finally—we were ready to form our supergroup.

# 7

# BAKER FOGERT
# APPLESEED

In which Drummerdude ignores Rod Stewart's warning to steer clear of Jeff Beck, forms supergroup BBA, observes orange-helmeted lesbian action, receives dreadful medical care from Dr. Robert, incites a flag-related riot in Germany, and is baffled by the Strange Case of the Vanishing Jeff Beck

*Tim and I could hardly have been more* excited about teaming up with Jeff and opening a new musical chapter. However, not everybody shared our enthusiasm.

Few people knew Jeff Beck as well as his old friend Rod Stewart, and when we shared our plans with him, Rod was horrified. "Why would you want to do that?" he asked us, baffled. "Cactus is a great band, and if you stick with your current lineup, you will do really well. Whatever you do, don't go with Jeff—it won't last. He never sticks to any band. That's the way Jeff is."

I guess sometimes in life you get good advice and you just don't listen. Or, rather, you don't want to hear it.

Tim and I had touched base with Jeff again just before we split from Cactus. Legendary British music producer Mickie Most invited us over to London to do some studio work with a new artist he was pushing, which was a good chance to catch up with Jeff.

The trip didn't go smoothly. Mickie had put us up in a very exclusive hotel in Mayfair, and Tim and I called a few of our English friends to hang out with us. Faces tour manager Pete Buckland came up to our room and after a few drinks reverted to his default mode of trashing the joint.

For once Tim and I were blameless as we sat back and watched our furniture vanish through the window. I must say, Pete really went to town. When we peered down into the courtyard later, we saw people staring upward as they gingerly picked their way through the debris. We were lucky Pete left us our beds to sleep in.

The next morning we snuck out of the hotel without checking out and jumped into a cab. A couple of days later, Mickie Most put in an outraged phone call to Phil Basile insisting that we pay for the damage. We suggested he ask the Faces' road crew for the money, as they were a lot richer than us. For years after that, we kept hearing from Mickie demanding his money back.

Unsurprisingly, we didn't play on his new project.

Back in the States, my hot new hobby was my red De Tomaso Pantera. I loved that car. I first saw one after a Cactus show in Birmingham, Alabama, and was so blown away that I wrote the name of the car down so that I wouldn't forget it. Shortly after, I saw a pink one in *Playboy*; they gave it as a prize to their Playmate of the Year. It was an amazing hybrid of slick Italian design and American brute force—a bit like me, right?

So once I had seen a Pantera at a dealer in Long Beach, I looked at it in awe every time I went past. Finally I got up the nerve to go in and ask how much it cost. It was ten thousand dollars! In 1972! Despite this, I called on the sales guy, Saul, many times, until on one visit he asked me, "Why don't you take it for a test drive?"

"OK!" I said eagerly. He tossed me the keys, and I backed it out of the showroom and waited for Saul to get in. To my surprise, he told me, "Just take it. We have your XKE as insurance that you'll come back." Wow! A solo test drive!

The Pantera was amazing, just so fast, like a giant go-kart. I couldn't believe how cool it was. When I got back in my XKE, it felt like a kid's pedal car. I knew I had to have the Pantera; I also knew I couldn't justify spending ten grand. Shortly afterward I got a call from Saul—who was a good fucking salesman—saying I could have it for just under nine thousand and he would trade in my Jaguar. Man, I could not get down to the dealer fast enough!

Once I had the Pantera, I wanted nothing but to drive it twenty-four/seven, so it pissed me off that I had to leave for London two days later. But I was to have many amazing street races in that beauty. Everyone who got in it with me, from Rod Stewart to Jeff Beck to John Bonham, walked away either thrilled or scared shitless—usually both. I owned it for forty years.

In London, Tim and I began rehearsing with Jeff, and it soon became clear that this new band would be a very different beast from Cactus. Whereas Cactus were raw power and energy, now we were playing Motown chords that bordered on jazz. It was way more technically proficient and progressive.

We had decided to call the band Beck, Bogert & Appice, or BBA—but not straight away. We had seen so-called supergroups such as West, Bruce & Laing—Leslie West and Corky Laing from Mountain and Jack Bruce of Cream—launch with much fanfare, only to collapse under the weight of media hype and sky-high expectations. We didn't want to repeat the mistake.

So we agreed to play a few introductory US dates in the summer of 1972 as the Jeff Beck Group, then as the Jeff Beck Group featuring Tim Bogert and Carmine Appice, before going whole hog and switching to BBA. It gave us space to ease ourselves in, gave people time to get to know us.

We were still casting around for a singer and initially rehearsed with Bobby Tench from the second Jeff Beck Group. Bobby was a great guy and a killer soulful singer with a real cool, gritty edge to his vocals. I thought we sounded great, but Jeff didn't agree and fired him.

To replace him, Jeff brought in Kim Milford, an actor-singer who had played Rocky in the *Rocky Horror Picture Show* on Broadway and been Jesus in *Jesus Christ Superstar*. With Max Middleton on keyboards, we rehearsed a set that included Beck, Vanilla Fudge, and Cactus songs and set out on an American mini-tour.

It wasn't without its highs and lows. Our debut show as the Jeff Beck Group, in Pittsburgh, went well, and it was a rush to share a stage with Jeff and his incredible playing. Tim and I beamed at each other onstage as we realized that we were finally living our dream of being in a band with a genuine guitar hero.

However, our second gig, at Gaelic Park in New York, was delayed by ninety minutes when Jeff's limo failed to arrive to pick him up. When we finally got onstage, the disgruntled crowd started throwing rocks at us. I could not believe my eyes: people were hurling stones at Jeff Beck! We had to cut the show short.

The bigger problem we had was that our fans did not dig Kim. He was a nice guy, but he was a slight, effeminate figure who looked like a female go-go dancer. Our serious hard-rock and blues fans were not into his flamboyant antics, and after six dates we had to let Kim go.

Bobby Tench, who was clearly either a very forgiving dude or just used to the way Jeff worked, rejoined and replaced Kim, and the dates got better. The other question for Tim and me was, what would life on the road with Jeff be like? He was quite a shy, private figure. Would he be horrified by the rock-and-roll shenanigans that we routinely got up to?

We soon got our answer. After a show in Tucson, we were all staying on the first floor of a very cool hotel with room doors that opened up to the pool area. It was a beautiful, hot Arizona night, and we were all smoking superstrong pot and jumping in the Jacuzzi with some friendly, naked local blonde women.

All except for Jeff. Mr. Beck never smoked pot (in those days his poison was strictly vodka), and he had retired to his room to get it on with a groupie chick. I had poked my head into his room and left his sliding doors open so we could bust his balls later, and after a while, stoned and giggling, we crept across to his room.

When we slipped in the doors, Jeff and the chick were sitting on the bed and nothing much was going on. That soon changed. As soon as we arrived, one of the roadies threw her across the bed and put his dick in her mouth. What the fuck? This was, to say the least, a rather direct approach.

The groupie girl was into it and started sucking the dick straight away. Jeff sat looking stunned, and Tim and I felt pretty much the same, but somebody else began playing with the girl's pussy and getting her off. The room filled with crew and groupies, and I was getting flashbacks to Zeppelin and Seattle.

Except—who needed a mud shark? Suddenly the scene got even crazier. I heard the roar of a motorcycle outside, and a chick in an orange helmet climbed off, strolled into the room, and cast her eyes over the unfolding orgy.

"Do you want to get involved?" somebody asked her.

"Sure," she said. She stripped off, headed over to the bed, where the first chick was lying on her back with her legs wide open, and went down on her. We were freaking out, and to increase the comedy value, we put her helmet back on her head.

The girl on the bed assumed it was one of the guys eating her out. Eventually she glanced down, saw a woman in an orange motorcycle helmet between her legs, and screamed as she jumped out of the bed and ran out of the room, leaving us all in hysterics.

Mr. Beck's plans for a quiet, romantic evening had been spoiled. But at least now he knew what he was dealing with in his new band.

Bobby had been great on the tour, but now it was all change once more. We decided we should carry on as a trio, with Tim and me splitting the vocals. We were fine with that, as we had both sung a lot in Vanilla Fudge. After a short British tour and a few more US dates, it was time to make an album.

Having finally adopted the Beck, Bogert & Appice name, we relocated to London to begin writing songs. This meant more time away from my beloved Pantera for me—as well as from Arlene, who had moved in with me in a house that I had bought in Cold Spring Harbor, Long Island.

I have to confess that I didn't let this new state of cohabitation interfere with my pleasures on the road. While working on the album in London, Tim and I rented an apartment just off King's Road. I was screwing a woman named Liz, who was ironically a Long Islander and who would sometimes bring her friend Sally around for threesomes.

Tim began dating a girl named Kristy, who worked at Equator, BBA's London management company. It's fair to say that Tim was rather more serious about Kristy than I was about my dalliances—they ended up getting married and having a kid.

We flew to Chess Records in Chicago to record the album with the producer and songwriter Don Nix, who the year before had worked with Jeff on his *Orange* album and with George Harrison on his Madison Square Garden Concert for Bangladesh. Having written five or six songs in London, we felt pretty good to go.

Our trump card was "Superstition," which had been written by Stevie Wonder with a Jeff Beck riff. Stevie owed Jeff a favor after Jeff had played on his recording sessions for *Talking Book* and gave him "Superstition" as a gift.

However, when Motown chief Berry Gordy heard the song, he made Stevie also include it on *Talking Book*. This made people think that our version was just a cover, which was a drag, even though our version had Stevie's original lyrics, which he had rewritten by the time he released it himself.

Chicago in December is seriously cold, and I will never forget how freezing it was as we made the *BBA* album. We had the heat on nonstop. Finding myself locked out of the studio one evening, I had to take a leak and had to relieve myself in the parking lot. My piss froze as soon as it hit the ground.

I also had a nosebleed one night that went on for hours, which I put down to the heat being on constantly in the hotel room and the Arctic conditions drying my nose out. Little did I know that it was the first sign of a condition that was to make my life unbearable many years later.

Chicago was freezing, but inside our recording studio, the sessions were a riot. Maybe Jeff, Tim, and I had let the term "supergroup" go to our heads, because we went through a prima donna phase of demanding everything yesterday. *Playboy* models from the nearby Playboy mansion and groupies ran around the studio every day. It was one huge fucking party.

One night I invited one of the *Playboy* girls back to my room, but after she got into my bed I smelled a noxious odor. I could not believe it—this absurdly beautiful woman had bad pussy smell! It was so strong that I couldn't get it on with her and got my tour manager to kick her out.

An easygoing Southern gentleman, Don Nix had worked with Jeff before, but it had never been like this, and I think he found it hard to cope with our musical and sexual excesses. In fact, I know he did. Speaking to a US magazine, he told the journalist, "I don't know how I got this job, but I'd sure like to get out of it."

Despite this, he did a good job and wrote a song for us called "Black Cat Moan," which we persuaded Jeff to sing. Jeff was no great singer, but his voice had a certain unique quality, and he had enjoyed a solo hit single in Europe a few years earlier singing "Hi Ho Silver Lining."

After we had finished, Don took the tapes to his home studio in Nashville to mix them. When we heard them, I thought Tim and I both sounded kick-ass, but I was shocked how buried in the mix Jeff's guitar was. Jeff said he had asked for his parts to be mixed low so he could hear us rock out.

The record got good reviews and nearly went top ten in the United States, so we were looking forward to touring it. And what do you know? BBA on the road turned out to be a total fucking circus. Jeff may have had the image of being a very serious and intense musician, but offstage it was nonstop rock-and-roll mayhem.

We began with some British college dates, and it was a kick to play Leeds University, where the Who had recorded their *Live at Leeds* album. After the show, Jeff vanished to his room with two girls, which seemed greedy, so Tim, our matronly manager's assistant Pam, and I tiptoed outside his door.

Banging hard on the door, Pam yelled, "Jeffrey! This is your wife! I know you have women in there—open up!" When Jeff didn't respond, we spotted a hotel food trolley in the corridor and smashed it hard against the door, at which point it flew open and two terrified women sprinted off down the corridor.

Jeff saw the funny side. Eventually.

Still in northern England, in Manchester a fan handed a big, fat English-style half-tobacco, half-dope joint to Tim while we were onstage. It was a huge Cheech-and-Chong job. Tim took a hit and offered it to Jeff, who refused, and then passed it to me to toke on. I handed it on to the road crew.

When our set ended, I noticed that none of the crew seemed to be backstage and asked Jeff's manager, Ernest Chapman, who was a big London attorney, where they were.

"They've all been busted, darling!" he informed me. "And so have you and Tim!"

Busted in my absence? This was a new one on me, but Ernest explained that the police, who had witnessed our onstage joint-smoking from the audience, had decided to allow us to finish the show before reporting to the police station to get booked.

It proved to be a very British bust. When Tim and I got to the police station, they showed us the offending joint in an evidence bag and politely took our photos and fingerprints. We were expecting to get thrown into a cell, but instead the cops offered us tea and cookies and sat chatting with us. Ernest did some legal magic, and we got off with a conditional discharge.

One major problem I had on that tour was a blister I got on my left thumb on an early date. I taped it up and did all I could to turn it into a callus—I even pissed on it every day after someone told me that would help. It kept getting worse, became more and more painful, and after a couple of weeks was a blood blister on top of a blister. Ouch!

Our show in London was going to be a big deal, with Zeppelin, Deep Purple, ELP, and others coming down to see us, so I decided to get my wound sorted once and for all. Our management got me an appointment with a Dr. Robert—yes, the very same guy immortalized in the Beatles song! Or so we assumed.

In a dingy office like something out of the 1950s, the now middle-aged Dr. Robert glanced at my ugly-looking thumb and said he would inject it with Novocain. It seemed to work, and I felt fine at that night's show, even though it was weird to be hitting with a numb thumb.

In fact, the London date was a blast. We rented out some tuxedo tails to wear during the encore, as a goof, and after the show, when the crowd was yelling for more, we turned the stage into a sea of dry ice and drove into the middle of it in one of Jeff's hot rods! After the encore, we threw paper plates of whipped cream into each other's faces and tore our tuxedos to shreds.

Over the next few days, however, I noticed my thumb wasn't getting better. In fact, a giant volcano-like pimple was growing on the end of it, and a red line was spreading up my arm. By the time it reached my elbow, the pain was excruciating. Like the trouper I am, I never missed a show.

I finally took it to a provincial English doctor, who was horrified at what she saw. Telling me that my whole arm was getting infected, she lanced the pimple with a sterilized scalpel. It sent gross green and white pus oozing everywhere. The doc said that in a couple of days the infection would have got into my heart and could have killed me.

"How did you get the infection?" she asked me. I told her about Dr. Robert, and she explained that the needle he used to inject me with Novocain was probably dirty. I learned a lesson right there: don't mix with rock-and-roll doctors!

The tour continued to the States, and we were getting along great. We had one goofy part of the set where Jeff played a big solo and then fell to the floor as if he were exhausted, and Tim and I would help him up. In Seattle, rather than pick him up, we hit him in the face with a whipped-cream pie. We repeated the trick at other shows.

What was cool was that my *Realistic Rock Drum Method* book was selling like crazy. I was selling copies as merchandising at the BBA gigs, and Ludwig had started buying a thousand copies a year to sell. The drum clinics were also attracting more and more people.

When we passed through Arkansas, we encountered a legend of the groupie scene: Connie from Little Rock. Well, actually, I didn't. I just heard later that she was hanging around backstage and at the hotel and that she serviced the entire road crew. Nice girl, huh?

In Charlotte, North Carolina, BBA played a ten-thousand-capacity gig with the James Gang. They insisted on closing the show, which seemed weird, as their main draw, Joe Walsh, had left the band and been replaced by Tommy Bolin. Surely Jeff's name alone was a bigger draw than them? At that stage, BBA were selling out ten-thousand-seaters on our own!

But we went along with it, decided to have an early night, went on first, and tore the place up. The crowd went fucking crazy for us. After we had showered and changed, we went out to check out the James Gang, and there were maybe two thousand people left in the hall. It was sad to see, but cool for us!

As we were pulling away from that show, a chick staggered up and banged on the window of our limousine so hard that we thought she'd break the glass. We opened it, and as she stuck her head in the car, we all smelled the breath of somebody who had been drinking for many, many hours.

"Which of y'all guys is . . . Jeff Baker?" she slurred, in the strongest Southern accent you can imagine.

She introduced herself as Suzie, and we pulled her into the car through the window and took her back to the hotel and one of the roadies' rooms. That's what we always did: took the group-ies to roadies' rooms so that we wouldn't get stuck with them afterward.

Suzie had her own bottle of booze and was swigging on it as she fooled around with us and led us to believe we were all about to have a very good time. Then she lay down on the bed and passed out. Inside a minute she was snoring.

We were all pretty horny and very stoned (except for Jeff, who was vodka fueled as usual), so we pulled up her tank top, fondled her bare breasts, and took it in turns to masturbate on her chest. Then we pulled her shirt back down and patted it with a towel to make sure that she would wake up with it glued to her.

Suzie woke up the next morning and pretty quickly asked us, "What is going on with my shirt? It's sticking to my chest and it's stiff!" We played dumb at first but then advised her to smell it, at which point she worked out what had happened. We then let her use the shower and gave her a clean shirt to wear. You know what? We probably thought that made us gentlemen.

Suzie was to enter into BBA folklore. After that night, whenever we checked into a hotel, we did so as Jeff Baker, Tim Fogert, and

Carmine Appleseed—and always in a Southern accent, as a tribute to our North Carolina drunken angel.

In Los Angeles I met a girl named Marlene in the Rainbow Bar on Sunset Strip, who told me she was a virgin. As she climbed out of my bed the following morning, I wasn't entirely sure I believed her. It seemed like a typical one-night stand. I had no idea just how seriously she was to enter my life again.

The first leg of the BBA American tour ended in Honolulu, where we had a few days' rest. We had gelled really well, both onstage around Jeff's amazing guitar heroics and as friends and co-adventurers. The band felt like a huge success. To celebrate, I decided to fly Arlene out, although I was of two minds, as I loved Hawaiian groupies. Somehow, miraculously, I managed to get the best of both worlds.

Arlene was in the shower in our room and I was enjoying the view of the turquoise ocean from the balcony when Jeff phoned me up. "Where's your chick?" he asked. When I told him, he sounded pleased: "Good—you've got to come down to my room!"

I told Arlene I was going down to see Jeff. When I got there, he was with a crazed groupie who was on a mission to have sex with all of BBA.

"My girlfriend is upstairs!" I told her, but she was determined to give me head there and then. Well, I can't pretend I tried too hard to talk her out of it. One blow job later, I was back upstairs with Arlene, feeling like an asshole but at the same time getting off on the sleaziness of what I had just done.

From Hawaii we flew on to Japan, and we were not expecting the reception we received when we got there. Unknown to us, BBA mania had kicked in! As we cleared customs, we were mobbed by hordes of screaming fans, and security guards had to pull us clear and help us run to the waiting cars. Suddenly I had a little insight into how the Beatles must have felt.

Phil Basile was out in Tokyo with us, although our manager's math was a little off on this Japanese jaunt. We were getting fifty thousand dollars for three shows, which was fine—except that flying our full PA system out to Japan cost us seventy thousand! But the crowd reaction at our sold-out show at the legendary Budokan was unforgettable.

The audience loved our set of BBA, Beck Group, Vanilla Fudge, and Cactus tunes and went mental for our solos. Tim was still heavily into fuzz tones and slapping his bass, everybody in the arena clapped along to my twenty-minute thunder solo, and Jeff was simply a god in Japan, particularly with his guitar bag that made his instrument talk. We were humbled to be told that BBA were the first band to sell out the Budokan.

Nevertheless, I can't pretend that the gig didn't freak me out. The Budokan had no proper light system, just four ten-thousand-watt search lights left over from World War II glaring at us from both sides of the stage. Also, it felt fucking weird to be entertaining ten thousand ecstatic Japanese people when just a generation ago we had been at war with them! But these thoughts passed; it was a magical night.

Naturally, the tour gave us the opportunity to extend our hotel-wrecking activities to a fresh continent. After the Budokan show, we somehow ended up in a room with some fans at our hotel. It was boring, so we left after five minutes, and as we walked down the hall, two guys followed us out of the room, shouted, "Jeff, Timmy, Carmine—bye!" and started blowing kisses at us!

Guys blowing kisses at us struck me as weird, so I grabbed a fire extinguisher off the wall, aimed it at them, and let fire. Instantly the whole hallway was enveloped in a thick cloud of smoke. We made a dash for the elevator and our rooms, but the hotel management heard what had happened, and, as usual, we got a hefty bill for the damage.

Obviously, we were also eager to import our sexual misbehavior into Asia. One night in Tokyo our tour manager had a hooker in his room and for some reason invited me, Jeff, Tim, and Phil to watch. The poor girl didn't appear to think this was part of the deal and kept demanding more money—not easy, as she was lying flat on her back with his dick in her mouth at the time.

The tour manager was squatting over the girl and unleashed three huge farts onto her tits. As she smelled the rank odor and heard us all laughing, she found the strength to push him off her, grab her clothes, and run out of the room. Whatever he paid that chick, she earned it.

My adventures in the exotic, erotic East continued with a visit to a traditional Japanese bathhouse. I was in heaven as I lay nude while a naked woman slid up and down me on the bathhouse floor, washing me with suds and her body, and giving me an amazing hard-on. She put me into a hot tub for the rinse off. Then after a fantastic massage on a padded table, she put a rubber on me with her mouth—she was so experienced that I didn't even know she'd done it!—then gave me head and sat on me until I came.

It was an amazing sensual experience, but ridiculously, at the time I remember feeling it was all a little too robotic. Well, what the hell was I expecting? To fall in love in a whorehouse?

BBA also played two nights at the Festival Hall in Osaka and recorded the shows for Japanese release on analog eight-track one-inch tape. We never got to hear it until it came out as *BBA Live in Japan*, and we were horrified to find they had left all of the mistakes in, rather than correct them via overdubs! We hated it, even though it became one of Japan's bestselling live albums.

On that tour we used a backdrop of three huge flags hanging at the back of the stage: two Stars and Stripes and one British Union Jack, to show that BBA was two American dudes and a British guy. This was no problem in the States, Britain, or Japan. Germany was a different story.

We flew to Europe from Japan and had some German dates, including a show in a huge all-standing arena in Hanover. We played our first number and became aware that some people in the crowd were yelling stuff at us. A helpful German roadie translated for me: "They are saying, 'Take down the flags.'"

We hadn't expected this! I got on the mic and said that the flags just represented where we came from and were not any kind of political statement, but as we played, the jeers and catcalls kept coming. "We're not here to do politics—we're here to rock and roll!" I said. The booing continued.

Ten minutes in, Jeff spoke into the mic. "We'll do another song, but if you keep yelling this crap, we're going to fuck off and split!" he told them. Things got no better, so he laid his guitar down. "Goodbye. We're out of here."

We walked off the stage, and a hailstorm of glasses and bottles rained down on us. I was wearing a thick Afghan coat that I figured would protect me, so when I saw a guy in the front row throw a beer bottle at my drum set, which lodged in the shell of my tomtom, I grabbed a bottle and threw it back at him, hitting him on the shoulder.

My drum tech grabbed me. "Are you fucking crazy?" he yelled into my face. "Get out of here!" As we leapt into a car and made a fast getaway, there was a full-scale riot going on in the venue. The roadies had to clear away our gear through an avalanche of missiles. By the end, the glass on the stage was two inches thick.

It was fucking weird. We played other shows in Germany with the flags up—including a big festival in Frankfurt the following day—and never had any problem. Before the Frankfurt festival, we had to take my whole drum set apart to clean out the broken glass and wine and liquor stains from between the drumheads. Deep Purple dropped by to see us, and their drummer, Ian Paice, could not believe what had happened and helped out with the cleanup. It was one of those crazy nights that you never forget.

We had an equally surreal, but rather more enjoyable, adventure when the tour hit Hamburg. The city has a famous red-light district, and after the gig we decided to go see what went on down there.

Jeff, Tim, Clive (our tour manager), and I strolled past windows where prostitutes in lingerie waved and beckoned to us to go in. We ended up in a club where guys and chicks were having live sex onstage. The audience in there was middle-aged business guys, so I suppose with our long hair and rockers' clothes we probably stood out.

Some girls came and sat with us at our table and told us to buy them drinks. Clive had our cash on him from the gig and so was paying for everything, and the women started getting friendly with us. The chick sitting next to Jeff suddenly vanished under the table, and when I glanced down, she had his dick out.

We had never been to a European sex club before, and this was quite the initiation! A gorgeous woman in nothing but a fishnet body stocking came and sat next to me, putting her tongue in my ear and fondling my crotch. I was getting a real buzz from all this and passed her a bottle from the table.

"Hey, what can you do with this?" I asked her, and she put one leg up on the table and started screwing herself, hard and fast, with the bottle. On the other side of the table, a chick sitting by Tim started doing exactly the same thing.

"Oh, we have to go on the stage now!" one of them informed us. We watched their act, which involved licking each other's butts, screwing each other with candles and double-ended dildos, and giving head to a guy who was dressed as a sheikh and had the biggest dick I had ever seen.

Jeff, Tim, Clive, and I just looked at one another. We could not believe what we were seeing. We had thought we were crazy rock and rollers with hundreds of girls and multiple orgies to our credit; now we felt like nervous, inadequate virgins.

After their show, the chicks told us they were going to another club. "Do you want to come? It will be a good time!" they promised. We kind of believed them and so followed them to a disco, where Jeff and I sat at a table and fooled around with two of the girls. Suddenly one of them grabbed my arm under the table and put my hand right on Jeff's dick. I had all of my heavy rings on, so Jeff knew straight away that it was my hand. I don't know which of us screamed the loudest.

"What's the difference?" asked the girl, with a deadpan shrug. "It's all the same. It doesn't matter!"

"Whoa! It matters to us!" we told her, repressed Anglo-Saxons that we were. "Are you fucking crazy?"

By now it was nearly 4 AM, and when the chicks suggested going to another bar—all of this paid for, of course, by Clive's dwindling gig funds—we tagged along again. This turned out to be a lesbian bar, where my girl proceeded to give me head at the bar, skillfully stopping before I could come.

Two hours later we left the bar and told the women, "OK, let's go back to the hotel." They looked at our moneyman, Clive, and told him, "It will be three hundred dollars each if you want us to do that."

Drunk, horny, and belligerent, we were outraged by this: "Three hundred each? We don't pay for chicks to come to our rooms—we're rock stars!" Plus, we had probably spent around two grand on booze already. It was dawning on us that we had been severely ripped off.

The women saw we were of no more use to them, abandoned us, and began hitting on early morning businessmen and commuters passing by. A guy in a suit carrying an attaché case seemed to accept their proposal, and as he walked off with the three chicks, we hurled a bottle of Jack Daniels toward them. It spilled all over them, and as they cursed us, we ran to our rented Mercedes and back to the hotel.

It was a fitting end to a bizarre evening. Tim went up to bed, and Jeff and I sat in the breakfast bar, reviewed the crazy night, and reflected on how much money we had wasted without even getting our rocks off!

Jeff, Tim, and I were having a great time in BBA, and this kind of escapade showed how tight we were getting as a gang. Everything was on the up for us. By now our gigs were a major production, with a trailer full of gear and a mini-army of road crew, and we flew back to the States for three more weeks of gigs that were all sold-out six- or seven-thousand-seat arenas: our biggest shows to date.

Which made what happened next all the more unbelievable.

A week into the US dates, Tim and I were eating breakfast in a hotel in Atlanta when Clive walked in to the room. We called him over and asked him what time sound check would be.

"There won't be a sound check," he told us. "The show has been canceled."

"Canceled?" I said. "What the fuck? I thought it was sold out!"

"The whole tour is canceled," Clive continued. "Jeff had a really bad argument with Celia on the phone last night, and this morning he got up, got a cab to the airport, and flew home."

a kid I thought baseball was cool.
Now I'd sooner watch grass grow.

This is where it all began: my first-ever
drum lesson, age eleven.

Family vacation at our summer house in Lakewood, New Jersey, 1961.
We had some great times there. Left to right: Frank, Vinny, Frank's
girlfriend Joyce, Mom, me, Pop. Front: my sister Terri.

Making a racket on the family porch on my very first Gretsch drum kit.

The 3 Beeets, 1963. The leopard-skin jackets made sense at the time (to us, anyway).

THE FABULOUS 3 BEEETS
TV and Recording Artists

DEE-DEE TALENT, INC
1639 Broadway N.Y.19
LT-1-1424
DON DAVIS Pres.

THE FAbULOUS 3 BEEETS
TV and Recording Artists

DEE-DEE TALENT, INC.
1639 Broadway N.Y.19
LT-1-1424
DON DAVIS Pres.

The 3 Beeets failed to sheikh up the music scene.

Monkees caps all round for the Pigeons, 1967.

Vanilla Fudge's first-ever promo photo goes a little too heavy on the ice-cream theme.

My famous supersize Gretsch kit, complete with twenty-six-inch bass drum. It was the talk of London's drummers when we toured in '67.

Working my big Ludwig double-bass-drum
kit on the *Ed Sullivan Show* in front of fifty
million people, 1969.
© Photo by Chuck Stewart

Cactus promo shot.
We were trying to look sexy.

Beck, Bogert, and Appice on tour in 1973. Infamously,
our backdrop of flags sparked a riot in Germany.
© Photo by Neal Slozower

Ray Kennedy     Carmine Appice     Barry Goldberg     Mike Bloomfield     Rick Grech

Exclusively On
.MCA RECORDS

GB, 1976. Some of my supergroups
rned out not to be so super.

Mom and Pop admire
my rock-star wardrobe
backstage at Madison
Square Garden after
I've played a Rod
Stewart show, 1979.
© Photo by Alan Miller

Rod and me receiving
awards for writing
"Do Ya Think I'm Sexy?"
© Photo by Alan Miller

"Sit on it!":
with my supercool friend
Henry Winkler,
a.k.a. the Fonz, 1980.
© Photo by Alan Miller

The strangest people used
to turn up at my gigs.
With Robin Williams.
© Photo by Alan Miller

The Sex Police:
Chief Stewart and Deputy Appice
at a crime scene.

The judges for a Carmine Appice Drum-Off in 1981. Left to right: Stan Lynch (Tom Petty and the Heartbreakers), me, Martin Chambers (the Pretenders), Bruce Gary (the Knack). Ten thousand people turned out to watch.
© Photo by Neal Slozower

It's a dirty job, but someone's gotta do it. Rod and the Sex Police on patrol, 1980. The band wore our "uniforms" in the video for a single, "Passion."

Back at the Budokan: the Super Sessions tour in 1982.
© Photo by Alan Miller

"The grossest thing I have read in years," complained a shocked reader: the notorious *Oui* magazine photo shoot, 1982.
© Photo by Mark "Weissguy" Weiss,
www.weissguygallery.com

Touring Europe with Ozzy, who may not be entirely sure which country we are in.

With my idol Buddy Rich at my drum-off on Carmine Appice Day in L.A. (yes, really!) in 1981. © Photo by Neal Slozower

With Robert Plant at the Atlantic Records fortieth-anniversary concert at Madison Square Garden, 1988. Twenty years earlier, I had advised him to "move around on stage a bit more."

My hair metal years: a 1984 promo photo.
© Photo by Neal Slozower

My master plan for world domination for King Kobra never quite worked out.
© Photo by Neal Slozower

Hanging out with Brian May after
an Aerosmith show. Brian played
on my *Guitar Zeus* solo album.

It takes a lot of balls,
with Pat Travers.
© Photo by Paul Latimer
and Sue Candia

Bringing sexy back? Meeting Justin Timberlake
in his NSYNC years.

'wo drummerdudes: with Foo Fighters' Dave Grohl.

Drumming is my life: playing live, 2013.
© Photo by Michael Sherer

The family that plays together: Vinny and me fighting Drum War
© Photo by Alex Solc

With my Jaguar Mark IX. I owned that car for forty years.
© Photo by Marco Soccoli

Do ya think I'm sexy? (Don't answer that!): me in 2015.
© Photo by Leland Bobbé

My father, Carmine Appice, a.k.a. Charlie, in his eighties—just a great guy.

An early Christmas with my amazing kids, Bianca and Nick.

It can take a long time to find your soul mate, but it's worth it: Leslie and me.
© Photo by Paul Latimer and Sue Candia

And that was that! Our tour was off because Jeff had argued with his model girlfriend, Celia Hammond, who was back home in England looking after their 122 cats, and had bailed out to sort things out—without a word to me or Tim or the road crew, drivers, sound guys, and light guys who were all depending on us.

I had one thought: *What an asshole!* Jeff was used to being the boss, the star guy, and doing whatever the fuck he wanted. Now he was in a band supposedly of three equals, but it hadn't made the slightest difference to him. It was what Jeff wants, Jeff gets.

It unsurprisingly opened up a deep division in BBA. Where we had all seemed tight, now suddenly it was hard to trust Jeff, and there was a definite feel of Tim and me against him. It was just too early in the band's career for this sort of shit to happen.

Nevertheless, Tim and I tried to swallow our resentment and got back together with Jeff in the second half of '73 to play a short European tour. We then returned to England to start work on our second studio album.

Initially we booked into a remote farm studio near where Jeff lived, but the sessions were crap. I was bored crazy being stuck out in the countryside. Jeff would turn up each day in a different car, from a Corvette to a Mini Cooper to a customized US hot rod. Nothing we did satisfied him, including his own parts—he was casting around for a new direction. The songs weren't happening, and after three weeks, we split and Tim and I flew back to NYC.

A second attempt in London with producer Jimmy Miller and engineer Andy Johns, who had both worked with the Stones, was no better. The first day in the studio, Andy was facedown on the studio board recuperating from a heavy alcohol- and drug-fueled party the night before. Things got no better from there.

Hoping that a change of scenery and producer might help, we headed to Sausalito, California, to try again. BBA all loved the songs and productions on Sly & the Family Stone's albums, so we tried Sly Stone as our producer.

This was a total fucking disaster. Sly may be a musical genius, but by then he was high on every drug going and in free fall. We hardly saw him in the studio, and even when he did physically turn up, he didn't bring his mind with him.

We would get a message at our hotel to go to the studio at two the next afternoon. We would turn up and wait for hours for Sly. He would fail to show or else arrive, play a bass riff, and growl, "OK, now get that groove." Then he would tell us he would be right back and vanish for the rest of the day.

With nothing else to do, we partied hard at the hotel, and I still have a fond memory of a gorgeous chick—who used to be married to one of Bad Company—waving my drumsticks and running around the hallways in just boots and her underwear. However, after ten days of getting nowhere fast, and having wasted twenty thousand dollars, we gave up and decided to record new material at live gigs—that was always where we were best, anyhow.

BBA might have temporarily stalled, but back in New York, my brother Vinny was doing amazing. Those Dick Benette lessons had paid off, and, still only sixteen, he formed a band called BOMF, who were managed by the owner of the Record Plant, where they rehearsed every day. Vinny bumped into John Lennon there and even did handclaps on Lennon's "Whatever Gets You Through the Night"! I could not have been more proud of him.

BBA had arranged a short UK tour at the start of 1974 and made some recordings of both new tunes and some of our classic tracks. However, the bad feeling in the band had not gone away, and it came to a head at the last date of the tour, at London's famous Rainbow Theatre.

Tim had caught a cold, as he often did, and backstage before the show he was complaining about how it was affecting his voice. Jeff made a sarcastic comment to him, and Tim punched Jeff right in the face!

Holy shit! I was getting flashbacks to Mark hitting Vince before Vanilla Fudge played the *Ed Sullivan Show*! I pulled them apart, asking Tim, "What the fuck are you doing?" We went ahead and played the show—in fact, it was two shows, which were recorded for a live album—but they were to be the last we ever did.

Tim apologized to Jeff, but the damage was done. Jeff went into lockdown, refusing to meet up or approve a second album. He was contracted to give Epic Records two albums and two world tours, and it looked like Tim and I would have no choice but to sue him.

The band was clearly over, but Jeff's people came back to us with a placatory offer that we could release the live Rainbow tapes as the second album and call it even. I agreed to that, as did Phil Basile and our lawyer, Steve Weiss, but then Tim went into his own meltdown.

Tim became obsessed with the notion that Phil was ripping us off and refused to sign anything unless we fired both Phil and Steve Weiss. This blocked not only the BBA agreement but also a lucrative offer from Epic to re-form Vanilla Fudge. We were two weeks into rehearsal with the Fudge when Tim put the blocks on everything.

How frustrating was this? Those two deals would have earned me around $150,000 each, but Tim dug in his heels and refused to sign either of them, instead quitting New York with his wife, Kristy, to start a new life in California.

To add insult to injury, the BBA Rainbow album became a very successful bootleg from which we never saw a cent. At that point, that was it for me. I was seriously fucking done with Tim Bogert.

Yet, oddly enough, I wasn't done with Jeff Beck. The previous year, while BBA was on tour in France, I had turned him on to a style of music I loved: jazz rock, as played by the Mahavishnu Orchestra, Billy Cobham, and Stanley Clarke. It was melodic, instrumental, and highly technical, and as a musician it was awesome to jam out on.

Jeff also got into it, and shortly after BBA split, I called him—figuring there was no point in bearing grudges—and suggested making an album of this style of music as Beck-Appice. We decided to record it in London and enlisted bassist Phil Chen and Max Middleton. Jeff loved the idea. He never actually said yes or no to the Beck-Appice name, but why should I doubt him on this one?

Yeah, right!

There was a further, amazing incentive to the project. The producer was to be the legendary George Martin, the man immortalized as the fifth Beatle.

The sessions were a joy, and George Martin was the absolute obverse of fucking Sly Stone: he was organized, meticulous, knowledgeable, and polite—the charming epitome of an English gentleman. Nevertheless, I was dealing with Jeff again, and as we rehearsed before going into the studio, I became more and more wary.

I had got Jeff into jazz-rock, I was cowriting a lot of songs—Jeff freely admits he is not a great solo songwriter—and he had still not objected to crediting the album to Beck-Appice, or at the very least Jeff Beck featuring Carmine Appice. If Jeff even agreed to the latter, it would secure me a fifty-thousand-dollar advance from Epic.

Nothing was sure, and I felt I had little choice but to—hard as it was—trust him and his people, do the recordings, and hope for the best. But I never felt confident; in fact, after the rehearsals I was secretly heading to another studio to hang out and write songs with two friends, guitarist Ray Gomez and bassist Ric Grech (Ric had been in Family and Blind Faith). I guess they were kind of my fallback plan.

Then, as I feared, Jeff's manager, Ernest, informed me that the project would be a Jeff Beck solo record. As I was reeling from this blow, Phil Basile and Steve Weiss got involved on my behalf. They felt being a sideman again would be too much of a step down for my career and told Ernest and Jeff I couldn't do the record.

Man, was I bummed! For me, this was the worst of all solutions. Not only would I not be paid, but I had lost the chance to play on an album I loved, produced by George Martin. Jeff hired a drummer named Richard Bailey to replace me. Years later, I read an interview with Richard, who said he had arrived at the studio and was handed a tape of the songs we had recorded and ordered, "Play as close to Carmine as possible."

To make things even worse, when the album, called *Blow by Blow*, appeared, I had no songwriting credits for the songs I had cowritten. The record was to hit number four in the United States and went platinum, so I maybe should have sued Jeff. But I didn't want to lose his friendship.

In a funny way, Jeff seemed to feel the same. Shortly after *Blow by Blow* came out, he called me to play with him and Stanley Clark in

Los Angeles on a track called "Rock 'n' Roll Jelly," which was cool. It's strange—even though Jeff has fucked me over more than once, we have always remained friends.

Despite that, there were many long nights in 1974 and 1975 when I reflected hard on my troubled dealings with Mr. Beck and wished I had paid closer attention to the wise words of Rod Stewart. It could have saved me a lot of grief.

In fact, maybe I should consider spending a lot more time with Rod. . . .

# 8

# ON PATROL
# WITH THE SEX POLICE

*In which Drummerdude forms another ill-fated supergroup, soundtracks a porn movie, gets married, joins Rod Stewart's band and enrolls in the Sex Police, cowrites a "Sexy" number one, befriends Buddy Rich, ends a rock cold war, gives Fred Astaire drumming tips, hangs out with Kojak, is bumped from the Muppets, and is canned by Rod Stewart . . . and screwed by Jeff Beck*

*I can't pretend,* given his lousy track record, that Jeff Beck or his people screwing me over on *Blow by Blow* had come as a total surprise. Nevertheless, it still left me feeling disoriented.

Things weren't great in my personal life, either. By the time I flew back to New York, I had been away in London for about two months. Arlene was getting antsy. She felt she was losing her identity and just being seen as Mrs. Carmine Appice (apart from the wedding band, of course). She had a novel solution to this dilemma: she wanted to become a stripper.

I was cool with this. I wasn't a possessive guy (given my lifestyle, that would have been rather fucking hypocritical). So I figured, why not? After all, she might spend her evening turning other guys on, but it would still be me who got to sleep with her at the end of the night!

Careerwise, I wasn't sure what to do next. Tim and I talked about hiring another guitarist whose name began with *B* so we could keep BBA going. I had even met up and jammed with Tommy Bolin, but while he was a great player, his name wasn't big enough to replace Jeff Beck. And now that Tim and I were done, so was BBA.

I played on a solo tour with Leslie West, who was taking a break from Mountain, supporting Kiss in arenas. It was the first time I had seen Kiss, and my jaw dropped. Their costumes, face paint, and five-inch platform heels were fantastic—pure rock-and-roll pantomime.

I got on great with Paul Stanley, who was a true native New Yorker like me, but was amazed when Paul admitted that he and Gene Simmons got the idea for Kiss from seeing Cactus support Alice Cooper in Long Island. Their concept was to marry the theatricality of Alice with the rock power of Cactus. They sure did that!

Touring with Kiss inspired me to pour lighter fluid over my cymbals so they would be set on fire during my big solo. It looked great, but when I hit them, the burning fluid flew up in the air, set the aisle in front of the stage alight, and the road crew had to run onstage with fire extinguishers. That was the end of my pyro experiment.

After the Kiss tour, my lawyer, Steve Weiss, told me about a new band in L.A. who were looking for a drummer. KGB was to be a supergroup along BBA lines, comprising vocalist Ray Kennedy, keyboardist Barry Goldberg, who had played with Dylan at the infamous Newport Folk Festival where he went electric, and guitarist Mike Bloomfield, who had formed the Butterfield Band and been with Goldberg in Electric Flag and had recently had his big *Super Session* album with Stephen Stills.

KGB looked promising. Their manager was Elliott Roberts, who had just finished partnering with David Geffen in a management company, Geffen & Roberts, and who managed Neil Young and Joni Mitchell. They also needed a bassist, so Ric Grech met me in New York, and we flew out to L.A. to check them out.

We all jammed, and it seemed to work. So Ric and I returned to London and New York, respectively, to get our gear and settled down for eight months in the California sunshine to make an album. It was much more of an L.A., song-based album than the edgy, jam-based tracks I was used to making with Cactus and BBA.

Making the record wasn't straightforward. Mike Bloomfield declared that he couldn't be in L.A., as he couldn't sleep in the city—talk about weird!—so the rest of us made the album with a studio guitarist before heading up to a studio near Mike's place in San Francisco for him to add his parts. Mike's pad was an eye-opener. It was pretty gross: his home and car were both overflowing with garbage.

One bonus side effect of this was that Mike co-opted me to help him make the soundtrack to a major porn movie titled *Sodom and Gomorrah*, by the Mitchell Brothers, who were the porn kings of the time. I even went to the movie's premiere at their San Francisco theater. It got the audience it deserved.

While we were making the album, I got an offer out of the blue to join Rainbow as Ritchie Blackmore looked to reshape the band. I thought about it but turned it down because I was legally committed to KGB and hoped that we would take off. This was not the best decision I ever made.

Being in California for the better part of a year reminded me of one thing: I loved Los Angeles. There was a great music scene going on, the beaches and sunshine were awesome, and as I flew back to New York and another gray winter, I knew the time had come to switch coasts.

This decision was made a lot easier by the fact that Arlene and I had finally split. She had met a biker in her strip club—well, you always meet nice guys in places like that, right?—and ran off with him. I could hardly complain—after all, I must have cheated on her a thousand times on the road—but we had been together seven years, so I was still kind of upset.

However, I guess you could say I got over Arlene fairly quickly. After she had moved out I flew female guests in to stay with me for a week or two each before I left New York. Sometimes it was two at a time: now that was fun! Then it came time to make my move to L.A.

As this point I also bade farewell to Phil Basile as my manager. Phil had started up a concert promotions company, Concerts East, which soon became the biggest promoter on the East Coast, arranging tours by all of the arena-filling bands, like Zeppelin.

One reason for Concert East's immediate success may well have been the ultra-intimidating Mob boss Paulie's involvement! Still, I was sorry to end my business relationship with Phil. We had been through a lot together, to say the least, and we'd come a long way since he put the Pigeons on a one-hundred-dollar salary each.

My brother Frank was by now living in L.A., and initially I stayed with him before Ric Grech and I moved into apartments in Oakwood. Having decided against joining Ritchie Blackmore's band, I coincidentally saw a little of his ex-wife Barbel, or Babs as I knew her. We started out as friends, and it became a fling.

The KGB album appeared, was getting loads of airplay, and was on the charts with a bullet. Things looked good—until Mike Bloomfield did a long interview with Robert Hilburn in the *Los Angeles Times* in which he said that KGB was just a project our managers had thrown together and that he had no faith in it and only did it for the money!

Ric Grech, who was a recovering heroin addict, then lapsed and started injecting the money he had got for the album into his arm, so we had to let him go. With our name guitarist and name bassist off the team, it kind of killed any buzz around the album, which stiffed.

KGB had a tour booked with Joe Cocker, so we quickly enlisted replacements in Benny Schultz on guitar and Greg Sutton on bass. The tour was hard work, and Joe Cocker wasn't on great form either—he was so fucked up on heroin and liquor that he was throwing up in a trashcan in the wings between songs.

At least my personal life in Los Angeles had taken an interesting turn. My thing with Babs soon fizzled out, but through her I remet Marlene, the supposed virgin I had made the acquaintance of a couple of years earlier when BBA were passing through L.A.

Marlene and I quickly became good friends. Apart from my brother, I didn't know too many people in L.A., and as a native Californian, she showed me the ropes. She took me to Santa Barbara and Carmel, and we took rides up and down the coast. I guess I was still on the rebound from Arlene, and Marlene and I quickly fell into a slightly crazy relationship.

Marlene was a little kooky, and my parents never liked her, but as we traversed California together in 1976, she kept on pressuring me to marry her. Eventually I figured, what the hell? It had been ten years since Marion. Maybe I was ready to try marriage again. Maybe.

We married in Las Vegas because you had to have a blood test to marry in L.A., and I used to hate needles. There was hardly anybody there, and I spent the ceremony and the day out of my head on Quaaludes. That probably tells you all that you need to know.

The new lineup of KGB made a second album, *Motion*, and went on tour, but we weren't happening and nobody really wanted to know. My brother Vinny's career was going great by now. He had joined Rick Derringer's band and was playing stadiums supporting Aerosmith at just age seventeen. I was proud, but I knew I needed another big gig for myself.

It was at this point that I heard through the grapevine that Rod Stewart was looking for a drummer for his band.

A drummer friend, Sandy Gennaro, mentioned in passing that he had auditioned for Rod, who had so far tried out twenty-five drummers. "You know him!" he told me. "You should go for it!" He gave me the name of Rod's tour manager, who was arranging the tryouts: Pete Buckland.

Pete Buckland! The man with whom I had shared countless on-the-road hotel trashings and sexual escapades and who had deposited the contents of Tim and my London hotel room all over the courtyard below! I called him immediately.

"Why the fuck didn't you tell me Rod was looking for a drummer?" I asked him.

"Because you're always busy!" Pete told me. I stressed that I would love to play with Rod, and Pete said he would call Rod in England and pass the message on.

The next day Pete called me back. "Rod would love to have you in the band. They're rehearsing at his place in Beverly Hills. He wants you to go to meet them to see if you like them." Which I thought was cool.

The next day I was gliding my red Pantera down Carolwood Drive, the location of some serious old-school Hollywood mansions. Pulling into Rod's driveway, I announced my arrival via the entry phone next to the elaborate wrought-iron gates and then headed up his driveway.

What a place! Just the exterior of his castle-like home took my breath away. A vast fountain dominated the circular courtyard in front of the mansion. Rod's many cars—a Lamborghini Miura, a Rolls-Royce Phantom, a Porsche—were parked around the courtyard. His guesthouse alone was bigger than my sizeable home in Los Feliz.

Pete came out to meet me and led me through the palatial Mediterranean-style interior, with its sweeping staircase and eye-wateringly expensive artwork on the walls. The bejeweled chandeliers and Galle lamps must have been worth tens of thousands of dollars. I had never seen wealth like this.

My eyes were wide as Pete led me outside to where the band members were all lounging by the swimming pool and the paddle-tennis court. Rod was on a flight back from London, but I met the rest of the band: guitarists Jim Cregan, Gary Grainger, and Billy Peek; bassist Phil Chen, who I had played with on *Blow by Blow*; and keyboard player John Jarvis. We headed down to jam in Rod's six-car garage, where they had instruments set up. It sounded awesome. Pulling out of the gates later, I looked back over my shoulder. Yep, this was a gig I *really* wanted.

The next day I was back at the mansion and Rod was there, jet-lagged from his overnight Atlantic crossing. We hung out and chatted with his girlfriend, Britt Ekland, and he casually told me to play just like I had in Cactus, and he would give me a solo every night, as he knew I had my own fans. And that was it!

Just like that, I was in the Rod Stewart band.

Incidentally, this was when I changed my name—or, at least, changed the way it was said. I had always gone by our family pronunciation, *Ah-pa-see*, although some people preferred the easier-to-say Anglicization *A-peece*, and I had got tired of correcting them. "What about sticking with A-peece, then?" asked Rod. I happily agreed. Carmine A-peece it was.

Britt Ekland was just as big a celebrity as Rod, of course, and truly looked like a Swedish goddess. It was clearly her influence that had transformed Rod from a bad-boy rock star to what they call Hollywood elite, and I'm sure her classy taste was behind his personal style and the house's immaculate art, furniture, and fittings.

Despite this, there was nothing haughty or aloof about Britt, who was as beautiful on the inside as on the outside and was always friendly and easygoing to hang out with. Of course, I suppose I had had a crush on her ever since I first set eyes on her in *The Man with the Golden Gun.*

Rod had European tour dates lined up for the end of '76, and we went into a Hollywood studio to rehearse. Although Rod had asked me to play like I did in Cactus, in rehearsal he told me to play a little bit behind the beat, in that lazy English style, rather than high-energy and right on the beat as I had in Cactus and BBA. It was no problem and easy to master.

When we were in the studio, I bumped into Tommy Bolin again, whom Tim and I had contemplated inviting to be the second B in BBA after Jeff quit. By now Tommy was in Deep Purple and had recorded two solo albums, one of which I had guested on.

He cut a sorry figure in the studio: he was so fucked up on booze and drugs that he was having trouble talking or even staying awake. I could tell he wasn't for this world much longer. Within a year, he was dead from a heroin overdose.

It took around six weeks before Rod was satisfied with our performances and arrangements. I enjoyed playing on "Losing You," a Temptations hit Rod had covered, and we decided since this song had a drum break in it, it would be the song for my big solo, when he would introduce me with my brand-new surname.

Frank Zappa was in the next-door studio rehearsing his own complex, crazy brand of music, and I hung out with him a little. I had hardly seen Frank since he had so kindly written that song about Led Zeppelin, Vanilla Fudge, and a mud shark.

My first tour with Rod's band swung through Scandinavia, with four warm-up dates in a small Norwegian theater before we got to Britain, ending up in London just before Christmas. The band was hot and real tight, and I was having a great time playing with Rod. I love his gravel-throat singing. He is one of the all-time great white rock singers.

We were also having fun offstage. Rod loved to mess about, as did the rest of the band members, who, being mostly English, were often drunk and ready to party. Rod initiated us into the Downstairs Supper Club, which basically consisted of visiting exclusive restaurants, placing our orders, then hiding under the table. On their return, the waiters would assume we had left, before one of us lifted the tablecloth and said, "Oi! Down here!"

I managed to make headlines for my bad behavior during a visit to our favorite London hangout, the Speakeasy. We were all there with our wives and girlfriends, and some drunk came over to talk to us and was swaying around, accidentally spilling beer on my jacket and on Marlene's fur coat.

When I asked him to take more care, he ignored me; when I tried to move his hand, he threatened to "chin" me—a weird English phrase.

"Fuck you," I said, and pushed the beer out of his hand. Then he punched me in the face!

The fight was on, and I had him in a headlock, beating him around the head, which must have hurt, as I had a ring on nearly every finger. Security threw him out, but the press got wind of it and went to town: "Rod Stewart Drummer Carmine Appice in Fight in London Bar!"

The tour wound up with four nights at the eight-thousand-capacity Olympia arena in London. We were in London for two weeks, and Rod took us shopping for cool band clothes: Fiorucci shirts; tight, straight-leg pants; scarves; and high-heeled shoes in red, blue, and black. Christmas in London was real pretty, kind of like New York.

The Olympia gigs were amazing. Rod was a god in England, and his fans adored him. It was the first time I heard a crowd sing along to the full verses of songs as well as to the chorus. After one of the shows, we had a party at a plush club with a champagne fountain flowing as freely as water. I hardly drink, but I did that night. My hangover lasted three days.

A host of big names came back to see us after the gigs, like Elton John and Ronnie Wood. Shit, even Prince Charles came to one of the shows! One night Paul McCartney turned up in our dressing room, and I conquered my nerves to ask him to confirm a rumor. Was it true that George Harrison used to be a Vanilla Fudge fan?

McCartney nodded. "Yeah, he used to carry your first album around everywhere. He'd turn up at parties with it under his arm and ask the host to play it." So there we had it. Maybe George had recognized us when he dropped in on Cactus in the studio, after all.

Back in L.A., I was hanging out a lot with Paul Stanley. I told him I was looking for a new manager, and he suggested Kiss's manager, Bill Aucoin. A meeting with Bill and his business partner, Alan Miller, opened up a raft of possibilities.

Bill and Alan told me they wanted to turn me from being a well-known musician into a "rock personality." Their plan seemed to mainly consist of having me hang out at Kiss shows and events to get photographed, to up my profile and help me get onto TV and radio shows and into magazines. I thought, *Why not?* and said I was ready to give it a go.

Bill's plan kind of worked and had a few unexpected side effects. One night, Paul and I went to Long Beach Arena to see Angel, who were a kind of Kiss rip-off band that was doing pretty well at the time. We said hello to them backstage and then settled into our seats out in the auditorium.

It wasn't long before we noticed fans congregating nearby and pointing at us. Why wouldn't they? It was Paul from Kiss! To my amazement, when they finally got up the courage to come over, it was my autograph they wanted! I guess that it kind of figured—my face was being seen around, whereas without their makeup, Kiss were anonymous.

Around the same time, I was hanging out in the Starwood Club one night with Todd Rundgren, whom I had also become friends with. Todd ran into some guy he knew and introduced me: "Hey, Carmine, this is Bruce."

"It's nice to meet you, Carmine," Bruce told me. "You know, my band opened up for you one time in Asbury Park when you were in Cactus."

"Really? What was the name of your band?" I asked him.

Todd gave me an exasperated look. "The same as it is now, Carmine—Bruce Springsteen!"

"Oh, *that* Bruce!" I blurted out, embarrassed. But come on, he had just cut his hair and shaved his beard off. Anybody can make a mistake, right? Anyway, his band's name was Steel Mill back then. How was I supposed to know it had been him?

Back in Rod's band, it was time to get to work on a new album, the record that was to become *Foot Loose & Fancy Free*. This meant return visits to Rod's mansion—which was never exactly a hardship—to write new songs in his garage before fine-tuning them in the studio.

Sadly, at this point Britt was no longer around. Rod had cheated on her during a trip to New York, and the *New York Post* ran a story about it. As soon as Britt heard about it, she was out of there. I thought it was such a shame; they always seemed great together. Of course, rock-star relationships are like dogs' ages: every year is worth seven years of a normal marriage!

When it came to recording, Rod always knew exactly what he wanted, and perfecting the songs took a long time. He liked very precise arrangements. Doing his vocals was a slow process. He didn't like a lot of people in the control booth and would often clear the studio out, but he sometimes let me stay, as I was a singer and could suggest background harmonies and stuff.

I enjoyed the recording process with Rod's band. Andy Johns, our engineer, worked with me to develop my drums via different microphone positions and compression. It was the sort of shit many engineers couldn't be bothered with, but it helped me to get some of the best drum sounds of my career as Andy and I spent hours together experimenting at Rod's expense.

One day Rod told me he had loved the Vanilla Fudge version of "You Keep Me Hangin' On" and wished that he had done it. "Well, why don't you do it now?" I asked him. "You've got one of Fudge in your band—it's the perfect excuse!" He laughed and agreed—and bang! It was on the album.

The big singles off the album were "You're in My Heart" and "Hot Legs," and we made a video for the latter track around a small town north of L.A. called Fillmore. There were railroad tracks, disused gas stations, and a model who never showed her face—most of the video was shot through her legs. It was the first video I had ever done, and I couldn't believe how long it took. We were there for three days.

As the new kid in the band, I didn't feel able to suggest any of my own songs for *Foot Loose & Fancy Free*, but that had changed by the following year when we came to record the *Blondes Have More Fun* album. Rod used to study the top one hundred singles chart very closely so he knew what was number one and so we could write songs similar to whatever was going on at the time. He liked the Rolling Stones' "Miss You" and told us he wanted a track with a similar groove and vibe.

I worked up a few chords at home on my electric piano and went over to my Cactus buddy Duane Hitchings's house, where he had a home studio. We got the idea down using just a drum machine, a bass, and keys, and when I presented it to Rod, he loved it. That song was to become "Do Ya Think I'm Sexy?"

As usual, we recorded the song over and over until it was right. I played with a click track for the first time, and the album's producer, Tom Dowd, added a full orchestra, a sax solo, and production doo-dahs until its big rock sound had gone and it was very much a disco track.

In truth, I still preferred the more basic version, but what did I know? "Sexy" was released in November 1978 as the lead single from *Blondes Have More Fun* as we set off on an eight-month world tour to promote the album. I had no idea how the song would do, but suddenly it began shooting up singles charts all around the world.

In no time at all it was platinum everywhere. I had written songs for Vanilla Fudge that had gone gold and had hits with BBA, but this was something else! I got a royalty check for eighty thousand dollars just for three months' sales. I made sure I gave Duane a credit and a share of the bucks—I guess I'd learned from Jeff Beck how not to do things.

While in L.A. I also took a few weeks to produce an album by a Japanese singer, Carmen Maki. She was a fan from my Cactus and BBA days and asked me to write and produce her *Night Stalker* album and assemble American musicians to play on it. She was cool, and I enjoyed the project.

Even more exciting than having a huge hit single and becoming a record producer, I finally got to meet one of my all-time idols and inspirations: Buddy Rich.

Our first meeting didn't start auspiciously. I heard that despite hating rock drummers, Buddy was to play some rock-oriented songs with his new big band at the Starwood in Hollywood. I asked my manager to get me some tickets for the gig, and he called me back saying he and the Starwood manager had had a great idea: I could jam with Buddy onstage, and we could film it for a cable TV show!

I could not believe what I was hearing and asked him, "Are you nuts? This is Buddy Rich—he is the best, and he hates rock drummers!" Eventually I got talked into the idea, but it all fell through, to my great relief, and I headed off with my brother Vinny to see the Starwood show.

At the gig I bumped into Buddy's daughter Cathy, whom I had met in New York a few years earlier. She greeted me and then told me, "My father is really mad at you because you have been challenging him to a drum battle to get press and headlines, just like Ginger Baker did."

It was true that Ginger had mouthed off about Buddy in the press a few years earlier, but I had done no such thing, and I tried to explain to Cathy that the aborted drum battle had not been my idea. "OK," she said, "why don't you come backstage and tell him yourself?"

This sounded like a fucking awful idea to me. Buddy was a fearsome character, and now he was mad as hell at me. Why should I want to go backstage and have my head chewed off by my childhood—and current—hero? No way! No. Fucking. Way.

Cathy kept chipping away at me, and eventually I agreed to go back as long as Vinny came with me for backup. Vinny was wary as well but eventually agreed. As we walked through the dressing room door, I was more nervous than I was when strolling onstage in front of ten thousand people.

There he was in the corner. Buddy Rich. Cathy marched us over to him and introduced me: "Buddy, I have Carmine Appice here, the drummer who was supposed to play with you tonight—the *rock* drummer."

Buddy narrowed his eyes and looked me up and down. "What, the kid who was looking for headlines, like that other rock drummer, Ginger Baker?"

We were up real close now, and I started gabbling as I explained to Buddy that the contest was not really a contest, had not been my idea anyway, and I had been reluctant from the start—and anyway he was my idol. Buddy listened, nodded, and asked me, "Do you smoke?"

"Cigarettes? No."

He sighed. "I said, 'Do you smoke?'"

"You mean pot?" I asked nervously. He nodded, as though humoring a slow child. "Yeah!" I told him.

At which point Buddy reached into his shirt pocket to produce a joint wrapped in chocolate papers. We smoked it until it was gone as Vinny and I stared at each other and shared a silent message: "Holy shit! We're smoking a joint with Buddy Rich!"

Buddy bade us farewell and hit the stage. Vinny and I watched the gig from the VIP bar in a stoned trance. Had we *really* just smoked a joint with Buddy Rich? And had he *really* been nice to us? It was a night I would never forget.

Meanwhile, Rod was getting bigger than ever. *Blondes Have More Fun* was topping charts around the globe, and our 1978/1979 tour promised to be an absolute blast. It wasn't just that: it was a master class in musical and hedonistic excess. It would be hard to imagine a tour that was more fun, or wilder.

Just before it began, Keith Moon from the Who died, and my manager phoned to say he had heard I would be invited to replace him. This was an intriguing prospect, and I was definitely interested, but nothing came of it—and it's hard to believe I could have enjoyed it more than I did touring with Rod's band.

This was partly because the group gelled so well. Rod was always up for fun and games. We all had our offstage pastimes: Phil Chen liked to show us his black-belt martial-arts abilities, Gary Grainger drank as only Englishmen can, and baby-of-the-band keyboard player Kevin Savigar liked his weed.

Rod was also very laid-back about my extracurricular activities. Sales of my *Realistic Rock Drum Method* book were now up to a staggering 150,000 copies, and he didn't mind me doing drum clinics, which by now were pulling in as many as a thousand people at a time. The clinics were big news, and when I gave the proceeds of the ticket sales to UNICEF, I was able to hand over fifty thousand dollars.

There was one activity, however, in which the Rod Stewart Group came together as one. This was when we all donned our uniforms and became the fine body of men known as the Sex Police.

How do I explain the Sex Police? They were our main offstage passion on the *Blondes* tour, and basically their sole purpose was to sabotage anybody—band member, tour manager, road crew, support band—who got lucky with a girl on the road. We were kept extremely busy.

The routine was this: If word spread that somebody had taken a chick back to his room, the rest of us would congregate and don our bespoke Sex Police T-shirts. We would then charge down the hotel corridor to that person's room, singing our theme song as we went, to the theme of the old black-and-white TV show *Dragnet*: "Sex Police, we're the Sex Police! Sex Police, we're the Sex Police!"

Once we got into the room, we would cause as much mayhem as possible. Beds might get tipped over; sometimes the chick would be thrown out of the room without her clothes. Normally she would take one look at the ten to fifteen guys bursting into the room and leave of her own accord anyway.

The Sex Police were a very resourceful and diligent force. Our official slogan was "Cruel but fair." In advance of a raid, we would try to get ahold of a spare key to the room we were targeting. If we couldn't do that . . . well, we would get the job done by any means necessary.

Rod was very involved in one raid when we spotted a band member sneaking out of the hotel bar to his room with a chick. We pictured the seduction scene inside the room—the soft lights, the music, the glass of wine—and decided to kill it with a cautious and patient approach.

We didn't sing the theme song this time. Instead we switched off the main electric breaker for the room and gaffer-taped the door up so nobody could get out. We banged hard on the door to freak them out, and it worked: we could hear the girl flipping out because she couldn't open the door. Then Rod and I proudly posed for photos in our Sex Police T-shirts, another "crime" successfully thwarted.

It wasn't so much fun being the person getting raided, of course. One time I had taken Kirsty, a really nice chick from our record company, back to my room to fool around. As usual, one thing led to another, and we had just started having sex when I heard a dreaded noise from down the hotel hallway, quiet at first but gaining in volume: "Sex Police, we're the Sex Police! Sex Police, we're the Sex Police!"

Shit! They were coming for us! I stopped dead, my hard-on suddenly limp with fear, and whispered to Kirsty, "It's the Sex Police! Lie still and don't say a word until we know if they know about us!" She had no idea what I was talking about, but she did as I said.

My heart was beating fast as the chants got louder and louder . . . then passed as the Sex Police raced past my room to interrupt some other poor sap. I was then very ready to carry on, but Kirsty had other ideas: "You must be kidding! I can't have that happening to me—I might lose my job!" The Sex Police did their job that night without knowing it, and I wasn't even their target.

In Stockholm I was in bed with a young Swedish girl and had just got my rocks off when I heard the unmistakable sounds of my comrades gathering in the corridor. I bade her farewell, jumped out of bed, put on my Sex Police T-shirt, and joined them.

On this job, the Sex Police had a tip-off. Pete Buckland, who was on the fifth floor of the hotel, had taken a chick back to his room and was showing her a pretty good time, judging by the moaning going on behind his door. We didn't have a spare key, but he had told us that he would leave his window open.

Pete's room was on the fifth floor? The only access to his window was a narrow ledge that ran around the edge of the building? It was refrigerator-cold, the ice was slippery, and most of the guys were drunk?

No problem!

One by one, we climbed out of the window of the room two doors down and inched along the ledge to Pete's room, freezing in our Sex Police T-shirts. We didn't sing the Sex Police theme: we wanted it to be a surprise attack.

It was no surprise to Pete, who was expecting us, but the poor chick was shocked as the first guy jumped in their bedroom window and said, "Hello, Pete."

"Hello, mate," Pete said back, continuing to screw the girl.

The next sex cop did the same, and by the time there were five or six of us in the room, the girl was seriously freaked out and ran out of there. I can't say I blamed her.

The whole of the *Blondes Have More Fun* tour was awesome. We played six nights at Olympia in London around Christmas 1978.

We were staying at a hotel near Harrods in Knightsbridge, and one afternoon before one of the shows, I was strolling around and saw a familiar figure coming toward me: Tim Bogert!

Tim and I had not spoken since he had cost me a fortune blocking the Vanilla Fudge reunion and BBA live album projects, but he had seen me in the street, too, so it was kind of hard not to speak. He told me he lived right across the street and invited me up for a cup of tea.

As we sat in his small apartment talking and smoking hashish, he told me he was playing in some obscure European music project. It became clear to me that his career was not going as well as mine, and all of my bad feelings toward him fell away. After all, if he had not blown out Vanilla Fudge and BBA, I would never have gotten to join Rod's band and had the time of my life. In a funny way, he had done me a favor! Tim and I made up right then and have been friends to this day.

Our time in Australia on the *Blondes Have More Fun* tour was particularly special. The first leg was in Perth, where I met a gorgeous Aboriginal chick named Jade. I asked her how old she was, she told me she was eighteen, and off we went to my hotel room for the night.

The next day we went down to the hotel restaurant to breakfast together, and a waitress, who was also an Aborigine, came over to our table. However, she didn't take our order. Instead she smiled at my companion, said, "Hi, Jade. Did you have fun last night?" and wandered off.

"Oh, you know the waitress?" I asked Jade.

"Yes," she replied. "It's my mother."

I was still reeling from this as Jade casually dropped another bombshell: "Oh, by the way, I'm only sixteen."

Wow! She clearly came from one very enlightened family!

While we were in Australia, "Do Ya Think I'm Sexy?" went to number one in the States, and Rod said that he and I, the two songwriters, should take the whole tour party out to dinner to celebrate. That meal cost me fifteen hundred Australian dollars before we'd even seen a dime in royalties. But it was typical of Rod to want to do something classy like that.

In Sydney we played a thirty-thousand-capacity stadium. I had seen a pretty reporter on TV and was delighted when she came to interview the band. We got flirting, and she stayed in my hotel room for our first few days in the city. The stadium show was weird for me, as I had an inner ear infection that rendered my hearing incredibly sensitive and messed with my equilibrium as I played.

We were staying at the top-end Sebel Townhouse, and I was astonished to discover that, coincidentally, Jeff Beck was also there. By now things were going so well for me in Rod's band that the whole BBA and *Blow by Blow* debacle felt like history, so I decided to visit Jeff's room and surprise him.

He was certainly astonished to answer a knock on his door and find me standing there, but we shared a laugh and a joke—and even, later that night, a cool Australian chick. As ever, I couldn't stay mad at Jeff, but some falling-outs had proven harder to mend.

Rod had left the Jeff Beck Group very pissed off with Jeff and his management over some money issues, and the anger had festered. It had been many years since the once best friends had been in the same room, and when either mentioned the other, it was always negative. I wondered if I could play peacemaker.

Jeff was initially hesitant when I suggested he come to our gig the next night but eventually agreed. That evening I spoke to Rod and got the same reaction: wariness followed by the agreement to give it a go.

Before the following night's show, Jeff arrived and I went out to meet him. I led him into the hospitality area of the dressing room. It was packed with friends, roadies, record-label staff, and well-wishers, all of whom knew about the legendary falling-out. The hubbub of conversation stopped as all eyes turned to the two former friends, who had not yet seen each other.

When I went over to Rod and pointed out that Jeff was on the other side of the room, you could have cut the tension in the air with a knife. Rod glared over at Jeff. Jeff stared back. Who would blink first? Then, after a few seconds that felt a lot longer, the two men smiled, stepped forward, and gave each other a big hug. That was all it took to end rock's cold war.

After the show, Jeff came up to me in a fantastic mood and said he had loved the gig, Rod sounded great, and I had kicked ass. He was just so relieved they had finally buried the hatchet.

Rod and I got very close on this tour. One day we were sharing a limo on the way back to the hotel in Sydney from a sound check. There had even been screaming girls outside the sound check, and Rod turned to me with a faux-weary sigh.

"It's a drag being a legend," he reflected.

"I know what you mean!" I deadpanned back.

A laughing Rod nodded. "Yeah, mate, you are the only other person in the band who could say that!"

I didn't feel like a fucking legend, but I did feel on top of the world. Australia was bathed in glorious sunshine, I was playing to stadiums with one of the biggest rock stars in the world, the single I had cowritten was number one in the United States—and in Australia—and I had chicks throwing themselves at me every day.

Yes, life felt perfect. The last thing I would want to do was meet a girl, fall in love, and go and complicate everything. So, naturally, that was exactly what I did.

At the end of our stay in Sydney, our record label threw us a yacht party. It was paradise: everybody was getting stoned, the drinks were flowing, and the boat was full of model-looking young Australian babes in tiny bikinis all dancing to our album. One of them was Ruth.

She was in her early twenties, blonde with blue eyes and a fantastic figure, and I was a sucker for an Australian accent. We clicked right away, and I fell head over heels for her. For the rest of the Australian trip, Ruth and I were inseparable.

Of course, I was still married to Marlene, but that union had been going downhill rather rapidly. When we first got married I had not been too bothered about the kooky part of her character. Quickly that side of her began to take over, until I wondered if she was out-and-out crazy.

Marlene had always favored bizarre clothes but lately had taken to wearing outfits that looked like costumes from some kind of kid's play. It was like being married to Cinderella. Yet I could live with her clothes. What really did my head in was Marvin.

Marvin was a kids' toy, a lion hand-puppet, and Marlene took to carrying him everywhere and producing him at inappropriate moments. (Actually any moment was inappropriate!) We would be having dinner with Rod and the band in L.A., and she would whip out Marvin and make him talk in everyone's faces. The band just thought she was weird, and it embarrassed the fuck out of me. It had been a relief to go out on tour and get away from Marlene, and I had met Ruth at just the right time.

Ruth was still on my mind as the *Blondes* tour hit Japan, but I had plenty there to distract me. I had told Rod that I had a strong personal following in Japan, where BBA had done really well and I always came high in polls for the best rock drummer, but I don't think he had totally believed me.

This changed when we played a gig early in the tour at an arena in Fukuoka. When it came time for my solo and I began smashing away at my kit to the applause of fifteen thousand people, Rod attempted to introduce me: "Carmine Appice on drums!" To his amazement, he couldn't hear himself speak over the screams.

After the show, Rod cornered me and conceded, "You really *are* big in Japan!" He asked me if I would sit next to him at the next day's press conference and take over doing some of the newspaper interviews. Naturally, I was delighted to do this. My standing in Japan was even higher than usual, as the Carmen Maki *Night Stalker* album was doing really well. Even I was staggered, though, when two thousand fans turned up at my Tokyo drum clinic.

It was a wonderful few weeks for me. We were playing four nights at the sold-out Budokan, "Do Ya Think I'm Sexy?" was number one in Japan, and I was on magazine covers both with Rod and with Carmen. I suspect this pissed one or two band members off. Jim Cregan seemed particularly jealous.

After the Japanese dates, the closing US leg of the *Blondes* tour found us at our peak. By now we were a luxurious and slick traveling company. Rod flew between shows by Lear jet, the band had our own Viscount private plane, totally tricked out inside, and an army of buses carried our crew and equipment—"the city on wheels"—from city to city.

I would love to say that I changed my ways on the road as I pined for Ruth, but old habits die hard. When we reached Pittsburgh, I met a beautiful chick with huge boobs, and after taking her backstage and hanging out with her, I invited her up to my room to party.

The girl said that her mom was at the gig with her and would have to come to my room, too, but explained that her mom was cool. My room was full of band and road crew members hanging out, drinking, and smoking pot, so I took the chick in the bathroom, where we had sex—after which she told me that she was only seventeen!

Wow! I gulped as I realized I had just unknowingly had sex with an underage chick, with her mother right outside the door. This wasn't looking good, and I was contemplating arrest as I suggested that the girl leave the bathroom first, saying I would follow her out a few minutes later.

A minute later there was a knock at the bathroom door. It was Mom, who looked at me accusingly as she slipped in and closed the door behind her.

"I know what you just did to my daughter," she told me.

I swallowed hard and waited for the retribution to begin.

"Can I have some, too?"

I was lost for words as she took me in hand and then gave me a great blow job. As I looked down on her, I could only think that she was sucking her own daughter's pussy juice off me. Being a superstar rock drummer had its perks, but fuck—we had gone through the looking glass here.

We played four nights at Madison Square Garden, and the *Blondes* tour finished with six sold-out nights at the L.A. Forum at the end of June '79. It's hard to explain now how prestigious this was. Most bands would be happy to do one Forum gig, and we were booked in for six!

That week in June, the climax of a sold-out world tour, we felt like returning conquering heroes. Here I was, in my adopted hometown, playing gigs that were the hottest ticket going, at the heart of one of the biggest bands in the world. It didn't get any better than this.

The shows were unbelievable. The high started as soon as we stepped onstage, to be greeted by the excited roar of twenty thousand fans. As we played the first note, the screams were so loud that they sounded distorted, as if we were in the middle of a jet engine or underwater. We felt like we were superhuman.

Of course, three-quarters of the audience at Rod's concerts is female, and so we gazed out night after night at a crazed army of screaming chicks. Many of them lifted their tops, showing their tits to try to grab our attention. Being L.A., there was a lot of silicon in the house. By the final night we could tell real tits from fakes from a hundred yards away.

The hysteria just seemed to build and build every night, through the *Blondes* tracks and Rod's monster hits, such as "Maggie May," "Tonight's the Night," and "Hot Legs." Halfway through "(I Know I'm) Losing You," Rod would run offstage to change, freshen up, and blow-dry his hair, leaving me to crash through my ten-minute drum solo.

The crowd would be clapping along when Rod returned to finish the song and introduce me: "Carmine A-peece on the drums!" I would join him at the front of the stage to take a bow, and we'd throw my drumsticks into the audience. Their ovation almost knocked us over.

The highlight of the shows, though, was always "Do Ya Think I'm Sexy?" We'd often play it twice, once in the main set and once as an encore, after Rod had kicked soccer balls into the crowd for "Stay with Me." We would fall offstage covered in sweat, exhilarated, and feeling like we had just had a two-hour orgasm or as if we had had sex with twenty thousand people.

Some nights we headed to the hospitality room for an after-show party. This was another kind of buzz, as the great and good of music and Hollywood gathered for the party where you simply had to be seen. No bullshit: we felt like kings, and this was our court.

I would glance around the room and see Freddie Mercury and Roger Taylor from Queen talking to movie stars like Tony Curtis or Valerie Perrine, or Ronnie Wood from the Stones or Paul Stanley from Kiss hanging out. Yet none of them had the same impact on me as seeing Gregory Peck in the room.

Gregory Peck! I immediately got a mental image of him as Captain Ahab in *Moby Dick*, lashed to the giant whale! He was an imposing giant of a man, about six foot three, and possessed of charismatic strength and intensity. I didn't dare go over to introduce myself.

Rod had recently married Alana Hamilton, former wife of George Hamilton. Tall and blonde, Alana looked a typical Rod female and seemed to know anybody who was anybody, making Rod even more of a Hollywood socialite than he already was. Alana and I got along fine, but she was never around the band very much.

Rod and Alana sure knew how to throw a party. One particular high-society event at their mansion took days to prepare. The band was rehearsing in his garage, so we saw the huge marquee tents going up all across the lawns in the back of his house as the day neared.

This event was to cause me grief. I was still hanging out with Paul Stanley—in fact, I had played on Paul's solo record when all of Kiss decided to make solo albums. I had flown back from my Far East drum clinic tour and gone straight to the studio, arriving jet-lagged to the point of exhaustion. To this day I'm still not entirely sure on which tracks I played in the studio—but I know only one of them made it on to the album.

Rod had invited all of Kiss to his party, and Paul was planning to go in a rented Rolls limo. When Paul asked me if I wanted to get a lift and head down with him, I happily accepted. It turned out that this was not my wisest move.

Rod always had this whole thing that his band was like a gang: we all worked, played, ate, drank, and partied together. When he asked me before the party how I was getting there and I told him I would be with Paul from Kiss, his eyes narrowed. It was almost like he thought I was switching teams.

The party was absurdly star studded and glamorous, but even among all the Hollywood and sports legends, I saw Rod giving Paul and me a few funny looks, especially when he noticed us leaving three hours in. The next time I saw Rod, he quizzed me hard about why I had gone with Paul and "left early." It was a side of Rod that I was sadly to see again.

Another great party came when *Grease* producer Allan Carr threw a huge extravaganza for Rod and Alana in Beverly Hills. This was pure

Hollywood Babylon—yet more A-listers and the kinds of exotic foods I had never even heard of when I was growing up in Brooklyn were as abundant at the party as were cocaine and champagne.

I had seen Gregory Peck from afar. Now I was to meet him up close. Suddenly there he was, walking toward me, his hand extended. "Hello, I'm Greg—" he began, in that inimitable Atticus Finch voice, only for me to excitedly interrupt him: "I know who you are, and if my mother were here now, she would *die!*"

I mentioned to Gregory that I had seen him backstage at one of our Forum shows. "I was sitting with Fred Astaire during the concert," he explained. "In the middle of your solo, Fred turned to me and said it was the best drum solo he had heard since Gene Krupa."

This was amazing for me. As I have explained, Gene Krupa was my childhood hero, the reason I got into playing drums. Now I was being told that Fred Astaire, of all people, thought I was as good as Gene—and the person telling me the story was Gregory Peck! Life just kept getting crazier.

Gregory told me that Fred Astaire had always wanted to play rock-and-roll drums but had never known how to start. I found myself telling him about my *Realistic Rock* book and offering to give him a copy to give to Fred. Gregory accepted the offer on Fred's behalf and asked me to drop the book off next time I was at Rod's house. Gregory was Rod's next-door neighbor. Well, of course he was!

At Rod's the following week, I called Gregory's house to see if he was home and walked around to drop off my book for Fred. I was seriously nervous as I got buzzed in the giant gates and walked up the airport-runway-length driveway to his mansion. Towering over me on his doorstep, Gregory asked me to sign the book, and I wrote:

To Fred,
Good luck with this book, and I hope it helps you.
Love,
Carmine Appice

Two weeks later I was back at Rod's place for rehearsals when his PR guy, Tony, handed me a letter. I assumed it was fan mail—but why would that go to Rod's house? Tearing it open, I read the following handwritten note:

> Hi Carmine Appice!
> Thanks so much for sending me your book with the nice message written. I was delighted to get it. You sure are terrific, and I've enjoyed your work many times!
> Sincerely,
> Fred Astaire

It sounds stupid now, but I could have cried. At that moment, holding that letter, I felt like I had arrived. I had certainly come a long, long way from Borough Park in Brooklyn.

I was living like a king in Rod's band, and when an offer came through via my publicist to join Black Sabbath, I never gave it more than a minute's thought. However, I did suggest an alternative to them: my brother Vinny. Tony Iommi liked his playing on a recent album he had done, *Axis*, and Vinny auditioned and got the job. I was delighted.

My career was going great, but my love life wasn't getting any easier. After meeting Ruth, I finally had enough of Marvin the puppet and told Marlene we were over. I hated telling her, and it was a horrible conversation to have—but when it was over, I felt incredibly relieved.

My only worries, if I had any, were Marlene taking me to the cleaners financially. Yet when I confided my fears in my father, he simply said, "Fuck the money—you'll make it back!" My mom and dad were as happy to see the back of Marlene as I was.

The same evening I told Marlene we were done, I went to see Elton John play the Universal Amphitheater in L.A. I bumped into a cool Greek chick named Angela, whom I had known ten years earlier when she was eighteen and going out with Joe Schermie of Three Dog Night. I was always attracted to her, and we started seeing each other.

So where did this leave Ruth? Well, I made a couple of weekend trips to Sydney to see her. Flying for twenty-four hours to spend forty-eight hours together was exhausting, but we got on great and the trips felt romantic and special. On one trip, we went to see Santana, and he asked me to jam with him—he turned out to be a big BBA fan.

Back in L.A., the band began writing the songs for Rod's next album, which was to be called *Foolish Behaviour*, in his garage as usual. However, as 1980 dawned he decided that we would make the record in London and booked the American band members into the Montcalm hotel near Marble Arch.

The recording sessions followed a very English pattern. We would meet in the pub at lunchtime before heading off to Olympic Studios to work with our producer, Tom Dowd, and engineer, Andy Johns, for a few hours and then return to the pub in the evening. I loved the recording, but as a virtual nondrinker, the pub routine was boring for me.

It may have been partly to relieve the boredom that I decided to start augmenting my famous Fu Manchu moustache by putting colors in my hair. I started off with blue, green, and red; tried silver, which made me look like a gnarly old dude; and settled on purple and black. Obviously, Rod reacted by busting my balls and giving me the nickname Parrot.

I flew Ruth out to spend a few weeks with me in London as we made the album. I was excited to see her and looking forward to her visit, but when she arrived—disaster! The thrill had gone. We didn't connect any more, and what we had seemed to vanish as fast as it had arrived.

Our anticipated idyllic reunion became an awkward ordeal, and one night I made an excuse and took refuge in the arms of Jane, an English chick I usually screwed when I was in London. As we lay in bed after sex, my mind made me an impassioned little speech: *You're in bed with Jane, and you have a beautiful Australian chick waiting at your hotel for you. Angela, who is gorgeous, is waiting for you in L.A., and your soon-to-be ex-wife is in your house. What the fuck is wrong with you?*

And the funny thing is, despite this embarrassment of riches, I was lying there feeling sorry for myself! Which I guess is the precise definition of a spoiled rock star. Anyway, the end of my infatuation with Ruth at least cleared the way for me to get serious with Angela.

As we finished off *Foolish Behaviour* in L.A. after the London sessions, I started a sideline band, Carmine and the Rockers, which featured soon-to-be ex–Kiss guitarist Vinny Casano, a.k.a. Vinny Vincent. We were booked to play two dates at the Whisky a Go-Go and wanted a way to promote the shows. I had a brainwave.

My idea was to stage drum contests wherein established and famous drummers would judge a live contest between aspiring drummers, who would win prizes, such as new kits. In truth, my original inspiration for this plan was my hero Gene Krupa, who had done something similar in the 1930s. We decided to call them the Carmine Appice Drum-Offs.

The first one took place on Mother's Day 1980 in the parking lot of Tower Records in Hollywood, after I had spent half the day in the studio with Rod and the band. The turnout amazed me. L.A. radio stations publicized it, and more than three thousand people came out, overflowed into the street, and caused the traffic to back up right down Sunset Boulevard. It was a huge success and a formula I was to replicate for years.

The Carmine and the Rockers show at the Whisky was also pretty cool. It sold out, and Eddie and Alex Van Halen came down, as did Bruce Gary from the Knack, Eddie Money, and Hollywood actor Robin Williams! Robin was definitely a rock fan and also a very funny guy.

Meanwhile, I was still doing my usual drum clinics, and in the late summer of '80 I embarked on a two-month European clinics tour. I was on my own at Amsterdam Airport when I read the newspaper headlines announcing that John Bonham had died.

He had died after drinking the equivalent of forty shots of vodka. It was hardly an unpredictable end, but it was a horrible shock to me. Bonzo had always been cool with me, and we had had so many great nights together, both out on tour in the Fudge's early days and later living it up whenever he passed through town.

Obviously, he also had his dark side, invariably brought on by alcohol. When he drank, Bonzo turned into the mad, bad, and dangerous-to-know character that became his caricature, and as I stood in that Dutch airport, my mind went back to one evening just a couple of years earlier in L.A.

Zeppelin were in town, and after a lively night in the Rainbow Bar & Grill, we had returned to their usual L.A. hangout, the Hyatt House hotel, a.k.a. the Riot House. We were partying in Bonham's suite, and some overexcited guy named Tony who said he drummed for a famous UK band (that none of us had heard of) was also there.

At first Tony was fine, telling me, "Man, I can't believe I'm sitting here with two of my biggest drum influences, Carmine Appice and John Bonham!" It was just normal fan stuff. But as the night went on, he started bad-mouthing Bad Company, who of course were signed to Zeppelin's label, Swan Song.

By now, Bonham was, as usual, getting monumentally drunk and heard what Tony was saying. He came over to me and asked, "Do you know that guy?"

"No," I told him, "he's a fan and a drummer."

"Well," said Bonham, "tell him if he doesn't button his fucking hole, I'm going to button it for him."

I told Tony that it wasn't cool to put down Bad Company in John's room, since they were signed to his label. Tony seemed to agree, but he was so drunk and excited that a minute later he was doing it again. Bonzo staggered back to me.

"Tell him he's got one more shot," he growled. "If he doesn't shut up, I'll drag him out by his hair and we'll beat the crap out of him."

I warned Tony again, "Look, dude, shut your mouth or leave, or you're going to get beat up!" He clearly didn't believe in the three-strikes rule, because he just kept ranting. The next thing he knew, Bonham was standing over him—and in those days Bonzo probably weighed 240 pounds.

Bonham grabbed Tony by his hair with one hand, yanked him off his seat, and pulled him across the room, still by the hair, caveman-style, punching him hard in the face with the other hand. He opened the door, hurled Tony into the corridor, and slammed the door behind him.

"Sorry, mate!" he told me. "I just couldn't take it!"

There was a knock at the door. A roadie opened it. It was Tony. "You don't want to come back in here," the roadie warned him, but Tony pushed past him, at which point Bonzo and the roadie really beat him to a pulp. He must have had a death wish—even after they threw him out the second time, he still knocked on the door again! Thankfully, that time nobody answered it.

So sure, Bonham was a flawed character, but what a unique guy—and what a drummer! Of course, on one level it was no kind of surprise that he had OD'd from drinking, as drinking was all he ever did. But at the same time he was such a bull of a man, such a giant, that he seemed like he could handle it. He had always appeared invincible.

One aftereffect of his death was that stories began to appear in the music press suggesting that I might take his place in Led Zeppelin. It definitely made sense, as Bonzo had admitted that I had influenced his drumming quite a lot, so we had similar styles.

I was flattered and excited by this idea, but at the same time I didn't want to piss off Rod and told him there was nothing in the stories. Rod seemed to find it all pretty funny. At the same time, there were rumors in the papers that he might be about to retire, and he told me, "Carmine, let's keep these stories going! They're great for selling tickets!"

*Foolish Behaviour* wasn't Rod's biggest album. The main singles off it were "Passion" and "She Won't Dance with Me." We shot videos for these at the start of the European tour with leggy blonde models—the kind of girls who were always in Rod's videos—which gave us the chance to pursue one of our favorite hobbies: bogging.

Rod was our leader in this sport of bogging, which essentially consisted of trying to spy on women as they were changing. Filming the "Passion" video, we discovered that the roof of the building we were in had a skylight with an excellent view of the girls' dressing room. So for every costume change, the models had a secret, very appreciative audience high above their heads.

The *Foolish Behaviour* tour kicked off in Scandinavia in late 1980 before swinging through Europe to Britain. Angela was with me in London, and we saw a lot of her Greek uncle—a certain Telly Savalas.

Telly was real old-school Hollywood but was world-famous at that time for playing TV detective Kojak. He was a nice guy to hang out with, really easygoing, and Angela and I would go with Telly and his wife, Julie, to dinner and then down to Park Lane for the Playboy Club and the casinos.

Rod was impressed that we knew Telly, and when Telly came to one of our four nights at Wembley Arena, we invited him to the after-show party. Every head in the room turned when Telly walked in; he just had that effortless star quality. Rod was by then married to Alana, and we took some great photos of the three of us with our women.

The next morning, I heard on the radio that John Lennon had been shot dead in New York City, and I told Telly the bad news when Angela and I went to his London flat. As I did so, the dumbest thing ran through my head: *This is a job for Kojak!*

When Rod played Manchester, we got a reminder of just how different Britain is from America. At the end of the shows, I always hurled my drumsticks hard into the crowd, and backstage I met a girl who was bleeding from a deep facial cut and holding the stick that had caused it. I felt awful, but she just thanked me for the stick! In America, she would have sued my ass off.

Back in L.A., I went into the studio to record a solo album to be released on Rod's record label, Riva. It was to be mostly original songs with a couple of cover versions, such as "Paint It Black" and "Be My Baby." One night after leaving the studio, I went to a charity event with Rod and the rest of the band, and the Fonz walked up to me!

For New Yorkers, the Fonz from the *Happy Days* show was a real dude, a big deal, so it was a thrill to meet Henry Winkler, the actor who played him. Henry told me that his eleven-year-old stepson, Jed, was learning the drums and was working through my *Realistic Rock Drum Method* book.

Henry said he'd love Jed to meet me, so I invited them down to the studio. When they turned up a few days later, the Fonz was carrying pizza and Jed was clutching my book. We had a great time. Henry invited Angela and me to his home in Toluca Lake, and we became buddies. He would sometimes come to see Rod's band. Hanging out with the Fonz! Who'd have thought it?

When my solo album was done, I was pleased with it, but it had an unexpected side effect. Rod wanted to shake up his band, and he loved my record's vibe and grooves so much that he decided to fire his entire band, except me, and replace them with the guys who had played on my album!

Being Rod, he just went ahead and did it, hiring my guitarist, Danny Johnson, and bassist, Jay Davis, and using Duane Hitchings as a session keyboards player. He didn't even tell Jim Cregan, Gary Grainger, Phil Chen, and Kevin Savigar that they were fired—they found out via stories in the press.

Rod quickly put the new band together, including guitarist Robin Le Mesurier and saxophonist Jimmy Zavala. It was a lot of change, and I persuaded him to bring back Jim Cregan so that we had at least one longtime member who knew all the chord changes for the songs. At that moment, unknown to me, I signed my own suicide note in the band.

Kevin Savigar was also back when we toured Japan, Hong Kong, and Thailand in the spring of '81. Bangkok was wild. With a few days to kill, we gave a young local guy twenty-five dollars in local currency to get us some marijuana Thai sticks.

The guy came back with fifty sticks, and we smoked ourselves silly before staggering off to a topless bar staffed by eighteen-year-old hookers who would spend the night with you and be your slave for just five dollars! The next morning I woke up with three of them. Before flying back to the States, we all got penicillin jabs.

I flew back from Thailand on my own for an event I could scarcely believe was happening. We had decided to stage our second drum-off, and my manager phoned to tell me that the day had been officially designated as Carmine Appice Day in Los Angeles.

Carmine Appice Day! Was this for real? It was: after an overnight flight from Bangkok during which I was too excited to sleep, I was met by a limo at LAX and taken straight to Griffin Park, where the event was to be held. The mayor of L.A., Tom Bradley, signed a proclamation in my honor, but I was even more excited by the news that one of the drum-off judges was to be Buddy Rich.

Buddy? Buddy, who hated rock drummers? Yes, there he was. It appeared his manager had heard that my first drum-off had been a success, and as Buddy was playing a show at Disneyland that week, he wanted some free publicity. He was even willing to play four-bar breaks with the other judges—except, of course, that nobody wanted to play immediately after him, because he could blow anyone away. So it fell to me, jet-lagged and sleep-deprived, to follow a Buddy Rich four-bar break in front of ten thousand fans. Thank God for my double bass drums and volume!

After the drum-off, Buddy and I got a helicopter to his show at Disneyland. There were news journalists on board, and Buddy introduced me to them on camera: "This is my friend, Carmine Appice. He's a great rock drummer—but what do I know?" It may possibly have been the proudest moment of my life.

Buddy and I then became good friends, especially after a funny incident that happened between us. I mentioned to my manager that I had seen Animal, the drummer on *The Muppet Show*, who some people had said was based on me.

That crazy puppet certainly looked pretty similar to me: the mountain of hair, the wild technique, flying sticks—he had everything but my moustache! As a joke, I added, "Maybe I should challenge him to a drum battle!" My manager thought it was a great idea and called the Muppets' company, Jim Henson Productions, who asked him to send them a press package about me, which he did.

A week later the Jim Henson people called my manager back and said they had good news and bad news.

"OK," said my manager. "What's the good news?"

"We love your idea, and we want to do it."

"So what's the bad news?"

"We're going to use Buddy Rich instead of Carmine."

What the fuck? I called Buddy at home. "What's going on?" I asked him. "You're doing *The Muppet Show*, right?"

"Yeah, I'm gonna have a drum battle with Animal—I'll kill him!" Buddy told me proudly. "How do you know?"

"Because it was my idea, and I was going to do it!" I yelled.

The reply was pure Buddy: "Well, they wanted the best!" It was kind of hard to argue with.

Back in L.A., Rod decided to produce the next album, *Tonight I'm Yours*, himself, with Jim Cregan and me as coproducers. We went into the Record Plant in L.A. and began some very work-hard/play-hard sessions. This was a recording process I wouldn't forget in a hurry.

We often used to party with Queen when they were in town. I had gotten friendly with their drummer, Roger Taylor, who had a place in the Hollywood Hills, and I would go there to hang out with him and talk drums. I was also friendly with Brian May and John Deacon. Freddie Mercury was surprisingly shy and quiet.

Queen were all there when we threw an all-night coke and booze party at the Record Plant during which Rod decided he wanted to drive his Lamborghini into the studio. It was a huge room, like a soundstage, with a thirty-foot-high door, so Rod had no problem vrooming into the party.

Things were finally winding down around eight the next morning when we reopened the giant door so Rod could drive out—only to discover a deep, six-foot-wide ditch right by the door! Workmen had begun relaying piping, and with all of us drunk or high, we could see no way of getting the Lamborghini back out. Eventually we laid planks of wood across the hole, and Rod inched out, nearly snapping them in two as he went.

The album was coming together OK, and we recorded a song I cowrote with Duane Hitchings, "Young Turks," which was to become the lead single. I didn't object when Rod suggested bringing in Tony Brock to guest on drums on some tracks, as I was coproducing the record—I had plenty to do.

Yet I wasn't enjoying the sessions as much as I had previous albums. We would spend hours in the bar each day, there was a crazy amount of booze and coke floating around, and as someone who hardly drank and never snorted, I felt itchy and excluded.

And there was another, bigger problem. Jim Cregan was in Rod's ear all the time, bitching about me and, from what I heard, saying they didn't need to give me a production credit. I wasn't quite sure what was going on, but one day I'd had enough: I slammed Cregan up against a studio wall and told him that if he didn't shut his mouth, I'd kick his ass.

That was the beginning of the end for me. The drink and coke were putting Rod into the same paranoid mind-set as Cregan, and he told me he was blowing out my production credit. I was royally pissed off about this, especially as I had hardly played on the record, but I had little choice but to bite my tongue and accept it.

We finished the album, got photographed dressed as sailors for the back sleeve, and mimed to the "Young Turks" single on a rooftop in Hollywood for a Dick Clark TV show. Next up was to prepare for the tour—which was when my manager took a call from Rod's manager telling me that I was out.

It was a total bombshell. I was out of the band and off the tour, where Tony Brock would take my place. And why had Rod done this? He was tired of hearing that I was about to join Led Zeppelin—the groundless rumors that he had actually told me to encourage a year before!

Looking back, I don't blame Rod for this betrayal. The drugs—and Cregan—were as much to blame as he was. At the time, I was devastated—I had spent months on the album but now had no production credit and no tour, which meant I would get a flat fee for performing on the record but would not get to tour, which I had kept my schedule free for. I decided to play dirty.

Rod had recently been the victim of a few tell-all stories in British tabloid newspapers, as former roadies and a makeup girl spilled the beans about the sexual shenanigans on tour. My manager called Rod's people and told them that if they didn't agree to a financial payoff for my missing the tour, I would do exactly the same thing.

I guess you could call it blackmail, and I felt bad doing it, but Rod had little choice other than to settle—I was an ex-member of the Sex Police! I knew a lot of dirty secrets! So we agreed on a settlement that was less than I would have got for playing the US tour, which was fine, but I felt depressed and used. All I wanted was to still be in the band and to play.

Rod resented the whole episode, and the separation got very petty and nasty. For the second pressing of the album, my face was removed from the photo of the band in sailor suits. Now Rod's arm was around my body with Tony Brock's face replacing mine!

The weird thing was I was still signed to Rod's publishing company, and my album, *Rockers*, was coming out on his label. This didn't stop

Rod badmouthing me in his interviews, where he enigmatically said, "Never trust a drummer with his name on the front of his drums." What the fuck did that mean? I hit back by telling journalists that Rod's music had gotten too wimpy and keyboards-based and he was forgetting how to rock.

Man, it was a desperately sad way to leave a band that had given me the best time of my life. It was embarrassing to me to get fired from a group I loved, and I was seriously down for a while. Yet I never can hold a grudge, and a year or so later, Rod and I made up.

Jeff Beck came over from London to hang out at my house in the Hollywood Hills, and after a few days' hard partying, we decided to make some music. We went to Duane Hitchings's house, where the three of us worked out a killer new version of "People Get Ready," the song that Vanilla Fudge had covered on our first album and BBA had played live.

Now we just needed somebody to sing it. "What about Rod?" wondered Jeff. We all looked at each other. Rod would *kill* this song.

We called Rod's office and tracked him down at a restaurant on Santa Monica Boulevard, where he was—surprise!—eating with a blonde beauty. Rod loved the song when we played it to him on the car cassette player, and a few weeks later we all met up in the Record Plant to record it.

I loved this session. As I had sung the song with Fudge and knew the lyrics and arrangement, I acted as producer and cued in Rod and Jeff when to sing and play. I have to admit, that felt pretty good. I programmed the drum machine, and we merged Jeff's solos and his rhythm guitar parts and put my sampled voice through a keyboard to make it sound like a multivoice choir, and I edited the end result while Rod and Jeff were in the pub next door. It sounded fantastic.

I half-forgot about that session until a few months later when Jeff's very posh, impeccably English manager, Ernest, called me from London to ask me, "Darling, how much do you want for that session that you did with Jeff and Rod?"

"All I want is a credit as the producer or coproducer," I said. "If it's produced by all of us, use all of our names."

"Of course, darling," Ernest said, and hung up.

So what do you know? When the track appeared on Jeff's *Flash* album, the credit simply read, "Produced by Jeff Beck" with a side-note: "Thanks to all the boys." What a bunch of bullshit! Yet part of me saw the funny side.

The moral of the tale? Whatever ups and downs I had had with Rod Stewart, I could always rely on Jeff Beck or his people to fuck me over.

# 9

# I COULD NEVER TAKE
# A PLACE WITH YOU, MAN

*In which Drummerdude finds himself sharing a house with Prince, stumbles in on him in bed with Vanity, tours with Ted Nugent and sees him beat up his audience, is a porn-magazine cover star, gets married, haunts an English mansion with Ozzy Osbourne, and gives career advice to Jon Bon Jovi*

*Here is a truth I have learned many times* in my career: it is a precarious life being a rock-and-roll drummer. One minute you are a cossetted superstar, traveling the world, entertaining arenas and stadiums, laying your head in the best hotels, and with countless beautiful women beating a path to your door.

The next minute—bang! You're unemployed.

I had not expected to get kicked out of the Rod Stewart Group. I didn't see it coming, and it was a blow to my self-confidence. But after I had lain low and licked my wounds for a few weeks, it was time to take stock. Just what, exactly, was I going to do next? Luckily, I had already glimpsed a possible way forward.

In January 1981 Rod's band had played the American Music Awards. Rod was getting heavily into the synthesizers side of things, and our performance that night was big on keyboards and very light on guitars. Afterward, my old friend Ted Nugent came up to me to critique our show.

"Man, that is really some wimpy-ass rock and roll you guys are playing there," he spat disgustedly. "Carmine, when you are ready to play real man's rock and roll, give me a call."

This conversation came back to me a few months later. I had played a little solo mini-tour of five-hundred-capacity venues, which was fun, but it was a big step down from entertaining packed arenas with Rod's band. I was missing the big time, so I decided to take Ted at his word and call him up.

He didn't seem surprised to hear from me. "Yeah, man, why don't you come up to Michigan for a few days?" he drawled on the phone. "We'll hang out for a few days, talk it over, and see if we can put something together."

Now, an invitation to Ted Nugent's house—or, rather, ranch—was not to be taken lightly. To say the least, his lifestyle was notorious. I knew Ted had never taken drugs, didn't drink or party, and when he wasn't on the road with his band, was all about shooting and hunting, sometimes even with a bow and arrow.

Let me level with you: I set off for Michigan with a degree of trepidation.

When I arrived, it was exactly as billed. Ted's sprawling farm-like home was set in acres of land. He had a custom-built dirt track, complete with big bumps, around which he would race his custom Ford Bronco trucks so hard they would literally go flying through the air.

Everywhere you looked inside the ranch, stuffed animal heads—Ted's trophies—stared out from the walls. I spent the night in his den on a foldout couch, and as I lay in the semidark trying to avoid the glazed eyes of deer, buffalos, and even a tiger, I counted seventy-five dead animal parts in my immediate line of vision. I hardly slept a wink.

Ted lived with his beautiful Hawaiian girlfriend, Pele, who had just turned seventeen when they met. Somehow Ted had persuaded her parents to give her their signed permission to live with him. Pele was a cool girl and a great cook, and every day began with a big breakfast in which red meat figured more prominently than is usual.

One day Ted announced that he was going hunting the next morning. I wasn't sure what was expected of me, so lamely suggested, "OK—maybe I should come, too?" Ted swiveled around, fixed his gaze on me, and itemized his intended schedule.

"I'll be getting up at about 4 AM," he began. "I'll be putting on all this camouflage clothing. I'll be out by 5:00 or 5:30. I'll be lying down in the wet leaves, waiting for some deer to come. I expect to wait an hour or two. Oh, and it's going to be mighty cold tomorrow."

I stayed home and had breakfast with Pele.

Another day, Pele had made us hamburgers, and I was finding mine hard to chew. It also tasted kind of weird.

"Man, what's the deal with the meat?" I asked her. "It's so black!"

"It's buffalo meat," Pele told me.

To my left, a huge bison head hung mournfully over a stone fireplace. "Is that him?" I asked her.

"Oh, no!" she told me. "This meat is really fresh. Ted just killed it." Call me squeamish, but I really couldn't finish that burger.

It was an interesting week, and also a productive one. In between Ted's hunting, shooting, and monster trucking sessions, we jammed in a big rehearsal space at the back of his property with singer Derek St. Holmes and bassist Dave Kiswiney. It felt good, and we decided to reconvene in a few weeks' time.

Ted and the rest of the band swung by L.A. to record the album that was to become *Nugent*. I quickly learned that there was no pretense at democracy in Ted's band: he wrote all of the songs, and we played 'em for him. Even so, I enjoyed being in a full-on rock-and-roll band again.

Ted had gotten hugely pissed off by the Iranian hostage crisis and wrote a song about it, "Bound and Gagged." We filmed a real pro-American video for it in Detroit, full of Stars and Stripes, missile strikes, and news footage from Tehran, and MTV played it to death.

As I mentally recovered from being kicked out of Rod's band, it was a great confidence boost to know that Japan still loved me. After I finished the *Nugent* album, some Japanese promoters offered to mount a tour under the name Carmine Appice & Friends. I was excited to do it to promote my solo album, *Rockers*.

My managers and I quickly assembled a mean supergroup. Rick Derringer, on vocals and guitar, was up for it, as was Eric Carmen, who had been in the Raspberries and enjoyed a solo number one with "All by Myself." On bass we had Tom Petersson, who had just left Cheap Trick—who were also huge in Japan. Duane Hitchings played keyboards.

The trip got off to a weird start. You can easily forget how small everything is in Japan, and I packed for the tour in full rock-star mode, with cases and cases of stage clothes. Angela and I saw the promoters' horrified faces when our stage trunks arrived at Tokyo's Haneda Airport. They had to hire another van to transport it and a spare hotel room to store it.

It's a measure of how popular we were out there that our first show was at the Budokan. The shows were great, except that Eric Carmen had a major drinking thing going on. Some nights I wasn't sure if he would get to the end of "All by Myself." At the Budokan, he fell off his piano stool halfway through.

On that tour, I debuted a special effect that I still use sometimes today. I would play a frantic drum solo during which a fog of dry ice would conceal my kit. Due to a miracle of technology, the drumming would go on until the smoke cleared to reveal an empty kit, Derringer would yell "Carmine Appice on drums!" and a spotlight would pick me out standing in the audience. It brought the house down every night.

We played a cool mix of tracks, including "Hang On Sloopy," which Rick Derringer had played with the McCoys, and Cheap Trick songs, such as "I Want You to Want Me" and "I Know What I Want." From my repertoire, we just played numbers off *Rockers*. Looking back, that was weird—I'm sure that the Japanese fans would have loved to hear some Vanilla Fudge, Cactus, or BBA songs, not to mention "Young Turks" or "Do Ya Think I'm Sexy?" I just felt kind of awkward playing those songs without Rod, Jeff, or Rusty up there with me. It took me years to realize how dumb those inhibitions were.

The Japanese tour was a great success and paid well, helping to make up for missing out on the Rod tour. When it finished, we played a few US dates. Eric and Tom couldn't make it, so Tim Bogert and Duane Hitchings stepped in. For support, I staged drum-off contests in the venues before the shows.

Back in L.A., I had moved out of the house Marlene and I had shared. Angela and I were getting along great, and I was spending most of my time at her apartment in Studio City. However, I also wanted a place of my own to use as a work base, keep my gear and cars, and occasionally crash.

I was very briefly with a management company called Cavallo, Ruffalo & Fargnoli (sounds like a bad Italian restaurant, huh?), and a friend who worked there, Jamie, had a two-bedroom place in Studio City. Jamie was having financial trouble, so we did a deal whereby I loaned her ten thousand dollars and in return could stay in her spare room rent-free. It made sense for both of us.

There was just one tiny catch: Cavallo, Ruffalo & Fargnoli were also managing a solo artist out of Minneapolis. He was pretty high-strung and didn't like staying in hotels, so whenever he was in L.A. he would also crash in Jamie's spare room. At the time, the guy was just starting to break through.

His name was Prince. And he was funky.

Let me tell you, I found Prince Rogers Nelson a very hard guy to figure out. We were just night and day. For one thing, he was a tiny dude, about half my size, and very quiet and introverted, whereas I have always been a typical Joe New York, loud and outgoing. He seemed to be intimidated just by being around me.

Despite our differences, though, we never had a cross word—we hardly had a word at all! I would bowl into the living room, where he was listening to music he was working on, and say, "Hey, man, what's up?" His answer would be a shy smile and silence. If he did speak, it was like somebody was whispering at me from two miles away.

His record label was giving him a big push, trying to make him into a superstar, and I remember they were calling the music he was making "punk funk." They even had little button badges made saying that. He was too shy to ever play it for me, but when I snuck a listen it did, indeed, sound funky and punky.

Prince and I made do sharing the room. As he rarely spoke, I never knew when he was going to be there. One time I drove up, marched into my room, and found him in my bed with Vanity, his backing singer and sort-of girlfriend. I apologized, backed out, and gave them time to get decent before collecting my stuff and splitting.

Jamie went with Prince the day he supported the Rolling Stones at L.A.'s Memorial Coliseum. The Stones' fans didn't know what to make of his stage gear of stilettoes, stockings, and panties, and booed him off. I was at the house when Prince came home freaked out and in tears.

Jamie and I were trying to calm him down and explain that it was only one show and that Stones fans were not his natural audience anyway. I told him about my own bad experiences, like Vanilla Fudge not going down great when we supported the Mamas and the Papas. But we were wasting our words; Prince was inconsolable.

Prince and I were so different that we didn't really socialize, but one day he asked if I could give him a lift into Hollywood. We climbed into my Pantera, and I gunned it hard and fast along the Hollywood Hills' winding roads and bends, chatting away and getting no reply, as usual. I glanced over and saw Prince pinned to his seat, pure terror on his face—I guess he just wasn't used to my driving.

In the meantime, my manager Alan's campaign to turn me into a "rock personality" had begun to bear fruit. I was getting offered some interesting shit to do, including an article for *Oui*, a soft-porn men's magazine like *Playboy* or *Penthouse*. *Oui* had begun interviewing rockers like Ozzy and Mötley Crüe, and after talking to me to promote my solo album on Rod's label, they asked if I would be interested in being the cover star of a special insert within the magazine.

Fuck, yeah!

The idea was that I would tell my sex, drugs, and rock-and-roll road stories over ten pages, accompanied by a photo shoot by a photographer friend of mine, Mark Weiss. The pictures would combine my two main offstage preoccupations: trashing hotels and sex with as many groupies as possible.

The *Oui* interview and shoot happened in Jacksonville, Florida, after I held a drum-off. My PR person persuaded the local radio station to run an appeal for chicks to shoot a photo session with me, neglecting to mention that the results would appear in a soft-porn magazine. The girls paraded before the drum-off crowd, who chose the lucky winners.

The shoot happened in a local Holiday Inn. Before the girls arrived, Mark and I "wrecked" the room: chairs and sofas all tipped over, shades removed from lamps, pillows and cushions strewn over the floor among beer bottles, album sleeves, and drum parts. I had never trashed a hotel so artfully.

The two chicks turned up with their boyfriends in tow, but all four of them were OK when Mark explained that the girls would have to get topless and get up close with me. We did shots with the three of us in bed and me feeling up the boobs of both girls at once. Even with their partners watching and harsh camera lights trained on us, I still felt a hard-on straining against my usual bikini underwear!

Over the next two to three hours, we did all kinds of sexy shots. The weirdest was one of me actually sucking on one of the girl's nipples. I felt that was a bit over the top and asked *Oui* not to include it. Naturally, when the issue appeared, they had totally ignored me.

It all looked outrageous. The insert cover proclaimed "Carmine Appice's Rock Confessions" alongside enticing cover lines such as "The International Musician's Guide to Hotel Wrecking," "Mud Shark Mayhem," and "Jeff Beck and the Great Semen Race of '72." The interview and photos were pretty gross, but who cared? It was great publicity for my album, and I was stoked to see it.

So I was having fun, but I was also itching to get back on the road with a full-on band and was pleased when the Ted Nugent tour rolled around. It was all I had expected. The raw energy reminded me a lot of Cactus, and I got into the habit of swinging on my gong stand. Press releases billed me as the "Drum City Rocker" after a song on my solo record. Ted, of course, was the "Motor City Madman."

Ted may not touch alcohol or weed, but he is that rare rocker who doesn't need to: a natural wild man. His adventures on the tour included crashing our rental cars into each other at seventy miles per hour and taking postshow showers with two different chicks. Pele, it seemed, was no longer on the scene.

When we passed through Little Rock, the telephone in my hotel room rang. I picked it up to hear a female Southern drawl: "Hi y'all! This is Connie—as in Connie from Little Rock. I think it's time that us two legends got together."

"Well, that would be OK as long as you don't fuck the rest of the touring party!" I replied, remembering how she had done the whole of the BBA road crew. "I don't care for sloppy seconds!" Connie agreed. I wasn't sure I believed her.

She was true to her word. The next day she showed up, looking pretty sexy for her age, and stuck by my side all day long (but not so close that the rest of the band knew what I was up to). After the show, she came back to my room, and while I was wary of sex with her—dude, I knew where she had been!—she gave me a kick-ass massage and one of the best blow jobs I had ever had. I was in the mouth of an artist.

Connie was an interesting character. It turned out that she was a schoolteacher by day, and she told me she had also been with that other famous, highly sexed Little Rock native, Bill Clinton. Was that true? I have no idea, but it was certainly cool that we two "legends" had gotten together.

While I was out on the Ted tour, *Oui* phoned me to tell me that the special edition of the magazine had sold more than three million copies and they wanted to throw a party for me in New York and present me with a special prize: the *Oui* Spill the Beans Award.

This was awesome! The party was during the week of Fourth of July, while the tour was on a break. Ted had invited the band to his ranch, where his idea of an Independence Day celebration was firing assault rifles and machine guns into a giant dirt mountain purpose-built on the property. He even had a bazooka! If ever an enemy were to invade American soil, Ted Nugent was ready for 'em.

*Oui* flew Angela and me from Ted's place in Michigan to the amazingly swanky NYC party. We did all the red-carpet shit, and Linda Blair, the star of *The Exorcist* and a friend from rock gigs in L.A., presented me with the award. For some reason Joe Frazier, the former world-heavyweight boxing champion, was also there.

Back on the tour it came as no surprise that Ted Nugent was big in Texas, and we played six shows in a row in El Paso before falling afoul of the craziest tour routing I had ever come across. After the last El Paso gig, we had to fly out at 3 AM to make a gig the next night . . . in Hawaii.

Arriving fried in Honolulu at breakfast time, we went straight to the hotel beach before being dragged away from the white sand, turquoise sea, and gorgeous girls to sound check. We had no sleep and did a load of press. I was definitely in an altered state during the arena gig—until I suddenly saw Ted pointing and yelling at someone before dropping his guitar and leaping into the crowd.

We all stopped playing, and running to the front of the stage to see what was going on, I was greeted by the sight of Ted beating the shit out of a fan in the audience. As I gazed open-mouthed, a security guard pulled Ted off the guy and threw his victim out as Ted climbed back onstage.

"What the hell happened?" I asked Ted.

"The guy was giving me the finger and telling me to go fuck myself all night, so I went down and kicked his ass!" he grunted before picking up his guitar and appropriately firing into a new track, "Fightin' Words." Say what you like about Ted Nugent (and people do), but he walks it like he talks it.

After the show, we partied into the early hours with some sweet local chicks who knew how to give a great blow job, but the weird routing was not done yet. By eight in the morning we were on a plane to Alaska. Arriving in Anchorage, it was so cold that it was like we'd flown from paradise to the Arctic, so we bunkered down in the hotel to chain-smoke strong Alaskan weed.

A few weeks after it appeared, the *Oui* article was to get me into shit. Ludwig Drums was still sponsoring me, and one of the firm's customers came across *Oui* (as it were) and wrote a horrified letter to the company's aged president, Bill Ludwig Jr.:

Dear President,
Being a concerned drummer and proud to be part of the music business, I was appalled by an article which interviewed one of your top rock drum stars.

While I was sitting in a barbershop, waiting my turn, I happened to pick up the latest issue of Oui magazine (which is not a trade publication), to read an article on Carmine Appice (photos included). It is the grossest thing I have read in years, but I'm even more shocked to think a company with your status and name would allow such a person to endorse Ludwig Drums, one of the biggest drum companies in the world. Perhaps you are not even aware of this article. It would certainly behove you to look into this matter.
Sincerely,
Disgusted.

Shortly afterward I bumped into the venerable Bill Ludwig Jr. at a drum event, and he wouldn't even shake my hand, looking at it as if it harbored some kind of unspeakable sexual disease (in fairness, it was when AIDS was first hitting the headlines). I left Ludwig soon after, but it wasn't because of *Oui*; it was because their drums were going downhill.

By contrast, *Oui* could not have been more pleased with me, and I was to figure in four more issues of the soft-porn mag over the next year. They even produced a calendar for my birthday, with pictures from the notorious hotel shoot. It was just what I had always wanted.

Of course, some girlfriends might have objected to their partners constantly turning up in titty mags, but Angela wasn't fazed at all. She was an actress herself—she had done the *BJ and the Bear* TV series and a load of ads—and didn't take it seriously. In fact, she and I were getting on so well that I decided it was time for marriage number three.

The wedding day was a blast. Telly Savalas came through for us. He was involved in the Riviera Country Club in Beverly Hills, a real upmarket joint, and arranged for us to marry there. My accountant told me that if we got a load of rock-star guests and press coverage, we could write it off our taxes as a promo party. So I got people like Ronnie James Dio, Quiet Riot, and the guys from Ratt to show up.

Workwise, I was between gigs again. Rick Derringer and I made an EP and did a few shows as DNA, but as Angela and I moved into a new place in Sherman Oaks, I knew I needed a big band to play with again.

My manager got me a deal with the Mattel Toy Company to be a spokesman—along with Buddy Rich—for a new Synsonic drum they were producing. I was promoting this in Cannes, in the south of France, when Ozzy Osbourne and Sharon got in touch to ask me to join Ozzy's band for the *Bark at the Moon* album and tour. Their timing was perfect.

After the initial meeting in which Sharon was all sweetness and light, I came away totally stoked. One big part of the deal for me was that I could be involved in finishing off the *Bark at the Moon* album. I wouldn't actually play on the record, but I was to get a credit as production assistant, which I hoped might help me get production work in the future.

Ozzy and I went into the Hit Factory studio in New York. The producer was Tony Bongiovi, which was funny for me, as he had been the engineer on Vanilla Fudge's *Near the Beginning* album back in '69. The studio was state of the art, but recording Ozzy's vocals was a seriously s-l-o-w process. Some sessions, he was so unfocussed that he would just sing one word at a time.

Ozzy was cool, but he really wasn't streetwise. Late afternoon every day, he and I would walk from the Helmsley Hotel on Forty-Second Street to the studio. (Find a cab that time of day? Forget it!) New York was a jungle in those days, but Ozzy would shamble through the dusk in his huge, flashy diamond rings, oblivious to potential muggers hiding in the shadows. I would try to warn him, but he never listened.

We flew supersonic to London on the Concorde to shoot the "Bark at the Moon" video. The flight was amazing—we got from JFK to London in just three and a half hours. A speedometer on the jet wall told us how fast we were going: Mach 1, Mach 2, and so on. The only disappointment was that it was too cloudy to see the curvature of the Earth, as you sometimes could.

The video was crazy, as in Ozzy crazy. We filmed it in a huge, wild old building that looked like an English castle but had once been a maximum-security mental hospital. Talk about creepy! The location manager who sourced this place was a twisted genius.

You could sense the suffering that had gone on in that hellhole. One day we found a wrecked old room with a table with straps to prevent patients from escaping while they were given electric shock therapy. In another, we came across jars with human embryos in them! Some of the rooms—well, they were more like cells—had a simple, plaintive cry scrawled on the walls: "Help me!"

It freaked us out, but "Bark at the Moon" was to become one of Ozzy's most popular videos. He spent hours every day in makeup being transformed into a werewolf as the rest of us prowled the house of horror, then we stood outside in the freezing cold as the production team drenched us in pretend rain from hoses for the cameras. What an experience!

Yet my time with Ozzy seemed ill-starred from the start. After the video, the band moved to a studio to rehearse for the tour, but I had visa problems and had to fly back to the States after one day. I practiced at home to live tapes of the show but never got to rehearse with the band, which was weird.

Like I said back in the introduction to this book, the tour started off well. We were all getting along, and if you discounted Ozzy and Sharon sporadically knocking seven shades of shit out of each other, the vibe was cool. I was enjoying rocking out, my solos kicked ass, and I felt part of the team.

Ozzy and I hung out a lot in the daytime and had some fairly deep conversations. He'd tell me how he loved acting and wanted to do movies or TV. He didn't say anything about becoming the star of one of the biggest TV reality shows the world had ever seen—but those shows didn't exist back then!

I had a cool image in the Ozzy band, with my streaks of purple dye in my dark hair, accessorized with a black fur coat. Ozzy was usually in a mink coat, with blond streaks in his hair. We were quite the pair. More than once we walked into a hotel lobby only for a confused receptionist to hand me Ozzy's key and say, "Here you are, Mr. Osbourne, sir!" I noticed that Sharon never liked that.

Ozzy was great early in the day, but he would get fucked up in the afternoons, drinking during his press interviews. This was partly to relieve the boredom, partly to alleviate the stage fright he used to get before the shows, and I guess mainly because he was a functioning alcoholic. By the evening he'd be telling me he was "knackered" (English slang for super-tired).

Before the shows, as we put our eye makeup on side by side, I could hardly tell what he was mumbling at me, drunk, in his thick Birmingham accent. In Europe the heavy metal audiences are all male, so I would tease Ozzy: "What are we, gay? Putting on eye makeup to go play for an audience of guys?" That made him laugh.

Ozzy was a great showman even when he was hammered, but you didn't always feel like he was in control. On the nights he was particularly "knackered," we would stick his song lyrics on the back of Bob Daisley so that Ozzy could read them as he lurched around the stage.

One cool thing on that tour was that my brother Vinny was playing the same circuit with Dio, and he and I would leave each other handwritten messages on the walls of the dressing rooms. Thankfully, unlike in the mental hospital, they didn't say "Help me!"

When we got to the American leg of the tour, Mötley Crüe were the support. They were really on the up. As you might expect, Mötley were totally opposed to Sharon's no-groupies rule and iron-fist control of the tour and were constantly looking for ways to get around it.

I guess drummers always gravitate toward one another, and I spent a lot of time hanging out with Tommy Lee. He was young, really powerful, and, even at that age, a great showman, and was just so flattered when I was the first person to write about his drumming in a drum column I used to write for *Circus*.

Tommy and I would watch videos of Gene Krupa, Buddy Rich, and "stick trick" drummers. Live, Tommy did a stick-twirling and cymbal-grabbing move that he told me he had picked up from watching John Bonham. When I explained that he had indirectly got it from me, Tommy stood his ground: "No, dude, I got it from Bonham!"

Eventually I showed Tommy the video of Vanilla Fudge on the *Ed Sullivan Show* in February 1968, way before Led Zeppelin existed, and told him how Bonham used to goof off by copying my shtick on the road. Tommy was amazed, but like I say, that is the way it goes in drumming and in music in general: moves get passed on down the generations.

When the *Bark at the Moon* tour hit New York, Mötley's infamous manager, Doc McGhee, whom I had first met on the Nugent tour, was backstage at the Nassau Coliseum and called me over to introduce me to a long-haired, good-looking, and clean-cut young rocker. "This is my new artist," Doc told me. "Maybe you can give him some career advice?"

The newcomer and I shot the breeze, and I told him that if his first album didn't make it, he shouldn't get disheartened. In return, he mentioned that I had been working with his cousin, Tony Bongiovi.

As the guy I was talking to was called Jon Bon Jovi, I guess it's fair to say that things worked out for him.

After the Nassau gig, Ozzy and I were in a limo when he suddenly decided that he needed a burger. I used my local New York knowledge to direct the driver to White Castle, a cool hamburger joint that specialized in mini-burgers known as "belly bombers."

Fuck, you should have seen people's faces when the two of us marched in! We munched our belly bombers in the limo. Ozzy was clearly impressed: two days later when we played Madison Square Garden, White Castle Burgers had taken over the backstage catering operation.

I had really thought things were going great on the Ozzy tour, and that was why it came as such a crushing shock and a blow when Sharon kicked me off the tour. It hurt real bad, but the sole consolation I had as I headed back to L.A. and seethed resentfully was that I knew it wasn't because of my playing, and it certainly wasn't down to Ozzy. It was just Sharon being Sharon.

As I lay low and got myself together, though, I got an offer that was going to allow me to go back to where it all began, to relive—or at least revisit—those extraordinary, halcyon days of my youth when my life turned upside down. I decided to take the tempting course that many a seasoned rocker has followed over the years.

I decided to go back to the future.

# 10

# IF YOU'RE NOT BLOND, YOU'RE NOT COMING IN

*In which Drummerdude finds the Fudge still can't get along, says farewell to loved ones, becomes a hair fascist in King Kobra, backs the wrong snake, drums with Pink Floyd, screams Blue Murder, discovers the English Coney Island, gets married, becomes a father, and cuts a fucking umbilical cord*

*When you've been part of any success-*ful band, the offers to re-form just keep on coming. There is never any shortage of record-label executives and live promoters trying to tempt you to milk your history as well as hoping that—who knows?—you may just find that original magic all over again.

When Atlantic Records came in with an offer for the four original members of Vanilla Fudge to reunite and record a new album, the timing felt right. It had been fifteen years since we had split, and the old enmities had been forgotten (or so we thought). We were older, maybe wiser. Shit, Phil Basile was even going to come back and manage us again! What did we have to lose?

So we booked into Pasha Studios, which had a cool drum sound that I had helped them to develop after being dissatisfied with it on the *Nugent* album. Mark Stein and Tim Bogert were already living in L.A., with only Vinny Martell still based in New York. So Vinny flew out to join us and used his advance money to buy himself a poky little motor home to live in. That seemed weird—and Vinny proved the odd man out in more ways than one.

185

Spencer Proffer was to produce, having just sold five million copies of Quiet Riot's number one album, *Metal Health*. We talked about updating the Fudge sound and making a contemporary rock record along the lines of Phil Collins and Genesis—at which point we began butting heads with our guitarist.

Vinny had never moved on from the sixties. He still wanted to do what he did, and that was it. From the get-go, he resisted any new idea that Spencer suggested, resorting to his default-mode comment from our first time around: "I just don't feel it, man."

It was frustrating, and eventually Spencer drafted in a session guitarist, Ron Mancuso, to Vinny's horror. As a bonus, I flew over to the UK and persuaded my old sparring partner Jeff Beck to guest on a couple of tracks. He agreed—I guess it was my karmic reward for not suing him for screwing me over on *Blow by Blow*—although for weird contractual reasons, we had to bill Jeff as J. Toad.

As a nod to the Fudge's big break, we covered a different Supremes song, "My World Is Empty Without You." But when the album, *Mystery*, was done, Vinny had only played on one or two tracks and done a few backing vocals. He got mad and slapped an injunction on the record.

That was the death knell for the album. Atlantic just could not believe what was going on. Their view was basically *Fuck, it's been fifteen years, and these guys* still *can't get along!* So they washed their hands of us, and *Mystery* died—which was a shame, because it was a good album.

Around this time I also caught up with a couple of old friends. Buddy Rich invited me to a show he was playing at Disneyland. Angela had broken her ankle in a fall at home, so I pushed her around the theme park in a wheelchair before we arrived at the venue to pick up our tickets.

A Disney worker at the ticket gate took exception to the purple streaks in my hair, refusing to let me in because I was "a punk rocker." We argued for twenty minutes until finally he agreed to call Buddy in his dressing room to vouch for me. Buddy informed him that if I were not let in immediately, he would pull the show!

Suddenly the attendant could not be more helpful. As I pushed Angela into the dressing room, Buddy greeted me with yet another joint! In drug-free Disneyland! This was getting to be a habit.

I also caught up with my ex-roommate. Since we had stopped semisharing the pad in Studio City, Prince had become one of the biggest pop stars in the world, right up there with Michael Jackson, and I went to see him headlining a show at the Universal Amphitheatre.

I could not believe my eyes. This sex maniac pretending to screw an invisible woman on the stage floor, this crazed, dry-humping extrovert showman was the same guy who was too shy to speak to me or even look at me when we were roomies? Well, I guess they say it's always the quiet ones!

After the show, I got to have a quick word with Prince when I presented him with a Synsonic drum machine for Mattel. He was cool with me. He asked me to the premiere of his movie, *Purple Rain*, and I made friends with the woman sitting next to me. She turned out to be Sheila E. We still talk occasionally.

Around this time the radio station KLOS promoted a Carmine Appice Drum-Off at Hollywood's Palace Theatre. It turned out to be the last one I did, but it was a blast. Eric Singer was in it, who went on to play drums with Lita Ford, Black Sabbath, Kiss, and Alice Cooper.

A kid called Steven Adler also entered. I got his name wrong and announced him as "All-der," and he didn't make the finals. Steven was upset by this setback. Eric told me that he saw him crying. About three years later, of course, he was in the world's biggest band: Guns N' Roses.

Yet all through the missed opportunity of the Vanilla Fudge reunion and everything else I was doing, I was still seething at the unfairness of being thrown out of Ozzy's band. In particular, one phrase Sharon had used as she sneeringly dismissed me had lodged in my head: "Your name is too big. You should start your own band."

*OK*, I figured, *maybe you are fucking right, Mrs. Osbourne. Maybe I will.* And I didn't just form a band. I dreamed up a whole concept.

You have to remember how things were in the eighties. Heavy metal in America, and particularly in L.A., wasn't just about the music. I knew that I wanted any group I formed to be musically tight and great performers, but I also knew that the image would be all-important.

I got the idea from watching Mötley Crüe when they were on tour with Ozzy. They had Vince, the blond singer, prancing around in front of Nikki Sixx, Mick Mars, and Tommy, who were all dark-haired, and I suddenly wondered, *What if we did the opposite?* What if we had me, with my black mop with purple patches, and a band of blond guys who also had color streaks?

I was on a mission. Like a musical Nazi from a bad-taste Mel Brooks movie, I set about recruiting a band made up entirely of blond musicians. I had been jamming and hanging out with a cool singer, Mark Free, and we found a guitarist, Mike Wolfe. The three of us started writing songs.

I had had a rehearsal space built into the big place in Sherman Oaks that I had bought to live with Angela, and as we practiced I advertised for more musicians. An avalanche of demo tapes and photos poured in to my manager, Alan, but I insisted that as well as being great players, they had to look good, too. We needed chicks to dig this band.

A succession of young blond hopefuls arrived to audition at my house. I recruited a keen young second guitarist, David Michael-Philips, from Phoenix, and he moved in with Angela and me for a while. A crazy bassist, Johnny Rod, flew in from St. Louis, and he fit the bill.

Johnny wasn't short of confidence. On his bass it said "BAD," short for big-ass dick. (He also introduced to the band his own idiosyncratic slang to describe chicks: LAL for long-ass legs, BAT for big-ass tits, and so forth. What can I say? It was the eighties!)

Mike Wolfe started getting an ego problem before we had even done anything, so I fired him. (It was a nice change to be doing the firing for once.) Through ads, I found a replacement guitarist, Mick Sweda. One problem: Mick had brown hair. I explained my concept. Brown hair was a deal-breaker. Mick bought peroxide.

I had my band.

I called us King Kobra, and Spencer Proffer, undaunted by the Vanilla Fudge comeback fiasco, offered to produce us. Spencer was good, but he didn't come cheap. He got us a five-hundred-thousand-dollar, two-album deal with Capitol, but we had to give half of it to him, as well as large chunks of our publishing money. We knew he could do a lot for us, though, so we sucked it up.

King Kobra got down to business. In those days hairspray and attitude mattered as much as the music, so I made Mark Free take lessons in karate-dance so he would be a great agile front guy. Spencer produced our first album: it rocked, it had some killer songs, and it broke into the charts. Things were looking good.

I had learned from Ted Nugent that it made more sense to buy the motor vehicles you toured in than to rent them, so we spent advance money on a motor home, a van, and a truck. The band parked them up at Mates Rehearsal Studios in North Hollywood and set about painting them all white, to tie in with the blond thing.

I was taping up the windows of the motor home one afternoon when I glanced up and saw Ozzy shambling across the parking lot toward me. He was at the studio to audition drummers! It was pretty ironic. It could also have been very awkward—at the time, I was still suing Ozzy and Sharon.

"I know that you have problems with my missus, mate," Ozzy said dolefully. "But I hope we can still be friends?"

"I know it wasn't you," I told him, truthfully. Ozzy cheered up and asked if he could help me tape the windows. In no time he was up a ladder and wielding masking tape. Now there was a sight!

My manager, Alan, did a great job on prepublicity for King Kobra. When we got invited to play a festival in Mexico, he suggested that, rather than take our wives and girlfriends, we invite the editors of *Circus*, *Cream*, and *Rock Scene* magazines plus big-name photographers.

Naturally, we got loads of press as a result. You would have thought we were as big as Mötley Crüe, except that Mötley were multiplatinum, whereas we had sold one hundred thousand records. King Kobra hadn't even had a hit.

Our first tour was supporting Autograph. With our lighting and show production guy, Larry Boster, we designed a badass set. Everything was red, black, and gold, including my drum kit and the amp line; aircraft-landing lights lit up to spell out *KK* on both sides of the stage; and we had walkways on top of the amps. On the first two dates, we blew Autograph off the stage, so their manager told us we couldn't use our set. Assholes.

We went out with Kiss on their *Asylum* tour, and they were way cooler. They let us use the full stage set every night, partly because Paul Stanley and I were so tight, but mainly because they had confidence in themselves not to be upstaged.

That was a pretty insane tour for groupies. The rest of the band members were all fifteen years or so younger than me and were good-looking dudes, but I still had my name, so we all got plenty of action. These were the days when AIDS and sexual diseases were becoming big news, so my tour manager, Andre (yes, he got promoted), came up with a plan.

Chicks would wait in line to screw the band in the motor home or at the hotels, and Andre was our sex police—but he was on our side! We drew up an agreement for girls to sign to party with us. It stated that they were over eighteen, they didn't have VD, and they did what they did at their own risk and wouldn't sue us.

After a show, Andre would adopt his Viking stance at the door of the motor home, handing out these forms, and chicks would just glance at them, sign them, and pile in to party the night away. So like all the glam metal bands, King Kobra got lots of pussy. I still have crazy videos of our sex parties!

In Detroit I hooked up with a cool chick named Sarah who was wild and a lot of fun. We partied together, and we would hook up whenever I was in town. Yet again, it was a chance encounter that was to lead to a whole lot more, further down the road.

Around that time, at a party I ran into two British metal musicians I knew, David Coverdale and John Sykes from Whitesnake. They were about to make a follow-up album to *Slide It In* and wanted me to join the group. I told them I was busy with Kobra: "I have my own snake to deal with!"

Of course, their next album, just called *Whitesnake*, was fucking huge in America and worldwide. Murphy's law! However, for King Kobra, things were not going quite so well.

Here is a cast-iron rule of the music industry: when your band is enjoying success, the record company sucks your dick. If you're not, they make it clear that they own you. I was pleased with the first King Kobra record, but when it didn't go massive, Capitol threw their weight around when we came to record the second album.

They were blunt, telling us, "Look, we can't sell that heavy metal shit. We can sell singles. As long as you make one side of the record singles, you can do whatever the fuck you want on the other side."

It was their way or the highway, so for the second album, *Thrill of a Lifetime*, we went in a softer, lighter direction. A track called "Iron Eagle" was recorded for a movie of the same name, and the record did OK in Europe, but Capitol never got behind it in America, where even a Kiss support tour couldn't prevent it from stiffing.

Things weren't great in the band, either. Mark Free had changed and was wimping out on us. He only seemed to want to sing love songs and weak shit. I had no idea that he had a major personal issue: he wanted to be a woman! Meanwhile, Johnny Rod was doing mountains of coke and all sorts of drugs and was all over the place.

We played dates with W.A.S.P. and Ted Nugent, but it was all going downhill. Johnny was coked out of his brain, and when W.A.S.P asked him to join them, he jumped ship. Mark also left after the tour to do what he had to do. Years later, he got a sex change, and now he—or rather, she—sings soft rock as Marcie Free.

Capitol dropped us, but I didn't want to give up on King Kobra just yet so I brought in a new singer and bassist in Marq Torien and Lonnie Vincent. We headed off on a tour of Spain, where we went down well, and wrote a load of new songs together—at which point things took a shitty turn.

The two new guys plus Mick Sweda suddenly quit the band and started up a new group, the BulletBoys. I guess they must have been planning it for a while, because King Kobra's merchandise guy, Dave Kaplan, was to manage the new band, and quickly secured them a deal with Warner Bros.

I was hurt by this desertion, but I just figured, *Well, shit happens!* But I was shocked when the debut BulletBoys album appeared a few months later. Half of the record was made up of songs King Kobra had written, except they gave us no writing credits.

The BulletBoys hit big with their debut single, "Smooth up in Ya," which had started life as a King Kobra song. Its follow-up was a cover of the O'Jays' "For the Love of Money"—a song that I had suggested Kobra should cover. It left me seriously pissed off, and I would have sued the asses off them had I not learned from the Ozzy and Sharon debacle just how much it costs to go to court.

What you gonna do? There are times you get ripped off and all you can do is swallow it. The BulletBoys must have felt guilty, because a while later, they came to my birthday party and gave me a gold record for sales of their first album to thank me "for my help." Well, their other albums didn't do nearly as well—maybe because they had to write all of their own songs. . . .

But just as the music industry can be a total bitch, it can also drop beautiful surprises into your lap. Around the time I got my back stabbed by the BulletBoys, I got a message on my answering machine from rock producer Bob Ezrin, who had produced huge albums by bands like Kiss and Alice Cooper.

"Carmine, I'm making this album, and it is *screaming* 'Carmine drum fills' at me!" Bob's excited voice said. He didn't say who the band was.

I rang him back, and at first he was coy, but then he came clean: "It's Pink Floyd."

"Pink Floyd?" I repeated, baffled. "So what happened to Nick Mason?"

Bob told me that Nick had been getting heavily into racing cars and his calluses were soft, and Floyd wanted some full-on heavy drumming for a track called "The Dogs of War." Wow! What an opportunity! I headed down to A&M Studios in L.A., where they were in Studio A—a really massive room.

Nick and David Gilmour were in the studio, and we hung out and chatted. Nick told me all about his cars and his racing. Bob Ezrin taught me a great trick that I use to this day: to put tissue paper in my ears to hear the click track better and prevent recording headaches. We filled up two twenty-four-track machines of drum parts.

I couldn't wait to hear what it sounded like and kept calling Bob while he was editing to ask him. Bob would give me all of these enigmatic one-word answers: "In a word . . . daring." I'd call him again a few days later. How was it? "In a word . . . energetic."

Around this time I also started a—very short—movie career. I filmed a movie called *Black Roses* up in Canada, playing a guy called Vinny Apache, who fought the movie's hero in a monster costume! It was a weird film, but it got a kind of cult status. (Maybe it was so bad it was good?) It was also the movie debut of Vincent Pastore, who went on to play Big Pussy in *The Sopranos*. I imagine he doesn't talk much about it now.

While I was in Canada filming the movie, *A Momentary Lapse of Reason* came out, and I raced to a mall to buy a cassette of it. I put it in my Walkman and was blown away. It was, indeed, daring and energetic, and it was so cool to be on a Pink Floyd album. Later I saw a live video for "The Dogs of War," with Nick Mason emulating my fills. It made me proud.

For all of the ups and downs and occasionally being kicked out of bands, I felt as if I had a charmed life up until now—but we all have to live through dark times, and in 1987 death touched my life for the first time. One of the first people to go was one of my all-time heroes.

Buddy Rich and I had become tight over the years. He had balls of steel. I remember he had a quadruple-bypass heart operation and told me he felt twenty years younger. The next thing I knew, he called me up from Australia or South America, or some place a long way away, where he was opening up for Frank Sinatra. It was very bold and very Buddy.

But his health wasn't great. After collapsing at a big show at the Hollywood Palladium in early '87, he was diagnosed with a brain tumor. I visited him in the hospital in L.A., and it was so sad to see the world's greatest drummer lying in bed half-paralyzed. But he still had his spirit, and made an angry little speech to me: "You know, Carmine, us drummers, we get fucked all the time. Take me and Frank Sinatra and you and Rod Stewart. We play in the same band together with these singers, then these singer assholes go out on their own and play Madison Square Garden, and we get to play five-hundred-seat places! They make all the dough, and we get fucked!"

Singers? In my case it was guitar players—but I knew what he meant. I was shocked to hear such anger from Buddy, who was virtually on his deathbed. But I couldn't argue with a word he had said.

Buddy had the tumor removed, came through the operation, and went off to recuperate at a wealthy friend's mansion just off the 405 freeway. I visited him there, but Buddy was still paralyzed and depressed that he couldn't play gigs. When his heart gave out, on April 2, 1987, it was a merciful release.

His funeral was three days later—my mother's birthday—in a chapel in west L.A. It was an unbelievable day. They had set up Buddy's Slingerland drum set next to the closed coffin, and the air was thick with grief. The chapel was packed with Hollywood A-listers: Frank Sinatra, Jerry Lewis, Johnny Carson, Robert Blake, and many more.

Sinatra got up and told the story of when he first met Buddy, when they were starting out and playing with the trombonist and bandleader Tommy Dorsey: "Tommy called me over and said, 'Frank, I want to introduce you to another pain in the ass—Buddy Rich!'" Everybody was laughing and crying at the same time. It was a moment of pure emotional release.

After the cemetery, Johnny Carson's ex-wife Joanna Holland held a "celebration of Buddy" party in Beverly Hills. I met Mel Tormé, who was a nice guy and told me he was writing a book about Buddy. I hung out at the party for a while but then had to leave to see my mom on her birthday, so I went up to Buddy's widow, Marie, to say goodbye.

"You can't leave without playing with the band," Marie told me.

"Marie, I'll be too loud," I said.

"Buddy would want you to play."

There was no arguing with that, so suddenly I found myself sitting in a four-piece jazz band, trying to play really soft—not my forte! Somehow I managed it, and at a fast jazz tempo, too. It was my final tribute to Buddy.

After the party, I went to my mother's house, and we watched footage of Buddy's funeral on the TV news.

Twelve days later, my mother was dead.

It was the week after her birthday, and I was on the road on a short tour of drum clinics. I couldn't believe it when I phoned Vinny's house to chat and his wife at that time, Justine, told me that Mom was in the hospital, that she had had a heart attack. Those happened to other people—not to my mother!

My instinct was to cancel the drum clinics and fly straight home, but when I called the L.A. hospital in a blind panic, my sister, Terri, said she was there with my father, Frank, and Vinny, and my mom was doing OK. She said Mom should be out in three or four days, and I would see her at the end of the week, when I was home for Easter Sunday.

I spoke to my mother, who repeated that she was fine and that I should carry on working and see her on Easter Sunday. I called her every day that week up until Friday, when I was in Chicago. Mom was in good spirits. As we ended our conversation, she did a weird thing.

"I love you," she told me.

"I love you, too," I replied, and we hung up.

Huh? What was that about? We were a close Italian family, always had been, and we loved each other, but we never talked like that. I nearly called her back to ask why she had said that, but then thought nothing of it.

That night I went out in Chicago with some friends, took in a rock club, and even got me a little groupie action. Before I crashed I called the desk of the hotel to arrange a wake-up call to catch a flight to Pittsburgh for my last clinic.

The next morning I answered the wake-up call—but it wasn't the wake-up call.

"Carm, it's Vinny," said my brother, using my family nickname.

"Is everything OK?" I asked him. "Is Mom OK?"

"No. Mom passed away last night."

Vinny told me she had a coughing fit so bad that it triggered another, massive heart attack. I put the phone down in that Chicago hotel room, and I cried.

As I sobbed, I felt overwhelmed with sadness and despair, out of my mind with guilt. My mom had gone, and I never got to see her before she went. I would never speak to her again. What had I been thinking? I should have ignored all the advice and raced home, just like I had wanted to.

I went crazy in that room. I couldn't even change my flights and go straight home to L.A., as everything was booked up for Easter. Eventually I realized that there was nothing to it but to go to Pittsburgh. When the bellman came up to get my bags, he found me wild-eyed and still crying. Concerned, he asked, "You OK? You look like you lost your best friend!"

I must have looked awful, because my cab driver asked me the same thing, as did the stewardess on the plane—she even came and sat by me for the flight. I just rambled at them. I had to talk to somebody, anybody. At my Pittsburgh clinic I was a total mess and almost burst into tears on the stage. I had never felt sadder or more alone.

The funeral was another ordeal. In the Italian tradition, Mom was to lie in an open casket and we would kiss her goodbye on the cheek. I couldn't face doing it and refused even to go to the funeral home, but all of my family began getting on my case, telling me they had seen her lying there and she looked good, so eventually I agreed.

My feet felt like lead as I walked into the funeral home, and tears welled up in my eyes as Vinny and I laid drumsticks and our press photos in my mother's casket. Her face muscles had relaxed; she didn't look like herself anymore. When the Los Angeles earthquakes struck a few days later, I had nightmares of the quakes terrorizing her in her coffin.

She had always loved me, supported me, came to my shows, kept scrapbooks carefully documenting my career—she had been the best mother anybody could hope for. I hope, and I know, that today she is resting in peace.

They say that bad things always come in threes, right? Well, in 1987 I also hit my third divorce.

Angela's acting career had gone into a downward spiral, and she was getting no work, which had made her depressed. I was away on the road a lot, and unlike my previous wives and girlfriends, I think Angela always knew I was fooling around with groupies. Her attitude was more *Keep that shit away from me and don't bring any diseases home.*

In any case, our relationship had been growing difficult and no fun. If I had been more mature, I would have worked at turning it around, but my attitude then was still *OK! Next!*

Plus, I had already met somebody else.

Whenever I went on the road, I hung out with Sarah, the chick I had met in Detroit on tour with King Kobra. When she moved to L.A. to live five minutes up the road from Angela and me, our affair picked up pace. In no time we were an item.

Sarah was twenty-two, skinny, a good-looking blonde. She was full of life, and compared with the hard time that Angela and I had been having, she was a lot of fun to be with. So when Angela and I split, I sold our big house, bought a smaller place, and Sarah and I moved in together.

Musically, I was kind of kicking my heels. I put together a new version of King Kobra with Johnny Edwards on vocals, who had been in Foreigner, but our album, *King Kobra III*, released on my own label, Rocker Records, did nothing. It felt like it was time for a new project.

For once I knew exactly what this should be. After playing on the *Whitesnake* album that I had turned down, John Sykes was canned from Whitesnake and formed a new group, Blue Murder. The bassist was Tony Franklin, who was great in the Firm with Jimmy Page. Cozy Powell was the drummer for Blue Murder, and when I heard through the grapevine that Cozy had quit, I wanted in.

In fact, I wanted in so badly that I took off on a transatlantic mission. My brother Vinny was on tour with Dio, and they had four nights at the Hammersmith Odeon. I figured everybody on the British metal scene would be at those gigs—someone would know how to get in touch with John Sykes, right?

The weird thing was, my fiendish plan worked like a dream! I jammed onstage with Dio, then at the after-show party, I met an old journalist friend, Chris Welch from British music magazine *Melody Maker*, who had used to interview me in the BBA days. Chris had a number for John, and in no time I was talking to John's stepdad, Ron, who was part of his management team.

"Can you get to our recording studio in Blackpool?" Ron asked. "Sure!" I told him, despite not having the first idea where—or what— Blackpool was.

It turned out Blackpool was a seaside town in the far north of England, so the next day I rented a car and drove up there. It was a four-hour drive, during which I played Aerosmith's *Permanent Vacation* on nonstop repeat. If ever I hear any song from that album now, I remember my Blue Murder drive.

When I got to Blackpool, I hooked up at my hotel with Tony Franklin. It was 2 AM, so the hotel owner had locked up for the night and given Tony my key. Tony had clearly had a few drinks and escorted me to the deserted bar.

"Fancy a drink?" he asked.

"It looks kind of closed," I told him.

"I can fix that," said Tony, casually crawling through the bar hatch and breaking into the hotel's liquor stash. What a cool intro to a new band!

The next morning Blackpool blew my mind. There were tacky game arcades for kids, depressed-looking people on vacation, even a tattered boardwalk sticking out over a horrible, cold, gray-looking ocean—shit, this place was the English Coney Island!

My intrepid journey was worthwhile, though, because when we jammed that day, the chemistry was great. We smoked a little hash, started playing, and by ten minutes in, we were all grinning at each other. At the end, Sykes said, "Man, you have a great pocket!" (A big compliment for a drummer—it means your groove.) "You've got more fills than anybody, even Cozy! Do you want to be in the band?"

This was a dumb question, right? "Of course I want to be in the band! I came all the way from Los Angeles to Blackpool to be in the band!"

Blue Murder already had a record deal. As John Sykes had been so closely involved with the *Whitesnake* album, which had been a huge hit, Whitesnake's label, Geffen, had signed them up. The plan was to make the debut album in Vancouver at the start of '88, with Tony Martin from Black Sabbath on vocals and Bob Rock producing.

Tony Martin changed his mind and pulled out on the day we were due to fly to Vancouver, but we decided to go anyway, as the songs were so strong and we figured we could always find a singer later. In fact, John sang the demos, and after we had auditioned scores of vocalists, we decided to stick with him as Blue Murder's full-time singer. Sometimes, the right answer is right in front of you.

Vancouver was a fun city, not least because it had these insane titty bars where the girls would take a shower onstage in front of you. We went there pretty much every night after recording, and the band and crew would take strippers back to our rented apartments to party.

One night the whole band was out and decided to go back to the studio at 3 AM with a load of strippers and hangers-on in tow. We had been recording a track called "Jelly Roll," but I hadn't done the drums yet, and John decided I should do them right there. I told him no way—I was tired, drunk, and fucked. But he insisted, and to my amazement, it sounded so good that we used that take on the album.

The sessions went great, and we were really excited about Blue Murder and the album. Despite that, we were hitting snags, not least because we didn't have a manager. John's stepdad was still doing his best with his small team, but he was never going to be Peter Grant, or even Phil Basile.

We also made some dumb mistakes. We had an eight-minute song called "Valley of the Kings" and spent $150,000 on a video for it by Mary Lambert, who directed the movie *Pet Cemetery*. Our A & R man, John Kalodner, got MTV to play it a few times, but it was just too long and not commercial enough. We should have gone with "Jelly Roll" and my drunken fucking drumming.

In May '88 Atlantic Records staged a huge fortieth anniversary concert at Madison Square Garden. It ran for thirteen hours and was a major event, with appearances from groups like Led Zeppelin; Yes; Genesis; Crosby, Stills & Nash; Foreigner; the Blues Brothers; and the Bee Gees.

Vanilla Fudge decided that we could stand each other for one show and, like Zeppelin, re-formed just for the night. We played two songs, "You Keep Me Hanging On" and "Take Me for a Little While," and the night was a great trip down memory lane.

As we left the stage, Phil Collins stopped me and told me that he had always loved Fudge and we had been a big influence on his music. Then later that night we got to hang out with Michael Douglas plus loads of old faces from the past, such as Robert Plant. The evening was a blast, and a welcome reminder of more successful times.

On a personal level, however, my life was gearing up for one of its regular periods of turmoil. Within a few months I got married again—and I was about to be a dad.

When you have three divorces behind you, you don't just leap into a fourth marriage without a very good reason. Sarah and I were getting along well, but when we talked about getting married, I was pretty wary. "What for?" I said. "We're fine as we are. Why do we need to get married?"

But I had been thinking more and more about having kids. I guess as an Italian guy, family had always been important to me, and I didn't want to miss out. Sarah was OK with this, so I had told her if she got pregnant, we would get married.

At which point, she got pregnant.

We had to induce the birth, as Blue Murder were about to go out on tour with Bon Jovi, and I really didn't want to miss the birth. It was a wild experience—it is incredible to see your child born. Before the birth, I remember walking around the delivery ward looking at all the placentas, thinking how amazing it was that each one had helped a little human to be born.

Sarah was in labor for four hours. The doctor was a friend of ours, and at the crucial moment right after the baby came out, he turned to me and said, "Carmine, you want to cut the cord?"

It looked kind of messy, and I imagined blood spurting out of it. "No, you're OK," I told him. "You do it."

"Come on, cut the cord!" he urged.

"I don't want to cut the cord!"

"Look, this is the beginning of your child's life. You have to cut the cord!" he insisted. "What are you, a fucking wimp?"

This was one rock-and-roll doctor we had here! "All right, I'll cut the fucking cord!" I said, and did so. It was easy, like cutting a piece of plastic; nothing spurted out. And there I was holding my daughter, just a minute old. What an amazing feeling! She had jet-black hair and looked just like my mother. We decided to call her Bianca Marie, a good Italian name.

So here I was, a new dad, and two days later I was back on the road again. The Bon Jovi support tour was quite something. At the time they were massive, and it was weird to see the teenage girls in the audience, pulled in by their pop-metal hits and Jon's looks, going crazy for Blue Murder's sludgy Cactus/BBA-style jamming.

We also did a triple-bill tour with Billy Squier and Kings X, who I thought were a great band. However, it was becoming clear that Blue Murder just wasn't happening. The album only sold 150,000 copies in the United States, which would be regarded as a pretty good performance nowadays, but back then was seen as a flop. It did great in Japan, but that wasn't enough.

It was particularly bad news because we had all been so bullish about Blue Murder that we had not even considered the prospect of failure. I had agreed to a deal with John with no salary but with a percentage of the profits. It meant that our failure didn't just hit our egos—it hit our pockets.

My instinctive reaction to a disappointment like that is always to regroup, make another record, and try again, but John Sykes took it hard, probably because he was following a hit as huge as *Whitesnake*. He got depressed and just stopped returning calls from the rest of us about what was happening next. Eventually we all just got frustrated and drifted away from the band.

Why had Blue Murder failed? Well, one reason was that a wind of change was blowing through rock music, in America and in Europe—and it was going to do me no favors at all.

# 11

# GO EAST, YOUNG MAN

*In which Drummerdude feels like a dinosaur, makes a fist in Hollywood, finds he's still big in Japan, rocks out with Slash, Brian May, Steven Seagal, and John McEnroe, buries his Mafia manager, gets married, suffers a nose-related near fatality, sinks into a deep depression, and talks to himself in a mirror*

*In the early nineties, rock in America was* changing as a whole new music came out of Seattle and the Northwest. The grunge bands like Nirvana and Pearl Jam were young, angry, and alienated, and like the first-generation punks in England, they were all about a complete break with the past and everything that had gone before.

Specifically, that meant the kind of music I played.

After Blue Murder drifted apart, a few other old-hand musicians and I put together what I guess we imagined was a supergroup. We called ourselves Mother's Army, and with me on drums, we had Joe Lynn Turner on vocals, Jeff Watson from Night Ranger on guitar, and Bob Daisley from Ozzy's band on bass.

As we rehearsed the band, a couple of cool things happened. First, Bianca got herself a little brother, Nicholas, born when she was two. Then I got inducted into rock's equivalent of the Hollywood Walk of Fame, the Rock Walk of Fame on Sunset Boulevard.

This was a proud day. The Guitar Center on Sunset Strip, who organize the Rock Walk of Fame, did a drummers' special, and as well as me inducted Buddy Rich, John Bonham, Keith Moon, Ginger

Baker, Alex Van Halen, and my all-time idol, Gene Krupa, all on the same day. I was honored to be in such cool company.

A week before the ceremony, I was carrying Bianca and running for an elevator at my doctor's office when I tripped. To protect Bianca, I put my right hand out to break our fall. It worked, but my whole palm became a massive burn-blister from the carpet. No way could I ram that into wet cement—ouch!

On the day, the only other honorees in attendance were Ginger Baker and Alex Van Halen, for the good reason that everybody else was dead. It was such a cool day that even Ginger was in a good mood, but I had to put one handprint and one fist imprint into the concrete. We talked of redoing it later when my hand was healed, but the fist looked cool and was unique—and very me—so we left it.

It was ironic that I was getting honored as a rock legend as out in the real world I was having a terrible time. If my new bandmates and I thought our reputations might create a buzz around Mother's Army, we were quickly disabused of that crazy idea. Nobody wanted to know.

The grunge rock–mad music business, radio stations, and fans saw us four old-school guys as dinosaurs. That was what we felt like, too. Mother's Army was a disaster. When we toured, the money was crap, and we couldn't afford a bus and had to squash into a motor home. We made an album, but it was never even released in the United States, so gig crowds were sparse.

Suddenly, from being a former member of some of the biggest bands in rock history, I was a struggling middle-aged guy with two kids, finding it hard to make a living. John Sykes resurfaced, and I played on a second Blue Murder album, *Nothin' but Trouble*, but that flopped too, apart from in Japan.

As we made that record, I received another blow. Alan Miller, my manager of fourteen years, died. He was not only a lovely guy but also a man who had done amazing things for me and who lived and breathed Carmine Appice twenty-four/seven.

Alan died of the AIDS virus, which also gave me cause to panic. I had long known he was gay and so was surprised when I was with a groupie chick once and he came over to join in. "Huh, you're into women?" I asked him.

"Yeah, I'm bi!" Alan said. So we screwed the chick together.

Naturally, as soon as Alan told me he was sick, I raced to have an AIDS test. Thankfully, I was clean.

I visited him right at the end in the hospital, and he was hardly there—just skin and bones. He was comatose, and I went over to his bed and whispered in his ear, "Alan, it's time for you to go on to the next plane. This is no life for you. I'll be OK. Please, you need to let go." As I sat back down, a strong wind blew in through the window, and his back arched up.

Was it his soul leaving his body? Who knows? I said a prayer for Alan, kissed him on the forehead, and left. The next day the hospital called and told me he had died.

So I had no band, no manager, and was struggling to feed my kids, working in an industry that thought I was a relic. Was it really only ten years ago I had been playing stadiums with Rod Stewart? It felt like a lifetime!

When an offer came in, I was relieved to join the Edgar Winter Band. Edgar was of my generation and a great guy to hang out with. We toured a lot, and it was fun to play his old hits like "Frankenstein" and "Free Ride." The pay wasn't great, but I couldn't afford to quibble. He let me sell my own merchandise on tour, and we played cool places, including South America, where for some reason I was more popular than Edgar.

I had a big name, but now I was definitely just one more jobbing drummer. During some downtime from Edgar's band in 1992, I went on tour to Japan with Jeff Watson's solo band. It reignited a love affair with the country that was to last the best part of a decade. It also saved my career.

On the tour I met a guy called Lefty Shimano, who was with a drum company I was associated with, Mapex. Lefty was a big Vanilla Fudge fan and began to put together some drum clinics there for me. Because the Blue Murder albums had done well in Japan—shit, even the Mother's Army record had done OK—I was also asked to reprise my Super Sessions tour of 1982 with a new cast of musicians, including Tony Franklin, Kelly Keeling (a singer-songwriter who had worked with Blue Murder), and Mitch Perry of the Michael Schenker Group.

Life had gotten hard for me in the States, and it was great to spend time in Japan again. I had always enjoyed visiting the country and found the people polite and respectful—if I ended up with a girl after a show, we had normal sex, not the crazy shit that groupie chicks got up to in America and Europe!

People still wanted to see and hear me in Japan, and it was nice to feel valued again. The country was also to enable my next big musical break.

It was an idea that I had had germinating for a while as I tried to get a solo record deal after Blue Murder. Guitarists in big groups were getting solo deals way more easily than drummers, and one day I laughingly said to Jeff Watson, "I should make a guitar record with all of my guitarist friends on it!" That night, as I lay in bed, I realized my joke could become reality.

My plan was to cowrite an album's worth of songs and get a different big-name guitarist to play on each track. I figured if it worked, it might even expand into a series. At first I wanted to call it *Guitar Gods*, but then I hit on an even better name: *Guitar Zeus*.

It's always hardest to get the first people to commit to projects like that, but when I ran into Brian May—whom I knew from the Rod days—and then into Ted Nugent, they both immediately agreed to be involved. Armed with those two massive names, I knew I could pull in more stars.

I had hired a new manager, Warren Wyatt, to replace Alan, and he got to work. American record companies had no interest in the project, as we expected, but Warren got me a deal with a Japanese label. I called Kelly Keeling from Blue Murder, and we wrote some of the best songs of our careers for the record.

From there it was plain sailing. Slash from Guns N' Roses said yes, as did Steve Morse from Deep Purple, Doug Pinnick and Ty Tabor from Kings X, Neal Schon from Journey, Yngwie Malmsteen, and Mötley Crüe's Mick Mars. It was cool to get Leslie West, who had played gigs with us in his first band, the Vagrants, when Vanilla Fudge were still the Pigeons.

*Guitar Zeus* did pretty well in Japan and Europe, and Warren negotiated me another, better deal, again in Japan, for a follow-up. The lineup kept growing: Richie Sambora from Bon Jovi, Denny Laine from Wings, Zakk Wylde, Frank Zappa's son Dweezil, Bruce Kulick from Kiss, Vivian Campbell from Def Leppard, and Warren DeMartini from Ratt.

There were also two wild cards. I had met Steven Seagal at a charity gig, and the Hollywood star told me he'd love to come down to play some blues. John McEnroe also had his agent call to say he wanted to be involved. They were both excited to be on the record. McEnroe had a pretty simple rhythm guitar part, but he gave it depth and, well, balls.

To this day I think the *Guitar Zeus I* and *II* albums are two of the best records I ever made. Man, to me they sound like Blue Murder meets Soundgarden meets the Beatles! But I was still missing being part of a working band—and Japan was to fill that gap, too.

Tony Franklin from Blue Murder played bass on the two *Guitar Zeus* albums, and he and I got an offer from left field. A famous Japanese singer named Shota was re-forming her old band Pearl, who used to play huge venues in Japan—did we want to be involved?

What did I think? I thought, *Fuck, this is better than any offer I'm getting out of America! Why not?* So in 1996 Shota and a well-known Japanese guitarist named Kenji Kitajima came over to Los Angeles, and we recorded an album, produced by former *Star Search* music director Joey Carbone, titled *East Meets West*. We also made a couple of videos, and it was all very relaxed and fun.

Around this time, Phil Basile died. Phil had pneumonia, and when I flew in to New York to visit him in the hospital, he looked frail but still had the old spark in his eyes. I promised to go visit him again the next day, but the weather was horrible, and he told me not to bother. The day after that, he was dead.

It wasn't until Phil passed that I realized the full extent of his Mafia connections: that he was associated with the notorious Lucchese crime family; that he was arrested after giving Henry Hill a "no show" job at one of his clubs; and that he turned up in Nicholas Pileggi's novel *Wiseguy*, which *Goodfellas* was based on. Wow! Who knew?

Phil's funeral was packed with heavy-duty Mobsters, and his old sidekick, Chubby, pointed out a plain van parked outside the funeral parlor. "That's the feds, watching who's here." I felt like I was in a movie! But whatever his faults, Phil Basile had helped to make Vanilla Fudge. Right to the end, he was awesome with me. I loved him like family.

While I was on a break from Japan in L.A., Tim Bogert and I played on a couple of tracks on an album by an Argentinean guitarist named Pappo. He was a long-haired old hippie guy who apparently did well in South America. It only took a couple of days and was enjoyable but no big deal. For now, anyway.

Back in Japan, the *East Meets West* album came out in '97, and its success astounded me. I knew Pearl were big in Japan but had not realized how fucking big! It went straight into the top ten, selling two hundred thousand copies in its first week. It even went gold—the biggest record I had ever been on in Japan, including Vanilla Fudge and Rod.

When Pearl toured, we played major venues in eleven cities, including to five thousand people in Tokyo, and appeared on TV shows watched by fifty million people, like a Japanese *Ed Sullivan Show*. Our faces beamed down from the giant Times Square–like TV screens in all of the major Japanese cities. It was truly mind-blowing.

For some reason Pearl switched labels from Polydor to Atlantic, who wanted to put a record out quickly. Tony and I decamped to Japan for weeks to hook up again with Shota and Kenji and record *4 Infinity*. By now I was spending about four months a year in Japan—which often felt like an escape, as my marriage to Sarah was not doing well.

Sarah had dark sides to her nature that I hadn't seen when we first met and married. (Then again, that's true of everybody, right?) We had moved to Palmdale to give our kids a nice area to grow up in, and I guess it can't have been easy for her looking after them single-handedly while I was away working in Japan for months at a time.

When I was home we were arguing like crazy. I would yell at Sarah about running up credit-card debts when I wasn't earning the money that I used to. In truth, if it had been just the two of us, I would have ended the marriage; but I didn't want my kids growing up in a broken home, so I put up with it.

So things at home were pretty grim, and they got worse one day when I had a major health scare. It was a nosebleed. Ever since my first one in Chicago in '73, I had had occasional nosebleeds—once while having sex, once during a drum clinic in Australia. But this latest one took it to another level.

Sarah and I were home one afternoon when the bleeding started. An hour later, it was still coming, thicker and faster. I started having a panic attack, which got my heart beating faster and pumping the blood out even more. Before long there was blood all over the kitchen, and Sarah called 911.

In the ambulance the paramedics took my blood pressure, and it was through the roof. It was something like 204/101. Way high! I flipped out, which made things even worse. The blood was like a waterfall. Just as in that tiny plane over Switzerland decades earlier, I was sure I was going to die.

At the Palmdale hospital the medics cauterized my nose again and again, until finally the bleeding stopped four or five hours after it had started. I didn't feel at all well, but the doctors told me I was fine: "Just go home and relax." Yeah, right!

Exhausted from the loss of blood, I fell into my bed and into a deep sleep, only to wake at one in the morning. My nose was bleeding again. One more 911 call later, I was back in the hospital at Palmdale, but they had no idea what to do. "Fuck this place!" I told Sarah, panicking. "Let's go to the Tarzana Medical Center."

The Tarzana Center in the Valley is a great hospital, but when I arrived I got stuck in a nightmare limbo. They couldn't admit me without speaking to my doctor; my doctor was on vacation. My nose was still pouring blood, so they packed it with gauze and cocaine (believe it or not, some medics use cocaine to stanch nosebleeds) and left me sitting in an ER hospital bed for the rest of the night.

The next morning as I was near delirious and close to passing out, a record producer friend, Greg Hampton, called my cell phone by chance. Greg put me in touch with his nose doctor, who was based at Tarzana. All the bleeding so far had been through one nostril, but then as Greg's doctor checked me out, the other one started gushing.

Man, I was in a bad way. I had bled so much that I ended up swallowing a lot of blood; when I went to the bathroom, my shit was pitch-black. I had both nostrils blocked up with gauze and was breathing through my mouth. When I was close to needing a blood transfusion, they transferred me to ICU.

The doctor was honest: I could bleed to death. "If we pull these things out and they don't stop bleeding, we don't know what to do," he told me. For my two days in ICU, I was so sedated that the time is a blank for me now. The only thing I remember is seeing on TV news that Tommy Lee was in jail for beating up Pamela.

The hospital kept me under close observation for a week. Tony Franklin came to visit and brought me a picture of Christ, which I put on my closet door. "Pray to Jesus every day that when they take those things out of your nostrils, they don't bleed," Tony told me. I did, fervently.

When the docs finally came to remove the gauze, I was scared shitless. They gently, warily eased them out of my nostrils, and . . . nothing. No blood! As I sighed with relief and mentally thanked the picture of Christ, they told me to go home the next day, take it easy, and take my time to recuperate.

So that was when Sarah told me that she had met somebody else and she wanted out.

This bombshell devastated me. OK, we hadn't been getting along, but Sarah was the mother of my kids. This was a family we were breaking up here!

Even when things between Sarah and I had gotten bad, I was determined to make it work because Bianca and Nicholas were my life. When I wasn't on the road, I was a hands-on dad doing all the usual things: taking them to karate lessons and watching Bianca do ballet and Nick play basketball.

I loved giving them rides in my Pantera, putting them both in the same seat with the belt around them, and then going real fast to scare the hell out of them. We'd made sure they had awesome family vacations: Disneyland twice a year, Europe, Hawaii. I never wanted them to be from a broken home.

So the breakup was devastating for Bianca and Nicholas, for me—for all of us. I was still in terrible physical and mental shape from the nosebleeds, and the day I moved out of the family home to a nearby hotel broke my heart.

I had a minor distraction from my troubles when a good friend, Richard Mann, asked Kelly Keeling and I to write the music for a movie he was making, *Chasing Destiny*, starring Roger Daltrey. I became the movie's music producer, which meant I got to produce Roger, but I was under the huge, dark cloud of being separated from my kids and couldn't enjoy it.

I was still in emotional turmoil when I returned to Japan a few weeks later to promote *4 Infinity*. I was in absolutely no sort of mental place to meet a new woman.

So, of course, that was exactly what happened.

Atlantic held a launch party for the album, and I got talking to a Japanese woman named Mina who lived in London. She wasn't a music-industry person; she was on vacation in Tokyo and had tagged along to the party with a friend.

Mina was cool and charming and spoke English, and after talking all through the party, we spent the night together. For the next few days we were together most of the time as she came to gigs with me and translated at TV shows and interviews. I asked if she would be interested in coming back out to Japan to meet up with Pearl when we toured a few weeks later.

She was, and two months later we traveled up and down Japan as the band toured *4 Infinity*, with her and me growing closer and closer. At the end, I invited Mina to come back to L.A. with me for a while and try living together. I was delighted when she accepted.

My Japanese adventure was almost at an end—but not quite. In 1999 Vanilla Fudge were offered the chance to reunite and play Japan for the first time. Everybody was cool with it except for Mark Stein, who didn't want to do it because the dates were in supper clubs, and he thought Fudge should only play theaters. (He was probably right.) So we recruited another singer and organist, Bill Pascali, and did the tour without Mark.

During the Fudge shows we jammed with a virtuoso guitarist named Char, who was known as the Japanese Jeff Beck. Char had appeared on my *Guitar Zeus Japan* album, the latest in the series, which featured superstar Japanese guitarists.

Unsurprisingly, Char was a massive BBA fan, and he suggested that we re-form the band for Japan as Char Bogert Appice. Tim Bogert was up for the idea, so the three of us played a full Japanese tour, which included a show at the Budokan. It produced a TV special and a live album, *CBA Live in Japan*. Some of the scenes of hysteria even echoed my BBA days!

It had been a turbulent decade, but as the nineties ended, I felt as if I was back on the upswing. Japan had saved my career, my self-esteem, and probably my sanity, as well as giving me a new love. Mina had taken well to life in Los Angeles, and as a new millennium dawned, we settled down to a new domestic existence there.

Luckily, Bianca and Nicholas got on with Mina right away. I made sure the time we spent together was quality time because I felt so guilty that I couldn't always be there for them. Every weekend Sarah would leave the house in Palmdale, and Mina and I would move in, look after the kids, and take them out.

It wasn't ideal—but it was the best I could do.

I was also beginning to find more work in the United States, mostly with Vanilla Fudge, rather than everything coming out of Japan. When I got offered an album deal, Tim Bogert and I asked Rick Derringer to make a record with us, which we did as DBA: Derringer Bogert Appice. (I've always been real inventive on the band names, huh?)

We had the whole album done in about ten days, but Rick was getting into heavy-duty Christianity, which he insisted on reflecting in the words. A typical lyric ran, "When peace rains down from up above, the time has come for the dawn of love." It wasn't exactly what Tim and I wanted, but we went with it.

Rick was asking for divine intervention to show him the way to live and guide him through his days. A few months later, I was asking for God's help just to stay alive.

It was a late summer evening in 2001, and Mina and I were getting ready for a night out. Everything was totally normal, until my nose began to bleed. Again.

Mina put some ice on it, and the bleeding stopped within fifteen minutes. It would have appeared no big deal, if not for the fact that my attack three years earlier had made me ultracautious. "We'd better not go out tonight," I told Mina. I stayed home, very nervously.

The next morning I woke with a start at 6 AM with my heart pounding, in the throes of a full-on panic attack. Blood was again pouring from my nose. Freaking out, I called my brother Vinny. "Don't go to the same hospitals as last time!" he warned. "Go to somewhere good in Beverley Hills, where they know what the fuck they're doing!"

I was so scared that I took his advice. When I got to Cedars-Sinai, the blood was spurting thick and fast. The medics who saw me were worried. Instead of sticking gauze up my nostrils, they put a balloon in my nose and expanded it so it blocked the blood vessels while they tried to work out what was going on.

The main doc had also treated Ozzy and a bunch of other nasally challenged rockers and celebrities, but he explained that I was a whole other level of seriousness. He kept me in the hospital for a week, and the bleeding slowed to a trickle. Once it had stopped, he put a tiny camera up my nose but found that I had a deviated septum, so he couldn't see what was going on.

"I don't know what to do," he admitted. "I've never had this happen before."

This was terrifying, and it totally fucked with my head. By the time Mina and I went home, I was anxious and paranoid. I figured that I couldn't travel in case I bled again. I could never tour again.

This meant my career was over, right?

I never thought it could happen to an upbeat, outgoing guy like me, but I sank into a deep depression. Having moved out of my family home in Palmdale, by now Mina and I were renting a spare room from a female friend of mine, Chris, who had a two-bedroom apartment.

I would sit there and look around me. My whole life was in that shitty rented room: a bed, a computer, a few odds and ends of belongings. Had it really come to this? Carmine Appice, the supposedly legendary rock drummer, living like a broke-ass teenager and crippled by fear?

I became a total hermit and didn't leave that room for weeks. I couldn't do anything, and I didn't want to. I was lucky that Mina took such loving care of me, because I wouldn't even get in my car to buy groceries. Mina couldn't drive, but luckily there was one nearby store that she could walk to for supplies. If there hadn't been, I would have starved to death.

It was just the darkest, shittiest time. My accountant called and told me I had run out of money. All those divorces and big houses and cars had taken their toll, and I wasn't earning major bucks like I used to. Plus, now that I couldn't tour any more, what was I going to do?

To make matters worse, I was hiding in my one-bedroom cave and going through my personal meltdown on 9/11, when I turned on the TV to see the terrorist attacks on New York. As I sat with Mina on the bed watching the Twin Towers fall, it felt as if it wasn't just me but the whole world that was fucked beyond repair.

A few weeks later, I had to leave my hidey-hole when Vanilla Fudge played an early morning live biker-ride concert for Jay Leno. I was so twitchy and paranoid that I couldn't even hit the drums hard, because I was convinced it would give me another nosebleed. This was one dark place, and it seemed like I would be there forever.

Luckily, I found a way out. My nose doctor had suggested it might be a good idea to see somebody who could help me come to terms with my condition. Eventually I agreed and began to see a psychiatrist and a psychologist. It was the best decision I ever made.

The psychiatrist put me on Zoloft and Ativan for my depression. The drugs gave me a little more confidence, although when he doubled my dosage on the Zoloft from twenty-five to fifty milligrams, I felt like I was on fucking acid! I could feel my skin breathing. I had to ask him to knock it down again.

The psychologist's treatment ran deeper and went to the heart of who I was as a person—which I wasn't sure I knew anymore. She would make me do shit like stand in front of a mirror and say, "Carmine, I love you, and I'm going to help you get out of this!" It didn't come naturally to me, but I was willing to try anything.

The psychologist also pointed out to me that my life was a fucking mess. I had too many loose ends. Even with my fears for the kids, I had to face up to reality, officially divorce Sarah, and move on, because unless I tightened up my life, I would never be in control again.

Slowly, normality returned. I was still terrified of having more nosebleeds, but I got referred to a specialist at UCLA named Dr. Castro, who cut through the crap that all the other, clueless docs had fed me.

"Make believe that this room is your nose," he said. "There is a wall going down the middle. Your 'wall' is your septum, which is deviated. It also has a hole in it, so when you breathe in, the air gets turbulent, it dries out your blood vessels, and you bleed."

Dr. Castro outlined two options. I could either go on putting medicine and a saline solution up my nose, or he could do an operation whereby he would take skin grafts from my ears and put them in my nose. "We will cover up all the bad blood vessels, and you will never bleed again," he promised.

Fuck, that would do me! Where did I sign?

The only downside to this treatment was that I would have to shave off my moustache—for the first time since 1968! I was apprehensive and had no idea what I would look like without it: after all, I hadn't seen my face without it for more than a third of a century.

It probably sounds ridiculous, but my Fu Manchu moustache is so much a part of my image, and of me, that it felt like I was losing a leg. Some people think it is cool; some think it is comical. Some think it belongs in a cartoon; some in a seventies porn film. You know what? I agree with all of them!

Even so, I was getting near to another anxiety attack as I applied the razor. What the fuck would I look like? In the end, it wasn't so bad. I just looked like my brother Vinny.

The surgery went fine, once I got the hang of sleeping sitting up for a few days. It took a while for my fears to pass, though. At the start of 2002 I was due to fly to Japan and sought out Dr. Castro for a meeting before I left. What would happen if I had another nosebleed out there?

"You won't have another nosebleed."

"Yeah, but what would happen if I did?"

The doc patiently explained that if it were ever to recur, it would be far easier to treat, since my deviated septum had been corrected. My heart was beating fast as I boarded the plane, but the trip went fine.

I have never been able totally to banish my fears of the nosebleeds recurring, but I have at least put them to the back of my mind.

Mina had been a rock all through my personal crisis. I could not have been more grateful. By now she and I had been in and out of the States for four years, and she was having visa issues and finding it harder and harder to enter the United States with no green card or residence permit. So at the end of 2002, we had a low-key marriage in Las Vegas.

In truth, I didn't really want to get married again—maybe five times seemed kind of excessive—but it solved the visa issue, and, in any case, I saw no real reason why we shouldn't go on getting along nicely for years.

Well, that was what I thought.

# 12

# TUNING IN
# TO THE RADIOCHICK

*In which Drummerdude meets a sexy New York radio star, falls in love, learns she sometimes fakes it in bed, sees his sexual history turned into a spreadsheet, learns the art of fidelity, and reflects on a rock-and-roll life lived hard and wild but not always wisely*

*I knew about the Radiochick. When you* were in New York, it was kind of hard to miss her. Whenever I was passing through Manhattan early in the new millennium, I would see billboards bearing a cartoon logo of a big black bra barely holding up a pair of beautiful breasts and the name *Radiochick* written across it.

The owner of these luscious orbs, Leslie Gold, was the host of a popular morning show on a New York radio station, Q104.3, where she played a little music, conducted interviews, and took calls from her many listeners. Leslie was pretty outspoken, and I guess she wasn't too far off from being a female version of Howard Stern.

I first met her in 2002. I was in Q104.3 being interviewed by the late Scott Muni, who had been so supportive of Vanilla Fudge when we started out back in the day. After the interview, Scott's producer, Zach Martin, introduced me to Leslie and told her I would be a cool guest for her show.

Leslie was friendly but later sent a message back that she didn't think I was a big enough name to go on her show. Nevertheless, my

PR man and Zach kept plugging away at her, and eventually she agreed on one condition—that I would talk to her at 7 AM.

Still not excited by me as a guest, Leslie figured I was an inveterate old rock and roller who would never show up that early in the day. She didn't know me. I've always been a publicity hound, and so I was at the studio fifteen minutes before I was due on the air.

The interview went great, and after the show, I was able to help Leslie. She mentioned in passing that she wanted a big-name guitarist to judge a comedy air-guitar contest on her show, and I put her in touch with a friend, Vernon Reid from Living Colour. As a thank-you, she invited me to go back on her show a few months later.

We got along great during the second interview and, in fact, did some business together. Leslie was launching a local New York TV show, *Radiochick on the Prowl*, and needed a theme song. She liked a song on my *Guitar Zeus* album, "Days Are Nights," that Ted Nugent played on, so I suggested she use that. She did and in return gave me 108 TV ad spots to promote the album.

She also invested in the Guitar Zeus business, so we started talking on the phone regularly. A few months later I was on her radio show for the third time, and after the broadcast, somebody took a photo of Leslie and me. As we hugged, I was suddenly aware of my heart beating faster.

What the fuck was this? Suddenly I couldn't stop thinking about her.

By now I was back on the road with Vanilla Fudge as we toured *The Return*, an album of rerecorded old hits and covers, and I talked Leslie into helping to promote a gig that we were playing on Long Island. As she was involved, she came down to watch us.

When she got backstage, I asked if she would introduce us onstage—after all, she was a big star in New York. Initially she was reluctant, saying, "No, that's lame DJ stuff," but I talked her into it. She was surprisingly nervous but got a huge roar when she walked onstage, and afterward was glad she had done it.

I was less persuasive that night when I asked Leslie to come back to my hotel. She just smiled and said, "Nice show—well done!" and went home. Playing hard to get, huh? This made her even more exciting! A few days later I took her out for dinner to thank her for promoting the gig.

I learned a lot about Leslie at that dinner: that she was a Harvard Business School graduate and that before getting into radio she had run a multimillion-dollar window-manufacturing business. She was also charming, refined, and hyperintelligent as well as super-funny company. Yes, this was one smart cookie.

By now I had known Leslie for close to a year, and I knew that she was something special. That night after dinner, we went back to her apartment and sat on her couch talking for hours before going to bed together for the first time. She made me use a condom, which was kind of new for me, but I didn't mind—I thought we had amazing chemistry, not just sexually but intellectually and personally.

Meeting Leslie had come at an opportune time for me, as, despite having recently married, Mina and I were hitting problems. We had been together nearly five years, and she had always been a great, loyal partner, yet the language barrier between us was becoming an issue for me.

When I talked to Mina, I found I often had to repeat everything three or four times before she understood me. Some of my friends and family even told me I was speaking in broken English to them! It was frustrating for me, and I guess it must have been for Mina, too. Naturally, I should have been a man and told her that we were over. But I didn't.

The truth was I was falling head over heels in love with Leslie. I adored our phone calls and looked forward to them every day. Our talks could be kind of deep but were also fun and totally effortless. I realized that maybe, just maybe, she was something I had never had in a partner before—a soul mate.

She might have been a soul mate, but she was also somebody who didn't hold back from busting my balls. One day soon after we started dating, I was with Vanilla Fudge in a tour bus driving home from a gig in DC. We were listening to Leslie's radio show, and I felt proud that I was dating this smart, sexy Radiochick.

Leslie and her on-air sidekick, Chuck, started talking about faking it in bed. "Chick, have you ever faked it?" Chuck asked.

The Fudge guys were laughing and nudging me. "Not often," said Leslie. "But I admit, I have. Sometimes it becomes clear it's just never going to happen, despite the monumental effort being put in, and hey, I'm busy! I have to get up early in the morning! So I let out a grunt and moan and roll over. I had to fake it the first time I was with Carmine. He just wasn't getting the job done!"

"No?" Chuck was going nuts. "Not so good with his drumstick?"

Leslie's studio filled with hoots of laughter as her team began ridiculing me. Yet this was nothing compared to what was going on in the bus, where the band were busting my balls as only New Yorkers can. For a few long minutes, it felt as if the whole world was laughing at me!

As soon as the bus stopped and I could get some privacy, I phoned Leslie.

"What do you mean you faked it?"

"Oh, you were listening?" she asked, mock-surprised.

"Let me tell you something!" I said. "If you hadn't made me put those fucking condoms on, maybe it wouldn't have been so terrible!"

"Was it bad for you, too?"

"No!" I spat back. "It was good for me—but apparently not for you!"

But I can take a joke, and it felt great to have met a woman who was not only my intellectual equal but way ahead of me.

Then again, not all of our conversations were so enjoyable. Leslie and I had been dating for a few weeks and were sitting in her New York apartment one night when she posed a question I had been dreading—but which I knew had to come.

"Carmine, how many women have you slept with?"

You know what? I have never known how to answer this one, especially when it's a partner asking. Did I reply more or less honestly and risk seeing a horrified, disgusted look spread across her face? Or tell some bullshit lie that would probably be found out in the future anyway?

In any case, the true answer was that after forty years as a super-promiscuous rock star, I simply didn't know.

"Whatever it is, it is," Leslie went on. "But I'd like to know if it's dozens, hundreds, or thousands."

"Well, I have been on the road for a long time, and I never really kept count," I said lamely. She was never going to buy that! I tried to play for time.

"Let me ask you first, Leslie. How many guys have you been with?"

The Radiochick didn't miss a beat. "Seven," she said. It was clearly an honest answer and probably a typical one for people who haven't toured the world in successful rock bands. But . . . seven? Fuck, when I was in BBA or Rod's group, I might have seven chicks in two days!

Leslie wasn't letting me off the hook. In fact, she ratcheted up the pressure.

"Tell you what. I'll do a spreadsheet, and we'll work up an estimate," she declared, firing up her laptop.

Shit, this was going to be a challenging conversation, I told myself. It sure was. Leslie carefully divided her spreadsheet into columns: each year I was on tour, which band I was in, how many dates we played, and, in the all-important last column, how many groupies I had been with.

Wisely or not, I answered her questions as honestly as I could. "In the sixties the Fudge would play five or six days a week, and I had at least one . . . maybe two chicks each day," I began.

Leslie kept a poker face and began typing. There were things happening on the screen that I didn't understand.

Maybe there were things happening in the room that I didn't understand.

"Then when we got back home—well, I remember before I even made it and got famous, in 1963 and '64, when I first started having sex, I had maybe . . . three hundred women."

Suddenly I had the feeling that I shouldn't have said that. Leslie carried on typing and didn't blink an eyelid. After a minute she looked up and gave me a baleful stare: "Get off my couch."

"Why?"

"You might infect it."

Was she joking? I hoped so, but I wasn't sure. And it *was* a nice couch. I got up and moved to a chair. At least she hadn't kicked me out the door.

"What about when you were married?" she asked.

By now I was getting anxious. "Hey, we don't have to do this now. You want to go get some Chinese?"

"When we're done. So did you stop sleeping around when you were married?"

"Um, I guess it . . . slowed me down."

"What does that mean quantitatively?" she continued.

"Huh?"

"What does that mean in *numbers*, Carmine?"

"When I was married I was on the road about forty weeks a year," I figured. "Let's see. . . ."

"Shall we say five women a week?" Leslie suggested.

Well? Shall we? I sat back, looked at the ceiling, and started loosening my fingers, like I do pregig before picking up my sticks. I used my fingers to count as I tried to make sense of her question.

I snuck a glance at Leslie. She was staring at my fingers.

"Uh, maybe five in the beginning. Sometimes less. Sometimes a wife might be on the road with me, you know?"

Now there was another issue. At some point, I would have to tell her about my five wives. I took a deep breath and plowed on.

"So let's say two women a week. Oh, and we played a lot of weekend gigs, and you know what that means. . . ."

Did she? Did I? Leslie raised an eyebrow and typed in a few more figures. She shut the laptop, walked over to where I was sitting, and looked at me. She was giving nothing away, but I could see her dynamo brain churning behind her blue eyes.

"OK," I said quietly. "You gonna throw me out?"

"Get up. I'm ready to go get some Chinese."

I felt like I had dodged a bullet—but I knew this wasn't over yet.

The Chinese restaurant a few blocks away on the Upper West Side was cool, and so was Leslie, who was chowing down on chicken and noodles as if nothing had happened and she hadn't just conducted an exhaustive survey on my sexual history.

She was reeling me in, and I couldn't help myself. I bit.

"So, just how many did you figure out with that spreadsheet thing?" I asked, as casually as I was able.

"Four thousand five hundred," Leslie replied, equally offhandedly.

"Yeah, that sounds about right," I mumbled. Did I dare try to make a joke of it? "I was afraid that you would think I was some sort of a slutbag."

Leslie pointed a chopstick at me. "It's hard to look at that number and think otherwise," she sighed. "More important, I think we regard sex very differently. It's not *sport* for me."

She paused and looked me straight in the eyes.

"But if we're going to continue with each other, I guess I'll have to make my peace with it."

Forgiven! I was forgiven! I don't think I have ever felt more relieved. Instinctively, I reached across the table and gave her a big kiss. Leslie asked me one more question.

"I'd like to mention the 4,500 on my radio show. I think it might be kind of interesting. Are you OK with that?"

"Sure!" I told her. "I just hope the listeners don't think you're crazy."

Somehow I had dodged that massive bullet and survived. Now all I had to do was work out how to tell Leslie that back in Los Angeles, I was still married to Mina.

*A Note from Leslie Gold*

Several months had passed since the revealing "spreadsheet discussion." A discussion, by the way, that required some work on my part to come to terms with. It wasn't the number itself that was so troubling to me . . . although it was an absurdly, almost tragically high number. And a shock. It was—as I said that night—more an issue of how differently Carmine and I regarded sex.

For me it was always about intimacy, trust, and always in the context of a committed relationship. It's a rather old-fashioned notion, I guess, for someone known for interviewing porn stars and for her outrageous radio personality. However, if I was being honest with myself—which I was—it was a fundamental disparity between us.

There were others. At the time, I remember thinking that Carmine couldn't have been more wrong for me—at least on paper. He was wrong geographically, as I was based in New York City, and he was in Los Angeles. He was also too old for me, seventeen years my senior, not to mention that his relationship history stunk like week-old fish.

And I wasn't thrilled about attaching myself to someone in the music business who travels constantly, with ample opportunity to cheat. My experiences speaking to men on my radio show taught me most men are only as faithful as their options, and Carmine certainly had options. I had years of formal education; Carmine just about made it out of high school. In the part of my brain that was reasoned and analytical, it certainly seemed to me like a recipe for disaster. I could have blown it off. Instead, I waded in—but carefully. I always had one foot in and the other foot out of the relationship, because I was sure it would implode.

Why go in it at all? My day-to-day experience with Carmine was different. He was attentive. He called from L.A. several times a day just to talk, sometimes for hours. He found reasons—excuses, even—to come to New York. He was communicative, affectionate, and curious about my life. He was thoughtful in his advice to me. He was visibly excited to see me every time we were together. I was equally excited to see him. We laughed, we talked, we played, we enjoyed, and the sex was epic, imaginative, and fun (and, by the way, improved dramatically after that first time). So, on one hand, I was happy—joyous, even. On the other hand, I was always waiting for the other shoe to drop.

Then it did. But not in the way I thought. It was mid-July 2003. Carmine was rehearsing at fellow musician Randy Pratt's home studio in Long Island, before embarking on a three-week European Vanilla Fudge tour. As was always true whenever Carmine was in NYC, we were inseparable. So I tagged along to the rehearsal with a plan to drive him to JFK to drop him off for his trip. I met a bunch of new people at the house that day, including a singer named John Garner. John sang for the Lizards, who were to be the opening act for the Fudge in Europe. At this time, I had both a radio and a TV show in New York, so people knew my voice or my face and felt very comfortable striking up a conversation with me.

After I was introduced to John, he said to me, "Oh, so you're Carmine's cousin?" It was just an offhand comment meant to be some sort of a joke. I didn't really get it at first, but being a talk show host makes you fast on your feet, so I snapped back, "More like his niece," making reference to our age difference. I got a laugh, the desired result. The afternoon went on as planned, but there was something in John's comment that bothered me. Throughout the afternoon, I kept turning it over in my brain. It seemed to me something a married politician might say when being forced to introduce a woman who's actually his girlfriend. Even though Carmine hadn't said it, the reference made me uncomfortable.

*Could Carmine be married? No way*, I thought. In my head I went through all the reasons why not:

1. He takes my calls any time of the day and night.
2. When in New York, he stays with me and I never hear him get or make a phone call sounding remotely affectionate.
3. Most important, on our first dinner out together, I asked Carmine if he was married. He made a reference to an ex-wife, and I remember specifically saying the following: "Wife or ex-wife?" and "So you're not married now?"

I'm an interviewer by occupation. I know how to pin people down with specific questions. Perhaps that remark by John

Garner was just an ill-phrased or awkward joke. Probably, I told myself. But it still gnawed at me. I chewed on that comment over and over in my head for hours, until my stomach hurt. I was waiting nervously until I could speak to Carmine alone, and tried not to give anything away in my demeanor. I expected a lot of things to go wrong with my relationship with Carmine, but finding out he was married wasn't one of them.

Finally, after what seemed an eternity, it was time to go to the airport. This was my opportunity. Carmine was alone and trapped in the car with me for forty-five minutes. About ten minutes into the ride, after chatting about this or that, I brought it up. I'm a straightforward girl, so I just recounted the comment "So you're Carmine's cousin?" and why I thought it was odd. Then I calmly and sincerely asked, "Dude, are you married?"

I held my breath and watched him. Carmine had a toothpick in his mouth, and the only tell on him was that his mouth tensed up around the toothpick for a millisecond. Otherwise his face remained unchanged. There was a pause. Silence. I waited.

Then he said, "It depends on what you mean by married."

Jesus Christ. Oh no. Not good. Anything short of a flat-out "No" was not the right answer. I was crushed. I felt nauseous, and my breath went shallow. I was also dumbfounded. I didn't think I was in this relationship alone. It wasn't one-sided. Carmine had invested an immense amount of time, energy, thought, and effort into his relationship with me. I just didn't get it. He certainly didn't need to do that to get laid (as this book clearly illustrates). Why do all that if you're married? He knew me well. He had to know I wasn't the type of person who could tolerate a relationship with someone who is married? So why? WTF?

Miraculously, I kept my cool. I didn't get upset. I didn't yell. I really wanted to know what had transpired here, so I kept my poker face on and asked questions. Remember, I was always waiting for the other shoe to drop in my relationship with Carmine. While I didn't think this was "the shoe," I did always half-expect it all to fall apart. So I guess, on some level, I was braced.

Carmine told me he was married to a Japanese woman. He said he had gotten married primarily because she needed a green card, he couldn't communicate with her, and some other things, all of which were interesting but fairly irrelevant to me. He lived with her, they were married, and she knew nothing about anything. That made things very clear to me.

I asked him how he saw this situation playing out. He didn't know. I asked a few more questions, trying to assess where I went wrong. Where had I missed the signs? Carmine said he hadn't been completely sure I didn't know he was married. Still calm, I reminded him about the dinner when I had asked him if he was married. How could I know?

Then he said, "I didn't expect to feel this way about you."

That statement rang true to me. It was consistent with the effort and affection he had put into the relationship. It had seemed to me that he loved me, and I knew I loved him. It was at that moment I sort of got it. He didn't expect it to turn out to be a serious thing. Most likely he went into it like he went into all 4,500 of the others—for sport—and found himself entangled in something he didn't want to leave. So he just stayed in it, wondering how it would play out.

He was so sorry: sincerely remorseful and ashamed. I believed that, too. Now I understood a bit better. Regardless, I couldn't stay in it. "I have to be done," I said quietly. "I'm not some married guy's girlfriend. That's not who I am." He nodded. We were pulling into JFK airport. He apologized again and said that he really didn't want to lose the friendship we had. I told him I needed time, but I was sure one day we could be friends again. Just not today.

Carmine got out of the car and walked into the terminal. I drove back to Manhattan, shell-shocked. He called me one more time while I was on my way home to tell me he felt terrible. I believed him. It was—as it should be when a relationship ends—sad, painful, and over.

There was no contact, no e-mails or phone calls for the weeks he was in Europe. Carmine had been scheduled weeks before to appear on my New York TV show, *Radiochick on the Prowl*, after he returned from the tour. Sure, I could have canceled his appearance. The producers of the show would have understood, and we could have scrambled around and booked another guest without too much trouble. I didn't. I was a professional, and I felt I could handle it. I could get through an eight-minute on-camera interview with anyone, even Satan if need be. So I could certainly handle Carmine Appice.

I wasn't really even angry at Carmine. I was more angry with myself for ending up in this position when I should have known better than to be involved with him at all. *So, best to carry on*, I thought. In retrospect, if I'm being really honest, on some level I must have wanted to see him again, but I told myself it was just business.

Carmine arrived at the studio early and walked himself right into my dressing room, where I was making last-minute changes to the teleprompter script. In a ballsy move, he didn't knock, just burst through the door, grabbed me, kissed the belly showing out from the bottom of my leather belly shirt, and said, "Don't leave me. Everything is going to work out. I promise." Many times over the coming weeks, Carmine would say, "Don't worry, baby. It will all work out." I did worry . . . but truth be told, he delivered. He told the truth, got divorced, made good on every promise to me, and we've been together ever since.

Carmine proudly tells me that this is the only relationship to which he's been completely faithful. That statement always makes me nervous—after all, it shouldn't be such a monumental feat. But he has not given me a reason to worry, and he's remained as attentive, loving, communicative, and happy as he was thirteen years ago. The sex is still epic. He tells me he loves me every day. But more importantly, he shows me that he loves me every day.

I can't take the credit. I think I just got him at the right time, when Carmine (finally) could appreciate what you can get from a committed, monogamous relationship. Whaddya want? He's remedial. It only took him about three decades longer than the average guy!

One more thing—I should never have mentioned on the radio that Carmine had been with 4,500 women. For weeks after that, if I was doing a phone-in and arguing with a listener and I said something like, "Give me one good reason," they would say, "Oh, Leslie, there must be 4,500 reasons!"

I guess I asked for that one.

I'll never forget that awful conversation in the car with Leslie. I remember that as she was asking if I was still married, we kept passing giant billboards advertising "The Radiochick Show on Q104." They were like huge, taunting confirmations of just what I was about to lose.

So I left for Europe feeling hollow and confused, but I couldn't be without Leslie, and I knew what I had to do. I told Mina that our marriage was over—it was hard to do, because she was a great person and I hated hurting her in that way. Even after we got divorced, I tried to help her in any way I could. She had done so much for me.

But as soon as everything was straightened out and Leslie and I were back together again, life became great. We were like no relationship

I had ever had before, and we still are. She is the only woman I have never cheated on. When I say this, Leslie laughs and says she will notify the Nobel Peace Prize nominating committee. But the truth is, this is a big deal for me.

Why is everything so different this time? I guess it's the first time I am with a woman who is everything I want. I love Leslie's big boobs and great body, but even more than that—and I never thought I would say this—I love her amazing brain, and the fact that we have complete truth and understanding in our relationship.

It has also helped us to keep the spark that we're not together one hundred percent of the time. Leslie is very New York, and we're based there, but I still spend a lot of time in L.A. So for years I have been flying across the country two or three times a month. It keeps things fresh.

Despite sometimes having this geographical distance between us, Leslie has been totally supportive of me ever since we met. She has also been amazing with my kids from the start. When Bianca was applying for college and Nick was working out what to do with his life, Leslie was there with me, giving them help and support every inch of the way.

She also knows when to get involved in my dealings with my kids and when to stand back, looking amused. It was very much the latter when Bianca dyed her hair bright red and I started laying into her about it. Bianca calmly pointed out that as I was yelling at her from beneath purple hair, I didn't really have a leg to stand on.

Naturally, things are very different for me today from how they were. My career will never again hit the crazy heights of the sixties, seventies, and eighties, and I'm OK with that. I've done it all, and I've got so many memories.

In the twenty-first century, I've done loads of one-off projects, and I've enjoyed them. In 2004 I could have made another record with Rick Derringer. But you know what? I love Rick, but I couldn't handle any more Christian lyrics! So instead Pat Travers and I made an album called *It Takes a Lot of Balls* and toured the world.

I do interesting side ventures. I got involved with a charity called Little Kids Rock, going to schools and helping underprivileged kids to get into music. I also founded a touring show called SLAMM that was five drummers knocking hell out of oil drums, trash cans, and buckets. The critics called it "Stomp on steroids." That was about right.

Leslie has also been by my side in the bad times. In 2005 my father died. It was hard because he got Alzheimer's and was in and out of hospitals and nursing homes for his last few weeks, getting more and more sick and confused. It was a relief for him when he passed. He was a gentle, good man, and he is missed.

My last major health scare came in 2008. I was working on SLAMM in Los Angeles, where my son and daughter still live, and I woke up one morning with an itchy nose. I scratched it and it started to bleed. It had been seven years since my last attack, but immediately alarm bells went off in my head.

I phoned 911 and also called my son, Nicholas, who drove over with his mother, Sarah, in tow. The bleeding had stopped by the time the ambulance arrived, but the paramedics advised me to go to the hospital anyway. It was good that I did, because when I got to the emergency room, the bleeding started up again.

Sarah had a van and drove me down to the medical center at UCLA. I spent four hours there losing blood until their nose specialist arrived to put cocaine up my nostrils and pack up my nose. Leslie flew out from New York that day and was waiting for me when I got back to our L.A. home from the hospital.

We were back at UCLA the next day to consider my options. I was freaked out—after all, I had already had a state-of-the-art, high-tech operation, and now the problem was back! The doctor suggested that I get a procedure known as cerebral embolization.

"We go up your artery from your leg to the back of your nose, and we insert three surgical coils into the three main blood vessels of your nose," he explained. "Then if you do ever have another nosebleed, it will be a baby one—very small. We have been doing this for ten years and never had one person call back and say they were bleeding."

We did it, but I was pretty weak and insecure afterward. I kept thinking I tasted blood in my mouth and even started seeing a psychologist and hypnotist, who gave me tapes to try to relax my subconscious and stop it from being so fearful about my nose.

Weeks later, my paranoia really kicked in when I had to fly to Mexico to do a drum clinic. Leslie kindly came out with me. I felt anxious and broke out the antidepressant tablets, but it all went fine in the end. For eight years now, I've had no more bleeds. But it's always in the back of my mind.

I've also spent a lot of the twenty-first century re-forming bands for reunion tours. Vanilla Fudge get back together every few years and go out on the road. I did the same with the guys from Cactus. Even King Kobra are making records again. It's fun—I do it because I want to, not because I have to.

What's it like nowadays playing with the Fudge or Cactus guys? It's great. We're all older and smarter, so there are none—or, at least, not many—of the disagreements and tensions we used to get back in the day. Sure, we have words now and then, but underneath it all we love each other. We're family. It's just the way it is.

Once in a while I run into somebody who reminds me what a crazy life I've led. Sometimes I get invited to events where music and movie stars sign memorabilia for fans. In 2009 I went to one in Burbank, California, and across the aisle from me, between Eric Roberts and Pee-Wee Herman, sat Tony Curtis, looking old and frail.

I went over and asked Tony if he remembered hanging out at the parties at Rod's house and seeing us play the L.A. Forum. He did, and he remembered me playing drums. He gave me a copy of his book, which I asked him to sign. He wrote:

Carmine is a friend of mine.
—Tony Curtis

I knew Tony was from the Bronx, so I started kidding around with him, reminding him of an old saying we had in Brooklyn when I was a kid: "So-and-so is a friend of mine. He resembles Frankenstein." Tony laughed, because he remembered it, took the book back from me, and wrote in the back:

Carmine is a friend of mine. He doesn't look like Frankenstein.
—Tony Curtis

How cool was that? Sadly, within eighteen months, Tony was dead.

I have had a charmed life in so many ways, but sometimes I hear stories that remind me how differently things might have gone. When I was running with the gangs as a kid in Brooklyn, I used to hang with a guy named Louis Daidone, the quarterback of the school football team. He also played the trumpet in the school band with me.

What happened to Louis? Well, recently I found out that he became a major player in the Mafia, where he was known as Louis Bagels, was an acting boss in the Lucchese family, and is now in jail serving life for two murders. And part of me thinks that if I hadn't fallen in love with Gene Krupa and Buddy Rich, and picked up drumsticks, that could have been me.

Now I just hang out with pretend gangsters instead. Not so long ago, at a TV show pilot for Leslie, I met Steve Schirripa, who played Bobby Bacala, Tony Soprano's brother-in-law, in *The Sopranos*. Steve said he was a big Vanilla Fudge and Cactus fan and told me, "I grew up in Brooklyn, and when I was a kid, you were the shit! We were proud of you!" That was humbling to learn.

The music world can still surprise me. You remember how I made that album with the Argentinean dude, Pappo, back in the nineties? In 2011 I played with the Michael Schenker Group and went out to South America on tour.

Pappo had just died, and everywhere we went, people took me aside and asked me in hushed tones what it had been like to play with him. Bands were playing Pappo tribute gigs and selling out twenty-thousand-seat arenas—the sort of venues he used to routinely fill! Pappo had been a guitar god in South America. I had no idea.

What does please me nowadays is that I do so much with Vinny. Blood is thicker than water, and we have always stayed close. Nowadays we travel the world with a show called *Drum Wars*, and we hang out a lot. I just wish our mother and father were alive to see us working together. It would make them so happy.

I'm surprised to find myself saying this, but I'm glad that I have finally grown up. Looking back on my life to write this book has been an eye-opener, and with hindsight I confess that I haven't liked everything that has scrawled across my memory.

Man, the world has changed a lot in the fifty years since I gave up running with Brooklyn gangs to bang my drum and turned into a teenage rock star and a lusty kid in a candy store. At times I look back on the stadium gigs, the travels around the globe, and the thousands of groupies, and it all seems like a dream.

I know that I got lucky. I broke big at the start of the sexual revolution, when chicks were throwing themselves at musicians and two women per day was nothing out of the norm. Fuck, I did exactly what any young guy fortunate enough to be in that situation would have done.

But that doesn't mean we always behaved well.

Did we disrespect women back in the day? It's hard to say no. I'm a changed man now, and when I think back on memories of pulling down girls' tops backstage at gigs or sitting on the side of a bed laughing while they had a thrashing mud shark pushed inside them, I wince and I feel ashamed.

Those women chose to be groupies. They were willing players in a big, wild old game we were all playing, but sometimes the rules of the game were not very fair. Bianca is now the same age as the chicks we were fooling around with back then, and I'd hate anyone to treat her like that. In fact, I think I'd want to kill them.

So some of my old war stories may seem horrific in the cold light of the twenty-first century, but what can I say? Things were very, very different back then. I can't change the past, and I wouldn't want to. It is what it is.

When I started out, life was all about sex, drugs, and rock and roll. If I'm pleased about one thing, it's that I never got too involved in the drugs part of that equation, because I have seen far too many friends die young because of their love for coke, pills, or just plain old booze.

I remember losing John Bonham to drink, Keith Moon to drink and drugs, Jimi Hendrix—beautiful, shy young Jimmy James—to everything. I think of my friend John Entwistle, dying of a heart attack while taking coke with hookers, and I'm so grateful that I never went so far down that fucked-up road that I couldn't get back.

Nowadays when I go out on the road with the guys in Fudge or Cactus, it's all about the shows. I don't want to get trashed, and I don't want to screw around with women I've just met. I don't even want to throw televisions through hotel windows. I want to play music that I love, then get home to the family that I love even more.

I could not be more proud of my kids. Bianca works in movies doing amazing special effects and makeup, and Nick is doing great as an X-ray technician. They are wonderful people, and they know I love them and watch their lives carefully—as I do Leslie, who is still the woman of my dreams after thirteen years.

What can I say? Sometimes you have to go on a long, strange, meandering journey to get where you were always meant to be. Leslie asked me a loaded question, and the shocking answer was 4,500. But number 4,501 was the one that mattered most.

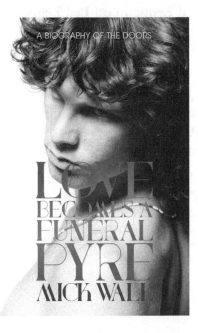
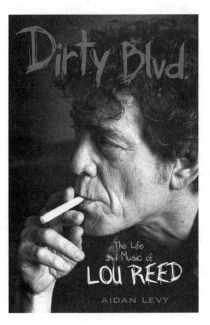

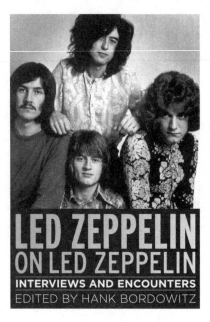

## Led Zeppelin on Led Zeppelin

Interviews and Encounters
Edited by Hank Bordowitz

"This is about as unvarnished a glance at the Led Zeppelin phenomenon as there can be—it's literally Led Zeppelin talking about Led Zeppelin—which makes it fascinating in and of itself." —*Rebeat*

Cloth, 480 pages
ISBN-13: 978-1-61374-754-4
$28.95 (CAN $34.95)

## Springsteen on Springsteen

Interviews, Speeches, and Encounters
Edited by Jeff Berger

"This collection . . . is a great illustration of how, when the appropriate subject is chosen, no one on earth can say it better than the subject himself. Impressively thorough . . . and highly recommended."
—Dave DiMartino, RollingStone.com

Trade paper, 432 pages
ISBN-13: 978-1-55652-544-5
$17.95 (CAN $21.95)

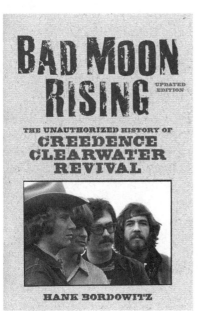

## Bad Moon Rising

The Unauthorized History
of Creedence Clearwater Revival
by Hank Bordowitz

"Bordowitz's recounting of all the acrimony is well detailed and not too hyperbolic. This is must reading for CCR-philes." —*Booklist*

Trade paper, 400 pages
ISBN-13: 978-1-55652-661-9
$16.95 (CAN $21.95)

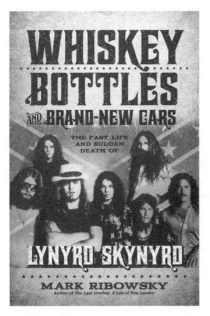

## Whiskey Bottles and Brand-New Cars

The Fast Life and Sudden Death
of Lynyrd Skynyrd
by Mark Ribowsky

"An excellent look at a band whose creative evolution was tragically cut short."
—*Booklist*

Cloth, 304 pages
ISBN-13: 978-1-56976-146-5
$27.95 (CAN $33.95)

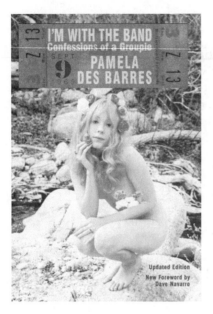

## I'm with the Band
Confessions of a Groupie
by Pamela Des Barres

"*I'm with the Band* is more than kiss-and-tell trash. Granted it's gossipy, but it's also a worthwhile document of the blossoming of an innocent California flower-child during rock's most exciting era." —*Star Tribune*

Trade paper, 352 pages
ISBN-13: 978-1-55652-589-6
$16.95 (CAN $18.95)

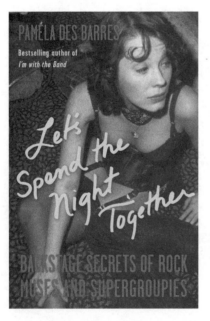

## Let's Spend the Night Together
Backstage Secrets of Rock Muses
and Supergroupies
by Pamela Des Barres

"The same kind of down-and-dirty details that made Des Barres's previous work so raunchily entertaining. Nasty fun from a bunch of sex kittens who've been there, done them." —*Kirkus Reviews*

Cloth, 400 pages
ISBN-13: 978-1-55652-668-8
$24.95 (CAN $27.95)